HOW WELFARE STA

CHANGING WELFARE STATES

Processes of socio-economic change – individualising society and globalising economics and politics – cause large problems for modern welfare states. Welfare states, organised on the level of nation-states and built on one or the other form of national solidarity, are increasingly confronted with – for instance – fiscal problems, costs control difficulties, and the unintended use of welfare programs. Such problems – generally speaking – raise the issue of sustainability because they tend to undermine the legitimacy of the programs of the welfare state and in the end induce the necessity of change, be it the complete abolishment of programs, retrenchment of programs, or attempts to preserve programs by modernising them.

This series of studies on welfare states focuses on the changing institutions and programs of modern welfare states. These changes are the product of external pressures on welfare states, for example because of the economic and political consequences of globalisation or individualisation, or result from the internal, political or institutional dynamics of welfare arrangements.

By studying the development of welfare state arrangements in different countries, in different institutional contexts, or by comparing developments between countries or different types of welfare states, this series hopes to enlarge the body of knowledge on the functioning and development of welfare states and their programs.

EDITORS OF THE SERIES

Gøsta Esping-Andersen, University of Pompeu Fabra, Barcelona, Spain
Anton Hemerijck, the Netherlands Scientific Council for Government
    Policy (Wetenschappelijke Raad voor het Regeringsbeleid – WRR)
Kees van Kersbergen, Free University Amsterdam, the Netherlands
Jelle Visser, University of Amsterdam, the Netherlands
Romke van der Veen, Erasmus University, Rotterdam, the Netherlands

How Welfare States Care

**Culture, Gender, and Parenting
in Europe**

Monique Kremer

AMSTERDAM UNIVERSITY PRESS

The publication of this book is made possible with a grant of the GAK-Foundation (Stichting Instituut GAK, Hilversum).

Cover illustration: Anna Ancher, *Pigen I køkkenet* (The Maid in the kitchen), 1883 + 1886, Oil on canvas, 87,7 x 68,5 cm, The Hirschsprung Collection, Copenhagen

Cover design: Jaak Crasborn BNO, Valkenburg a/d Geul
Layout: V3-Services, Baarn

ISBN 978 90 5356 975 7
NUR 754

Table of Contents

Tables

Acknowledgements

Nothing exists that does not touch upon something else
Niets bestaat dat niet iets anders aanraakt

Jeroen Brouwers, *Bezonken rood*

Once upon a time, women stayed at home when they had children. Today, the majority of European mothers work. The sociologist Arlie Hochschild (1989) has labelled this the biggest social revolution of our time. Still, uniformity is not the rule in Europe. The number of women who work and the number of hours they work vary per country. My own country, the Netherlands, is considered to be very modern in many respects but it has lagged behind when it comes to female labour market participation. Dutch mothers only started to enter the labour market in the 1990s. This is in stark contrast, for instance, to the Danish case. Danish mothers went to work in the 1960s and 1970s, and today most of them work full time. How to understand these changes and differences? And what is the role of politics and the welfare state? Is it really true that mothers in the Netherlands worked less because of a lack of state-subsidised childcare and the existence of financial compensation via tax policies? This book tries to answer questions that have preoccupied me for a long time.

The sowing. A book starts long before the first sentence. I think this one must have began in the early 1980s, when I was twelve or thirteen. When I came home from school I would find my mother waiting for me with the proverbial 'pot of tea', which has become the Dutch symbol of good motherly care. My mother only started to work when my younger sister reached the age of twelve, and often ended up in part-time, temporary, and poorly paid cleaning and home care jobs. While drinking tea, she – and my father too – urged us to have the best education possible, so we could have a good and rewarding career. And thanks to their incredible support (thank you!) we did. But I could not understand why my mother didn't work, while she clearly dreamed of a different life. She felt regret.

Later on, I asked her why she was at home with the pot of tea, she said: 'that's just what you did at the time'.

The growing. A Dutch feminist scholar once said that women start to become interested in emancipation not because of their jealousy or irritation at men, but because of the lives of their mothers. Indeed, for me, my mother's life puzzled me and her answer didn't satisfy me. When I went to school at Utrecht University, I quickly became interested in issues of gender, citizenship, and social policy. Luckily I encountered Trudie Knijn and later on Peter van Lieshout, so I could start the research project that has now become this book. I am grateful I met Trudie. She has played a crucial role in my personal and professional life. She is definitely my teacher in all the positive meanings of the word and I believe she will always be. Peter van Lieshout gave me a great sense of confidence and always posed pointed questions. Thank you both.

The flourishing. This is the best period: the time you collect data, ideas, and useless thoughts, especially when it is abroad. It is the period in which a thousand flowers bloom. I talked to many people in Belgium, Denmark, and the UK whose names cannot be mentioned here, as there are too many, although I still remember each and every one. Some scholars have been particularly important to me, especially because of their hospitality and guidance while I carried out my research in their countries. Special thanks go to Bea Cantillon, Ive Marx, Lieve de Lathouwer, Tine Rostgaard, Jon Kvist, Niels Plough, Hans Hansen, Finn Kenneth Hansen, Henning Hansen, Anette Borchorst, Birte Siim, Helga Moos, Peter Abrahamson, Jane Millar, Ruth Lister, Clare Ungerson, Jane Lewis, Wilf Nicoll.

The harvesting. This is mentally and physically the toughest period, as you have to make choices and restrict yourself to telling only one story. Discovery is generally much more joyful than discipline, at least for me. Many people supported and touched me in different ways. I had people who hiked with me (Els Aarts, Egbert Rentema, Arjan Schuiling, Paul Weemaes), people who helped me to forget about this book (Miriam Schram, Suzanne Tan, Sandra Kremer), and people who laughed and cried with me (Berend Jonker). There were also many nice people who worked with me (at the Netherlands Institute of Care and Welfare, the Department of General Social Sciences, and the Scientific Council for Government Policy), and people with whom I had interesting academic discussions (the PhD group 'TGV' and the Amsterdam/Utrecht reading group). There were also people with whom I could discuss all other social issues that are not in this book (Jelle van der Meer and the editors of TSS/ Journal of Social Issues, especially Loes Verplanke). Other people were crucial in the last months, when I knew I could do better but had no words and thoughts left. Anton Hemerijck, whose apt comments certainly improved some chapters; and Evelien Tonkens, who with a mixture of pep talk, funny metaphors, and convincing criticism pointed how to get to the end.

My love Shervin Nekuee has big shoulders, a golden heart, and a sharp tongue. In fact, he gave the most useful comments on this book without having read one single word. I hope it will stay that way, and that we talk less about policy and more about poetry. Sheyda, the sun in our life, has not noticed my preoccupation with this book. That makes me just as proud as finishing it. His arrival may have postponed the final harvesting but it certainly improved the quality. I became more convinced about what I had already discovered before he came: mothers do not work more hours per se when child care is cheap and available, or work less when they are financially compensated. They want to work when they have the feeling their children are well-cared for when they are not there.

When my own mother had young children, the moral message of the Dutch welfare state was: women's employment would harm children. The dominant ideal of care was full-time mothering. So, that is why staying at home is 'just what you did at that time'. Now, 25 years later, social policy is based on the ideal of parental sharing. Children are cared for well when both parents work and care part time. Indeed, at home we try to do it 'the Dutch way'. I am happy for myself, Shervin, Sheyda, and especially my parents that a social and cultural revolution has taken place.

1 Introduction: Working Women and the Question of Care and Culture in Europe

European governments are bidding farewell to the once-popular ideal of the male breadwinner model. Except for Scandinavia, this model has sat firmly in the welfare state saddle since the Second World War. But in the new millennium, the governments of Europe no longer expect women to be full-time mothers. In Europe, the icon of the happy housewife is fading. The European Union (EU) welfare states fully committed themselves to working women as part of the 2000 Lisbon Strategy, the EU's framework for action. If more women worked, this would contribute to the European aspirations of becoming 'the most competitive and dynamic knowledge-based economy in the world', while at the same time having 'sustainable, active and dynamic welfare states'. This has been underlined by the Kok Report, which assessed the 2000 Lisbon strategy. The report states that if Europe wants to show its social face, the focus should be on economic growth and employment (European Communities 2004).

The Lisbon targets – female employment rates of 60 percent by 2010 – have not been reached. In 2003, the European average was 55 percent, but there is time left. More striking are the huge changes and large cross-national differences. Denmark and Sweden already surpassed the Lisbon criteria in the 1970s, and today more than 70 percent of the women in these countries work. In the UK and the Netherlands the 'score' is around 65 percent, although British mothers participate much less when they have young children (ages 0-2), namely 52 percent. Germany (59 percent), France (57 percent) and Belgium (52 percent), and especially Italy (43 percent) and Spain (46 percent) are at the lower end of women's participation in paid employment. Part-time and full-time rates of employment also vary substantially. The revolutionary growth in women's employment in the Netherlands is mainly due to part-time work, as Dutch women rarely work full time (European Communities 2004; Eurostat 2005).

In 'Why We Need a New Welfare State', originally written for the Belgian presidency of the European Union, Esping-Andersen et al. (2002)

suggest how to raise women's employment rates. A new welfare architecture should bid farewell to the male breadwinner model and support women to work. 'In many countries women constitute a massive untapped labour reserve that can help narrow future age dependency rates and reduce associated financial pressures' (ibid., 94), and working mothers are 'the single most effective bulwark against child poverty' (ibid., 9-10). At the same time, as birth rates are low, European women need to be encouraged to deliver more babies. Gender equality policies should therefore not simply be seen as a concession to women's claims, the authors argue, supporting working women is a social investment. A new welfare state should emphasise affordable childcare services and good maternity and parental leave schemes. When the welfare state supports mothers, they will go out and get a job.

Seeing social policy as the cause of women's employment patterns has become the dominant paradigm among scholars and policymakers. Especially popular is what can be called the 'comparative welfare regime approach'. Esping-Andersen (1990, 1998, 2002) is indeed a well-known representative of this stream, as are Lewis (1992a, 1993, 1997b, 1998), Sainsbury (1996, 1999), O'Connor et al. (1999), and Daly and Rake (2003). The basic idea is that welfare states are not the same; their design differs across Europe. This is due to variety in the strength of social movements (working class and women) as well as historical, institutional legacies. Such differences in social policies also lead to different outcomes. In short, the composition of welfare states determines women's employment patterns.

It is also common to cluster welfare states in three 'models' or 'welfare regimes' along specific explanatory dimensions. Well-known are Esping-Andersen's (1990, 1999, 2002) 'three worlds of welfare' and Lewis' gender models (1992). Each regime or model has specific consequences for women, yet the explanatory logic is often as follows: the more available and affordable childcare services are, the more mothers work. The more work disincentives in taxation and social security, the less mothers work. The underlying notion is that women really want to work, but they can only do so when the social policy barriers are removed.

The main empirical concern of this book is whether this logic is true. Does the variety in welfare states' design really cause such a European patchwork of women's employment rates? In other words, to what extent and how are European diversity *and changes* in work rates shaped by different social policies? Have Danish women, for instance, started to work more because the state offers affordable and sufficient childcare services? And are Belgian women more likely to stay at home due to a lack of these facilities, or because of tax and benefit disincentives? Why do women's employment patterns change more in some countries than in others? Will all European countries meet the Lisbon targets if they have 'a new welfare state'?

To answer these questions, the study of welfare states will be linked to the concepts of care and culture. That is the main theoretical contribution of this book.

The Caring Dimension of Welfare States

The first contribution of this book is to link care to social policy. If we analyse how welfare states care, we may understand women and gender relations better (Anttonen and Sipilä 1996; Lewis 1997a; Knijn and Kremer 1997; Daly and Lewis; 1998; Jenson and Sineau 2001; Daly 2002; Daly and Rake 2003; Anttonen et al. 2003; Bettio and Plantenga 2004). Care in this book, as will be introduced in chapter 2, is defined as the provision of daily, social, psychological, emotional, and physical attention for people. This can be given paid or unpaid, informally or professionally, and within the state, market, or families. For women, care is crucial. It is not only an activity, it also shapes their identity. Women's decisions, especially when they concern work, are often made in the context of care. In other words, without looking through the lens of care it may be hard to understand women's work patterns.

Focusing on care has a different departure point than the exclusive focus on paid work. Care also urges us to rethink the normative assumptions about what a citizen is or should be. The concept of citizenship has become a popular yardstick by which to judge social policy outcomes, both in the political and the academic world (Marshall 1950; Esping-Andersen 1990; Hobson and Lister 2002). Traditionally, a person is seen as a full citizen when he is in paid work. Of course, women's employment is important – as Lisbon, Kok, and Esping-Andersen also stress – but not only in a functionalist, instrumental way aimed at saving the economy or the welfare state. Many women today desire to continue working even when they become mothers. Becoming a full-time mother is no longer a cultural given. This has not only changed the structure of labour markets but also the balance of power within families as women became earners too. The American sociologist Hochschild (1989) argues that women are involved in the biggest social and cultural revolution of our time.

But Hochschild also spoke about the 'stalled revolution': what happens to caring when mothers enter the labour market? During the industrial revolution, men moved out of their houses and lands into factories, shops, and offices while women moved inside the home. This became the dominant division of labour. But now that women are moving outside the home, men do not behave accordingly and move inside. As a result, many women now have two jobs: one outside the home and another one, when they come back, in the home, not only in the US, but even in Scandinavia (Borchorst and Siim 1987). To put it mildly, this is not the gender equality women wanted. Rather than a primary focus on women's participation in work, men's participation in care is important too. In that sense, care – surprisingly – also brings men into this book. What are European men doing? Can we see variety in men's participation in care across Europe?

Care is not just a matter of equal distribution: it is also an important value in people's lives. Both men and women like to give care and feel it is part of living the life of a social, human being. Caring time gives people the possibility to relate to children, parents, neighbours, friends, and significant others. In both the Lisbon Strategy and Esping-Andersen's (2002) new Beveridge plan, care is made subordinate and instrumental to the European interest of economic growth and employment. Care is primarily seen as a hindrance for working women. But is time to care not important in its own right – also with an eye to the social future of Europe?

This book will propose how care can be included in the concept of citizenship. If T.H. Marshall (1976 or 1949), one of the founding fathers of the theory of citizenship, were still alive, he could have easily included care in the concept. The focus on paid work and having 'a modicum of economic welfare and security' (1976 or 1949: 72) was also common in his time, but he also saw citizenship as living 'the life of a civilised being, according to the standard prevailing in society' (ibid., 72). For Marshall, citizenship meant the right to participate and be a member of society. Citizenship in this new interpretation offers people the right to participate in work as well as in care. In this book, participation in work is one indicator of citizenship, participation in care another.

Taking care seriously also urges us to study welfare states more precisely and study them as 'caring states'. In Marshall's view, rights are seen as admission tickets for participation in society. This book studies three caring rights. The first is the right to give care. This can include exemptions from work obligations, as lone mothers had in the Netherlands and the UK, or the more popular parental leave schemes. These rights may reduce women's employment rates but increase their (individual) income. A second right is the category of derived rights to give care, such as the so-called male breadwinner bonuses in taxation. Breadwinners receive extra income to allow their wives to give care. Such rights have the potential to reduce women's employment rates as well as their income. A third right is the right to receive care, such as home care for elderly or childcare services. Such services may increase the employment rates of potential carers and raise their income.

Studying these care rights crosses many social policy domains. For this reason, taxation, social security, leaves, and childcare services are studied and connected in this book. Welfare states make sure in different ways that children, the frail elderly and disabled people are cared for. They can provide or subsidise care services, or compensate caregivers financially via taxation, leave schemes, or social security. Together they show how welfare states care.

The question is: what has happened the last decades to caring rights? Can we see convergence or divergence in care policies? Does caring gradually become part of citizenship in all countries, as Jenson and Sineau (2001) argue? (see also Daly 2001). At the same time, in the last two decades many welfare states were in a state of permanent austerity (Pierson 2001), and the right and duty to work have become increasingly important – more important than caring (Lister 1997; OECD 2000b; Kvist and Jæger 2004; Orloff 2006). To put it differently, T.H. Marshall writes that civil rights like freedom of speech developed in the eighteenth century. Political rights, such as the right to vote, came into being in the nineteenth century. Social rights – the 'crowning stage' of citizenship – have been struggled for in the twentieth century. Will the twenty-first century go down in the history books as the age of work or that of caring rights?

The Cultural Dimension of Welfare States

The second contribution of this book is to include a cultural dimension in the study of welfare states. The Lisbon targets seem to show that European leaders still believe that politics can influence women's decisions: social policy matters. A 'cultural approach' stresses that the impact of welfare states is heavily overestimated. In contrast to the 'comparative welfare regime approach', it is said that women's own wishes and values can best explain the diversity in Europe. A cultural approach also claims it can understand change much better. Inspired by Giddens (1991), Hakim (2000, 2003a) argues that women in Europe are now free to choose to work or to care for the first time in history. Consequently, women's employment and care patterns are a direct result of their work-life preferences. Also Pfau-Effinger (1998, 1999) stresses the importance of the interplay between gender arrangements – the work-and-care practices of men and women – and gender culture, such as norms, values, and attitudes towards work and care.

The cultural approach states that changes in women's employment cannot simply be enforced by social policies or Lisbon strategies. Changes come, so to speak, 'from below': women themselves sew the European work-and-care patchwork. In the cultural approach, women are not held back by social policy bars. If mothers do not work it is because they do not want to: they want to care. This book tries to sort out empirically what best explains the changing gendered division of labour, care, and income across European countries: women's (and men's) own values or care policies?

Four countries are studied: the UK, the Netherlands, Denmark, and Belgium. A detailed analysis is made of citizenship and the changes in the last two decades: the gender division of labour, care, and income. What is the dominant work-and-care practice in each country, and what do women and men want? The focus is on mothers and care for young children. This analysis will be confronted with the cross-national study of the origins and mechanisms of social policy in four domains: taxation, social security, leaves (chapter 5), and childcare services (chapter 6). Let me summarise the conclusions in a few sentences: it is not true that the more abundant or cheaper childcare services are, the more mothers will work. Or that the more work incentives in taxation, the more women will work. But neither it is true that women (or men) behave according to their own, individual wishes and preferences. There is no straightforward, clear-cut relationship between womens' and mens' participation in work and care in welfare states, nor with womens' and mens' values and preferences. In other words, both approaches – the comparative welfare regime as well as the cultural – cannot be empirically grounded. Diversity in Europe cannot be explained sufficiently by either theory.

This book argues that what may help explain European diversity and change is when culture is seen as a dimension of welfare states (Rothstein 1998; Chamberlayne 1999; Clarke 2004; Van Oorschot 2003). While the cultural approach downplays social policy too much, social policy studies have little tradition of including culture in their analyses? To connect both, I propose using the concept of 'ideals of care'.

Ideals of Care

When I go to work, I feel guilty, is the title of a much-sold advice book for working mothers (Gilliband and Mosley 1998). According to the subtitle, this is a self-help book 'for sanity and survival', advising mothers on how to say goodbye at the kindergarten gates. This book was popular in the UK and has also been translated into Dutch. It points out that mothers' move into the economy is related to discussions around care. It also indicates that mothers do not feel the transition to employment has been paved with roses: their decision to work is surrounded by morality issues.

For mothers, to work or to care is a moral predicament. The feeling that their child is well cared for is a condition for being at ease at work. When mothers decide about work, they do not simply make a cost-benefit analysis – how expensive is childcare or what are my tax returns – as the comparative welfare regime approach tends to assume (Pfau-Effinger 1998; Duncan and Edwards 1999; Duncan et al. 2004; Lewis 2001). Their decision-making is based on 'a logic of appropriateness' (March and Olsen 1989). Appropriate childcare that fits parents' notion of what good care is helps working women. An ideal of care, as Hochschild (1995, 2003) points out, is an image of what is considered good childcare. In my view, ideals of care are moral images that are shaped culturally.

In each of the countries covered by this study, mothers entered the labour market in large numbers in different points in the period of time covered by this study but in each period and in each country mothers' interests were often placed against the interest of the child in the public debate. After the full-time motherhood ideal, new care ideals arose and old ones were revived. These new ideals softened the moral clash between working mothers and childrens' interests. In this study, four 'new' ideals, which came after the care ideal of the full-time mother, are distinguished: intergenerational care, surrogate mothers, parental sharing, and professional care. This book attempts to show that each welfare state promotes different ideals of care. In Dutch social policy, for instance, the ideal of parental sharing is dominant; in Denmark the ideal of professional care.

The concept of ideals of care may be useful on two levels. First, ideals of care may help us understand the origins and development of caring policies: they reveal why some policies are in place in one welfare state while others are not. Why do Denmark and Flanders have such high rates of state-subsidised childcare services? Secondly, ideals of care may help understand different policy outcomes, i.e., European variety in gendered work-and-care patterns. The Danish welfare state promotes the ideal of professional care. This means the belief that it is better for children to be socialised together, under the supervision of highly educated professionals, than to stay at home 'alone' with their mother. Such a care ideal may be the best guilt-reduction strategy for working mothers. Welfare states are often examined as structures of financial (dis)incentives – as if a mother was just a *homo economicus*. Studying ideals of care will help to examine welfare states as 'moral agents' or 'cultural catalysts'.

In short, this book will attempt to understand European differences and changes in women's work patterns and to link the study of social policy with two perspectives: care and culture. Both perspectives will meet in the concept of 'ideals of care'. Will such a study of ideals of care contribute to our understanding of why women across Europe are so different?

The Empirical Study

Studying the origins and impact of welfare states on work and care patterns requires a comparison, preferably across time and across countries. This book builds on a detailed country-by-country analysis of four welfare states – the UK, the Netherlands, Belgium, and Denmark during the 1980-2000 period, although it is sometimes necessary to go back further in history or forward to the present. This period is particularly interesting as welfare states were under permanent austerity and caring policies under a turbulent star (Lewis 1998; Daly 2002). At the same time, women's employment rates increased but still showed diversity.

The specific countries were chosen because especially mothers' employment patterns varied significantly among them. In the mid-1990s, Denmark had the highest employment rate fors of mothers, followed by Belgium, the Netherlands, and UK respectively. More recently, the Netherlands surpassed Belgium. In Denmark and Belgium mothers were more likely to work full time, while in the UK and especially in the Netherlands working mothers held predominantly part-time employment. In Belgium, mothers now increasingly work part time (ECNC 1996; Eurostat 2002; Eurostat 2005).

The four countries were also selected because they are representative of the dominant theoretical welfare state models. These models are clustered by specific explanatory policy mechanisms. Since generalisation power for case studies is relatively weak, using prototypes improves it: the mechanisms found may also apply to the cluster as a whole (Ragin 1987; Guy Peters 1998). Thus in Esping-Andersen's (1990, 1999) welfare regime approach, the UK tends towards the so-called liberal regime while

Denmark is seen as typically social democratic. Belgium and the Netherlands are examples of Christian democratic regimes (appendix I gives an overview of governments in the four countries between 1980-2000). In Lewis' gender models (1992), two countries represent the male breadwinner model: the UK and the Netherlands. Belgium stands for the modified male breadwinner model, meaning that both routes – to work and to stay at home – are in place, while Denmark can be seen as a weak male breadwinner model. This selection of countries offers us the opportunity to compare welfare states 'across families' and 'within families'.

It is important to note the specific situation of Belgium. In 1980, a crucial law made Belgium's three regions – Flanders, Walloon, and Brussels – responsible for 'personal matters' such as childcare and services for the elderly. This means that in this book sometimes Belgium is referred to, for instance when it concerns tax policy or social security, which are national responsibilities, and sometimes I refer to Flanders, when it concerns childcare services. I focus on this region because it can be fruitfully compared with the Netherlands, as it has a shared past and a shared language. For the UK, which is comprised of England, Northern Ireland, Wales, and Scotland, a similar story holds. When it concerns childcare services the focus is on England.

In cross-national studies one classic problem needs specific attention, the 'comparability problem': are we really sure that we are comparing similar things? (Guy Peters 1998). For this reason, it is important to use contextualised knowledge (Daly 2000) as well as the strategy of 'functional equivalences' (Dogan and Pelassy 1990). Functionalists have emphasised that different structures may perform the same function. Conversely, the same structure may perform several different functions. In one welfare state women may be encouraged to stay at home via taxation, whereas in another social security functions as such. In one country children are cared for by childcare services when parents are at work, whereas in another grandmothers care. This study therefore has a broad scope and is very detailed at the same time: it studies how welfare states care and how children are cared for.

Keeping this in mind, the first set of sources are cross-national statistics and studies, preferably those that have attempted to make data comparable (e.g., Organisation for Economic Co-operation and Development (OECD) and EU studies). Second, four-month stays in each country facilitated the collection of appropriate national data, such as studies of the origins and evaluations of social policies, with specific attention for social policy mechanisms. These stays helped me to gain contextualised knowledge. I nevertheless encountered many national-specific blind spots, often the inverse mirror of the dominant policy ideals. (In Denmark, for example, little is known about the male breadwinner bonus in taxation, while childcare services are studied abundantly.) More than 70 interviews were carried out with national experts to fill in these national gaps (appendix II). These interviews gave me the additional opportunity to verify or falsify my Dutch-biased interpretations of their welfare states.

Outline of the Book

Chapters 2 and 3 contain the theoretical and analytical framework of the study. In chapter 2, 'Cinderella and Snow White are Fairy Tales', care is linked to citizenship. I will show that care is often portrayed one-dimensionally and will try to offer a more adequate definition of care. Such interpretation of care is easily linked to citizenship, the dominant yardstick in welfare state research to measure outcomes. I will argue that if T.H. Marshall, one of the theorists of citizenship, were still alive he would have included care rights as part of social rights in a modernised conception of citizenship. Chapter 3, 'Policy or Culture?', outlays the two dominant approaches that help explain European diversity in women's work: the 'comparative welfare regime approach' and the 'cultural approach'. How do these theories explain variation? Special interest is given to the image of human decision-making that presuppose these theories: the *homo economicus* and the 'preference person'.

The next chapters are devoted to the empirical analysis of caring states and citizenship. Chapter 4 describes gendered employment, care and income patterns in Belgium, the UK, Denmark, and the Netherlands. I am especially concerned with (lone) mothers and the practice of (and wishes for) part-time work. These indicators of citizenship will be juxtaposed with caring policies in the four countries. Chapter 5 is devoted to the right to give care, financial compensations for care-giving, such as tax and social security arrangements, and leave schemes. What are the origins and consequences of these care-giving rights? Chapter 6 deals with the right to receive care: the state of childcare services. What are the origins and outcomes of childcare policy in these four countries? Together, these two chapters describe the cross-national history and impact of the right to give and receive care in the period between 1980 and 2000. These chapters show that there is no clear-cut relationship between welfare states and work-and-care participation of both men and women. Nor are womens' and mens' behaviour in line with their values when it comes to work and care. The existing theories fall short. Additionally, these chapters indicate a change of paradigm: the ideal of full-time mother care is no longer dominant practice.

Chapters 7 and 8 show which ideals of care have replaced the traditional one, why, and what the consequences are. Chapter 7, 'After full-time mother care', focuses on policy change. This chapter examines which new ideals have become dominant in public policy and how they originated. Attention is given to the women's movement – in its broadest sense – as its ideals of care have had an important impact. Chapter 8, 'How welfare states work', studies the practice and consequences of care ideals. It shows that culturally-shaped moral care ideals are more adequate for understanding women's decision-making in work-and-care than the images of human behaviour in the other two approaches (referred to in chapter 3). Care ideals can help to explain the European differences in women's employment and the differences between women of different countries.

2   Cinderella and Snow White Are Fairy Tales: Linking Care and Citizenship

The story of welfare states is also the story of citizenship. In general terms, citizenship describes the relationship between the individual and the state, but in welfare state theories it often acts as a yardstick by which progress can be measured. T.H. Marshall (1976 or 1950: 29), one of the concept's formative fathers, sees citizenship as 'an image of an ideal citizenship against which achievements can be measured and towards which aspirations can be directed'. Any interpretation of the concept is thus per definition value-led: it contains a normative definition of what a full citizen is, and the rights and duties that belong to citizenship.

A citizen, however, is often assumed to be a 'he'. The exclusion of women has been firmly imprinted within the historical template of citizenship. The question of this book is, then, how to refashion the yardstick so that it is not based on the lives and aspirations of only the male half of society (Hobson and Lister 2002).

This chapter will put forward how the concept of care can help to include women in the concept of citizenship. According to Daly and Lewis (1998: 4), 'care is one of the truly original concepts to have emerged from feminist scholarship'. Putting the focus on care brings gender into the study of welfare states. When care is linked to the social and political analyses of welfare states, new insights may be produced into the gendered outcomes of welfare states. In other words, studying caring states may contribute to an understanding of the citizenship status of care receivers – such as the elderly, children, or disabled people – as well as caregivers, who are primarily women. The main objective of this book however is to understand the latter, i.e., the citizenship status of (potential) caregivers.

This chapter will present a new yardstick with which to empirically measure citizenship. It is based on a reinterpretation of Marshall's legacy and shows how care rights can be integrated into his notion of citizenship. In other words, if Marshall were still alive, how would he integrate care into his conception of citizenship? Before discussing citizenship, the next sections are devoted to the question of how important care is and how to describe and define it.

What is Care?

At least at one moment during their lives, every person is likely to be in need of care. No matter how much money one earns, no matter how 'independently' one can live from family and friends, everyone has been a child in the past, has been ill, and may need help when they are elderly. The need for care is inevitable. In practice, nobody can be left to his own devices all of the time. Care, in this sense, can be seen as a process of care receiving, but it is also a process of caregiving (Tronto 1993).

Caregiving is a very gendered practice and gender is also about caring. Providing care is often considered to be an activity that requires feminine qualities, and femininity is often considered to have a caring nature. Whereas women are more likely to be caregivers and men receivers, caring is not only an activity – it is also a matter of identity. Women are approached as potential caregivers, often seeing themselves as such, and their identity is constructed in relation to caring. Men's activities and identity are constructed on the basis of the opposite premise, an absence of caring. Femininity and care are thus two sides of the same coin. Gender, however, is not equal to care; gender is broader than care. Conversely, care is not the only activity and identity that shapes gender relationships, but it is nevertheless a crucial one (Finch and Groves 1983; Graham 1983; Waerness 1984; Ungerson 1987, 1990; Knijn and Kremer 1997).

Care is also a multidimensional concept. Thomas (1993) distinguishes many dimensions to it: the identity of the provider and the recipient of care, the relationship between the two, the social content of care, the economic character of the relationship and of the labour involved, and the social domain and institutional setting within which care is provided. From a gender perspective it is impossible to separate the informal from the formal practice of caring (Ungerson 1990), therefore I use the following description: care is the provision of daily, socio-psychological, emotional, and physical attention to people. This can be provided by paid or unpaid work, on the basis of an agreement or voluntarily, and it can also be given professionally or on the basis of moral obligation. Caring can be done for different human beings: the frail elderly, children, and people with a handicap (Knijn and Kremer 1997).

Such a broad notion of care has several advantages, as it includes paid and unpaid labour across the politically decided boundaries of market, state, and family. This definition links British scholarship, which has had a strong focus on informal care and care for the elderly (e.g., Finch and Groves 1983; Ungerson 1987), with Scandinavian scholarship, which stresses the importance of public care (Waerness 1984; Borchorst and Siim 1987), and new European forms of marketised care (Lewis 1998). What they share is that the work of caring, paid and unpaid, is very unequally shared between men and women, and it is also undervalued (Daly and Lewis 1998).

Snow White and Cinderella

A broad definition of care goes beyond the highly normative debate on what care is about. In the political and academic debates on care, caregivers are often one-dimensionally portrayed as either Cinderella's or Snow Whites. This is problematic, as the debate on care should not be guided by fairy tales.

In the story of Cinderella, care is pictured as a burden, it is hard work. Cinderella sweeps the floor, does the laundry: caring means sweating. Poor Cinderella gets little recognition for her heavy burden: on the contrary, the caring work makes her dirty and ugly. She obviously does not provide this care of her own free will: she is forced to do so by her stepfamily. The only way she gets relief is by being saved by a prince, so she can escape from her caring duties. Snow White, on the other hand, loves caring for her little dwarfs. Her caregiving is not a job but a joy. Never portrayed on her knees sweeping the floor, she hangs out the wash in sunny weather while singing and whistling. In the image of Snow White, caring is more an attitude than an activity. She receives a lot of gratitude for her caring – the dwarfs caress and adore her. Caring makes Snow White beautiful, and it is because of her caregiving nature that a young prince falls in love with her. With tears in her eyes, she has to say goodbye to her care receivers. But she lives happily ever after and gives birth to a couple of children so she can continue caring.

Both images of care contain ideas about the content of care, the motivation to care, the relationship between gender and care, the qualification of caring, the role of the state, the role of care in family relationships, and an image of the care receiver. They are summarised in the table below.

Table 2.1   Models of care

Cinderella	Snow White
Burden/trouble	Joy/pleasure
Compulsory altruism	Free will/reciprocal relationships
Labour	Moral attitude
Oppression of women	Gift of women to society
Money-saver for the state	Protection against the state
Informal care is worse than formal care	Informal care is better than formal care
Economic value	Moral value
Disruption of family relations	Strengthening family relations
Negative image of care receiver	Positive image of care receiver

The fairy tales of Cinderella and Snow White have become real, both in political debates in various countries and in academic discussions. The social democratic welfare states, notably Sweden, Denmark, and Finland, are more likely to depart from the notion of Cinderella (see Ungerson 1990). Because of feminist intervention, strong labour movements, and a strong work ethic, caring is more likely to be considered work. When it is performed informally within the family, caring can become a real burden for women as well as for family relationships, as an excess of it is disruptive to individual lives. Women should therefore be relieved from the oppressive load of care, as it is compulsory and consequently not a free choice. In socialist-feminist language, the 'patriarchal societal structures' are Cinderella's stepfamily. Since caring resembles paid work, the solution to the problem of care is relatively simple: society has to value caring as such. Caregiving needs a wage, preferably paid by the state, Cinderella's prince. In the 'people's home' – as the Scandinavians see their state – professional care is warm.

Fairy tales about care are not only depicted in the political arena, academic contributions also contain similar stories. The Cinderella notion of care is particularly visible in the economic approach to welfare states, especially in the feminist and Marxist traditions, and can still be found in comparative welfare regime theories. Caring is then labelled as 'unpaid work', which immediately puts the focus on the socio-economic loss of those who care. These studies show that women would win economically and career-wise if they had no burden of care, and discuss care in terms of 'the cost of caring' (Joshi 1992), 'the cost of familyhood' (Esping-Andersen 1999) and 'child penalties' (Meyers et al. 1999). Liberation from care would give women the right to work and the right to economic independence. The representatives of this Cinderella notion focus exclusively on the economic aspects of caring and cannot imagine that caring can also be a choice.

The fairytale of Snow White is more likely to be told in Christian democratic and liberal welfare states. In the Netherlands in the 1980s, the Christian democratic answer to the crisis of the welfare state was the introduction of the concept of the 'caring society'. If people cared more for each other, this would benefit social cohesion. Mutual care is not only desirable, it is a citizen's virtue, a moral attitude – caring is not perceived as an economic activity. This caring society paradigm is similar to the British policy of 'community care'. Although the concept has existed for more than fifty years, during the Conservative Thatcher regime 'care in the community' changed into 'care by the community' (Finch 1990). This social philosophy of Snow White argues that women's caring is a credit to society. Conceptions of 'a caring society' and 'community care' stress that informal care is much better – warmer – than care by the cold state. A family is a 'haven on earth', which protects the individual from the careless state.

In the academic debate, Snow White is often implicit in the writings of communitarians and scholars concerned about morality (e.g., Adriaansens and Zijderveld 1981; Wolfe 1989; Etzioni 1993). For these scholars, Scandinavia is a living nightmare. A state that cares too much is a careless state, as it destroys the fabric of society. The American political scientist Wolfe, who studied the Danish welfare state, warns against 'public families'. He writes (1989: 142): 'A people's home suggests that the caring which characterizes the intimate sector ought also to characterize the public sector ... But the term raises as well the opposite possibility: if commitments in the home weaken, so will commitments to the people.' Wolfe warns against the social democratic welfare state, which he sees as the strongest 'moral state' in the world. If the state takes over care responsibilities, people have no moral energy left to care for each other. The most prominent communitarianist Etzioni (1993: 60) even distrusts care outside the family: 'We must acknowledge that as a matter of social policy (as distinct from some individual situations) we have made a mistake in assuming that strangers can be entrusted with the effective personality formation of infants and toddlers.' Historically, these scholars are neither concerned about Snow White's socio-economic situation nor with the gendered character of moral obligations to care. Today, however, Snow White storytellers – including Etzioni – may argue for a moral campaign to demand fathers to care too. The more care, the more morality.

For informal caregivers, caring can surely resemble work sometimes, and it can be a heavy load. Professionalizing care thus becomes very important. For others, caring is indeed a choice; caring full-time for their children or frail parents makes them happy. Sometimes caring is a joy, sometimes a burden. It can resemble paid labour – or not. It can be driven by moral pressure – or not. Caring can pull people out of the labour market, yet sometimes people happily combine paid employment with family life. State care can be warm while at home it can be cold, but it can equally be the other way around. Caring is not a heavy load or a joyful activity per se, warm or cold; it depends on the relationship between caregiver and care receiver, the conditions under which care is given, and whose choice it is. A framework to study caring states should therefore go beyond a priori Cinderella and Snow White notions of care.

The next sections will connect two issues that are not often linked: care and citizenship. If caring is so important, how can it be written into the concept of citizenship?

Rethinking Independence and Participation

When Marshall wrote his famous essay on citizenship, just after the Second World War, rights related to caring were not included; he spoke about the rights to work, housing, and social security. Like most of his contemporaries, he assumed that women would take responsibility for caring and be dependent on their husbands. Participation in the family was not questioned and considered as irrelevant. This is however a falsification of the past, as there had been public intervention into what is known as the 'private sphere' long before that. In the early twentieth century, for instance, rights connected to motherhood, such as maternity cash benefits, were developed all over Europe (Bock and Tane 1991).

In Marshall's essay, labour market participation was the entrance ticket to full citizenship. He saw it as a status vis-à-vis the (labour) market. As in most liberal theory, care was considered as part of the private domain and therefore irrelevant to the public sphere as well as public politics and the notion of citizenship (Pateman 1989; Tronto 1993; Lister 1997). The spotlight on care, however, pulls the so-called 'private domain' into the discussion of citizenship. Or, as Leira (1990: 208) has put it: 'What is lacking is a concept of citizenship which recognises the importance of care to society.' Linking care to politics and policies can yield more insight into gender relations within welfare states. At the same time, looking through the lens of care may also help to understand how the welfare state itself is developing. For this reason, nowadays many scholars propose placing care at the heart of a gendered analysis of citizenship and welfare states (Leira 1990, 1992, 2002; Anttonen and Sippilä 1996; Lewis 1997a; Knijn and Kremer 1997; Daly and Lewis 1998; Daly 2002; Jenson 1997; Jenson and Sineau 2001; Daly and Rake 2003; Bettio and Plantenga 2004).

Looking at citizenship through the lens of care has two merits. It helps us redefine the notion of participation, the topic of the next section, and it helps us rethink the concept of independence, which is so crucial to the citizenship debate. This will be discussed first.

Interdependencies

Citizenship theories often argue that an independent status is necessary to express political rights. The philosopher James (1992) shows that in liberal theory conditions for citizenship are not only physical and emotional, but also economic. Citizens need to speak freely 'in their own voice', free from bodily violation or the threat of it. It is important to take emotional distance to think and judge. Economic independence is crucial because citizens are not in the position to express their political views if by doing so they run the risk of losing the means to provide for themselves or their dependants. In this approach, independence is a condition for democratic citizenship.

Economic dependence can also trap women in a vicious circle within the family: their bargaining power in the family is low; they do not have the leverage to negotiate that caring is shared equally. At the same time, when their care load is high, their potential earnings and income in the labour market will be affected. Hobson (1990) describes this trap by using Hirschman's framework. The more dependent a person is, the less exit possibilities she has, the less of a voice. If a woman has a better job and brings more money into the family, she can more easily demand that her husband do the dishes or take parental leave. Conversely, the more a woman is responsible for the house and children, the more difficulties she will have in finding a good, well-paid job.

Independence, particularly economic independence, is thus considered to be crucial for citizenship (e.g., Lister, 1997; Daly 2000). Citizenship rights, as Lister (1990: 460) argues, need to be individual rights, and can never be family rights. Family-based citizenship rights are a contradiction in terms. 'It is not good enough that rights come to women second hand, mediated by their male partners, so that in practice, they cease to be rights at all.' Citizenship rights given to the family via the male breadwinner make women dependent and even disempower them.

Stressing the importance of independence and individualisation has had an important function. It was a wake-up call for those who fused the interests of families and individuals. The concept and practice of care, however, reminds us that we should not depart from the image of completely independent individualised people without ties. The problem with citizenship is that men have always been constructed as independent beings and citizens while women have been constructed as dependants. But men are of course also dependent on women's caregiving. Recognising the dependence of all human beings is one step forward in recognising women's activities. The keyword should not be independence, but recognising interdependencies (Pateman 1989; Fraser and Gordon 1994; Knijn and Kremer 1997; Sevenhuysen 1998).

An interesting empirical example of such an approach is provided by Sørensen (2001). She shows that the increase of women's economic independence in various countries actually increases the interdependence within the family, arguing that where women gained economic independence men also become more dependent on women's earnings for maintaining a satisfactory standard of living. They share more equally in the financial risks associated with the loss of one income due to the breakdown of marriage. This suggests that as a society moves towards more earnings equality between spouses, both husband and wife will gain 'some financial independence', yet at the same time will become quite dependent on each other. More independence for women, claims Sørensen, may not undermine interdependence between spouses but rather strengthen it. The study of care thus entails different shades of dependencies.

Moreover, the concept of care offers us a tool to study these dependencies within families. Care also puts the spotlight on informal relations between generations. A good example is provided by Millar and Warman (1996), who studied family obligations in Europe. They distinguish a category of welfare states in which family obligations are based on the extended family (Greece, Italy, Portugal, and Spain); a category based on the nuclear family, (Austria, Belgium, France, Ireland, Luxembourg, the Netherlands, and the UK); and Nordic countries, which have minimal formal family obligations (Denmark, Finland, Norway, and Sweden). An even more illuminating alternative would be to distinguish within the nuclear family and to study partner dependencies, dependencies between children and their old and frail parents, and dependencies between parents and their young children.

Such studies of horizontal and vertical dependencies are profound and come closer to reality than those based on a simple and unrealistic notion of independence.

Participation

The second merit of looking at citizenship through the lens of care is that it contributes to notions of participation. It is impossible to rethink citizenship without acknowledging the so-called Wollstonecraft dilemma, described by Pateman (1989) and modernised by Lister, who puts it like this (Lister 1997: 178):

> We are on the one hand torn between wanting to validate and support, through some form of income maintenance provisions, the caring work for which women still take the main responsibility in the private sphere and on the other hand, we want to liberate them from this responsibility so that they can achieve economic and political autonomy in the public sphere.

The main dilemma is, then, should women become citizen-workers, thereby achieving the corresponding rights and duties, or should the status of citizen-carer be upgraded so as to entitle women to full citizenship rights on the basis of caring?

When women behave just like men and take up paid employment, this may indeed give them full citizenship status. But acting like men may cause more problems than it solves. This is shown in very different ways in Scandinavia and the United States. When women work just as much as men, they still have more responsibilities at home. Even the Scandinavian welfare state cannot completely socialise social reproduction; individual management and responsibility in the provision of everyday care is still important (Leira 1993, 2001). This means that women have double work shifts (Borchorst and Siim 1987; Hochschild 1989). In the United States, where state intervention is lacking, this may also lead to a corrosion of care, as children do not get the care they need (Hochschild 2003). Besides, in this model, women have been integrated into a labour market that is structured by the male norm: working conditions and hours are related to male working patterns. At the same time, their wages are much lower, due to gender segregation in the labour market

The route to valorise caring and to pay for caregiving is equally problematic, as it has the tendency to capture women in the private domain so that they have less time and spirit to join the labour market or the political domain. This is not only problematic because individual women will lock themselves in, but also because caring will keep being ascribed to women. In addition, economic dependence seems to be an inevitable consequence of caring. When payments for caring exist, they are usually in the less generous league of benefits; payments based on employment are always more generous (Daly and Lewis 1998).

According to Lister, the Wollstonecraft dilemma is a creative one. The challenge is to go beyond the Wollstonecraft dilemma and acknowledge the importance of caring without downplaying the importance of work and income. One way of doing so is to go back to Marshall's notion of participation, which is central to citizenship.

Participation in Three Spheres

Marshall (1976: 72) has defined the social dimension of citizenship as 'the whole range from the right to a modicum of economic welfare and security to share to the full in the social heritage and to live the life of a civilised being, according to the standard prevailing in society.' This not only points to specific rights of social security, education, and housing but also to the right of participation. He sees social rights as admission tickets for membership and participation in society. Citizenship rights are rights of participation. Or as Barbalet (1988: 67) writes: 'Social rights may be required for the practice of citizenship in so far as they enable such participation.' In many welfare state approaches the onus is on income guarantees, which make it possible to exit working or caring. But participation is not only a route to income, it can also be considered a right on its own.

Citizenship is then a guarantee to participate in the various spheres of society, also including participation in income (Fraser 1989). These can be summarised as the spheres of the state, the market, and families (Evers 1987; Esping-Andersen 1990; O'Connor 1999). The first sphere is the state. Various rights are attached to participation in the state. The first ones are relatively old – as old as democracy itself – namely voting and participation in political parties. Locally and nationally, citizens should have a voice in public policy. This type of participation is in fact a condition for democracy. But when the 'state' became 'the welfare state', new rights of state participation came into being. Primarily Scandinavian researchers have pointed out how citizens participate in the state as clients of state services (Hernes

1987; Siim 2000). In the UK too a 'Citizens Charter' was introduced, and in various countries a national 'ombudsman' has been institutionalised – this to increase people's voice in the service state. Also client rights have been installed : rights to complain, rights to participate in client boards, etc.

The second sphere in which citizens have the right to participate is that of the market – or more precisely, the sphere of the markets, as there are two: the market of labour and the market of goods and services (Fraser 1989). A condition of citizenship is that every human has the possibility to participate in the labour market. Women, the lower educated, the handicapped, racial or ethnic minorities: they are included if they are in paid employment , not only because paid employment offers the possibility to earn a decent income but also because it facilitates having power in family relationships and public decision-making. The right to work is important, as Orloff (1993) and Lewis (1992a) also stress, but just as in the first sphere one also needs voice, thus power in the workplace. The second market is that of goods and services. Marshall describes this as the right to a 'modicum of income': low but qualitatively good. The practical translation is a claim for sufficient income, a claim against poverty. A woman-friendly interpretation is that this right should be an individual one – a modicum of income of her own. Women also have to be involved in 'earning', as Lister (1997) puts it, because when income is granted via a partner it is no citizenship right at all.

The third sphere of participation is the sphere of the family and intimate social networks. Citizens should also have the possibility to participate in the family and broader networks. Citizenship is about being able to live the life of a human, social being; to paraphrase Marshall (1976: 72), 'to live the life of a civilised being'. Having care relationships is part of such a life. Liberals have always worried about including the private sphere in the domain of citizenship, but the sphere of the family has opened up to the domain of citizenship exclusively for care issues. In other words, people should have the capacity to have time for care. As with the other citizenship rights, its practice is already visible in European welfare states. The right to parental leave, for instance, is now in place in many welfare states (see chapter 5).

Why it is Necessary to Include Care

Citizenship, in most theories – including feminist theory – means that individuals have an equal right to participate in the sphere of the market and that of the state. The often-called 'private sphere' is seldom recognised as a separate sphere of citizenship. Participants in the private sphere are considered to be supporting the participants in the two other spheres, mainly men. For Voet (1998: 24), for instance, it is 'equal participation of men and women in private care as a precondition of equal citizenship rather than as being itself a type of equal citizenship.' For many scholars, the right to work – the right to be commodified – has been much more pivotal.

This became clear again in the proposals of Hobson (2000) and particularly Kessler Harris (2002), who plead for a new dimension to citizenship: economic citizenship. According to Kessler Harris (2002: 159), this is a new category of citizenship that supplements social rights, which 'can be measured by the possession and exercise of the privileges and opportunities necessary for men and women to achieve economic and social autonomy and independence.' Economic citizenship embraces both the right to paid work and the social rights attached to paid work. Although Kessler Harris believes that economic rights should be attached to care, all the practical solutions she gives relate to outsourcing care or sharing the care. Solving the 'problem of care' seems a prerequisite for paid employment. Here the Cinderella image of care pops up again.

There are at least three reasons why care is not just a condition for paid labour and should be valued on its own terms. First, I reiterate that care has an important value to society: all people need care at some point of their lives. As Pateman (1989) already noted, it is most paradoxical that women have a lesser citizenship status whereas what they actually contribute to welfare states is welfare itself. Recognition that care is good for society is not enough though: policies should be put in place to achieve its valorisation (Fraser 1997; Daly 2002).

Secondly, care should be valued on its own because it contributes to its degendering (Knijn and Kremer 1997). Why is such a degendering of care necessary? If care is less strongly attached to the idea of femininity, women and men are freer to decide whether they want to be involved in informal or professional caregiving. They can do what suits their personal qualities and commitments, rather than being bound by gendered norms. Besides, if men were more involved in caregiving and felt responsible for caring at home, this would also support working women and decrease their 'double shift'. Finally, if men connected themselves to care – and this is a strategic argument – care would not be undervalued as much as it is now. 'Sullerot's law' stipulates that when women enter a specific profession, its status and wages decrease. The 'reverse law of Sullerot' means that when men perform a specific task, its status will increase (Grünel 2001). It follows that once men become involved in care, caregiving will be valorised and this would also be to the benefit of many women.

Thirdly, care is important in the light of the social and economic future of Western societies. Most European welfare states are confronted with the double greying of society ('younger' seniors and the very elderly), a decreasing birth rate, and increasing female labour market activity rates. What is left is a growing and worrying care gap (van Lieshout 1994; Esping-Andersen et al. 2002). How are we going to care for the frail elderly in society? If societies do not want people being left to their own devices, caring must remain attractive for all people, women as well as men.

Citizenship is Both Work and Care

Citizenship, according to Fraser, refers to a social world in which citizens' lives integrate wage earning, caregiving, community activism, political participation, and involvement in the associational life of civil society while also leaving some time for fun (Fraser 1994: 613). In the citizenship interpretation presented here, working, caring, and earning should be available and viable options at the same time. If one possibility is lacking, citizenship is second-class.

The right to participate in all spheres means that citizens should not be captured in one sphere, be it work or care. In incorporating care, we have to also acknowledge the importance of work (Orloff 1993; Lewis 1997a). If lone mothers only have the right to give care, this must be recognized as a denial of full citizenship. They should also have the right to work, by providing good quality care for children. If people only have the right to work and are not allowed to give care, full citizenship is also denied. People are captured in the sphere of the labour market. Inclusive citizenship includes the right to paid work as well as the right to care. The question now becomes: how can welfare states guarantee such an interpretation of citizenship?

Caring Rights and Duties: How Welfare States Care

A generous handful of social rights are defined in modern welfare states: rights to social security, rights to education, and rights to healthcare. Rights with respect to care are still less pronounced, but welfare states keep expanding and they often do so in the area of care. In other words, most European welfare states are redefining their care responsibilities. The question is: how do welfare states care? Can they guarantee inclusive citizenship?

Following Knijn and Kremer (1997), the different routes of participation can be reached via two rights: the right to give care and the right to receive care. Together, these rights guarantee citizens the option to be involved in paid work, receive an income, and participate in caregiving. They also guarantee citizens participation in families and social networks as well as in the markets of labour and goods. These rights can influence gender relations: they degender caring and paid work. Although the state needs help from the market and families, it has to guarantee this participation; citizenship is a status and a practice in relationship to the state. It is the only democratic and law-enforcing institution in society (Marshall 1976; Barbalet 1988). Moreover, rights only become rights when they can be used in practice. A right to childcare laid down in law becomes a citizenship right when childcare is indeed available. Rights to care and rights to receive care constitute what can be labelled as 'caring states'.[1]

The right to receive care and to give care

This first right is the right to receive care. This right implies accessible and qualitatively good institutionalised care to meet the demands of different groups of citizens who are in need of care. Not only are home care, nursing homes, and childcare part of this dimension, but also social services such as social work and day centres for the elderly. The right to receive professional care is only enforced when the services are good and affordable so all citizens can and will want to use their rights, which cannot be demanded from the family or the market. Of course, receiving informal care from a relative, significant other, or volunteer who has the right to caring time is often a good solution for both the person in need of care and the caregiver. But the person in need of care can never enforce this right because this type of care is conditional upon the character of the relationship with the potential caregiver. In other words, the family cannot and should not guarantee this citizenship right. Neither can the market grant citizens' right to receive care, as it is inherent to market logic that citizens in need of care but unable to pay will not be granted care services. The only possibility left is good institutional care financially organised by the state, the collectivity.

The right to receive care guarantees that citizens can participate in employment and earn income. A citizen may become a professional carer, but this will reduce the time that can be spent on caring in the private domain. Perhaps more important for women than for men, it guarantees people also having the right NOT to care. This is certainly not the same as turning your back on your family. It is quite possible to have a strong relationship with the family while deciding not to provide care.

The right to give care contains the option to do this for people one cares about. Clear and increasingly popular examples of the right to have time for care are labour market-related paid parental or care leave. This enables citizens to continue labour market participation while caring at home. Also, the exemption from the obligation to work for parents and carers on welfare should be considered as a citizenship right to time to care, just as other payments for care. In this case, the right to care full time enables citizens to (temporarily) give priority to care responsibilities instead of paid work.

The right to give care means the right to participate in both caring and earning income. In practice, this right will reduce employment. This right to time for care acknowledges that care is an aspect of interdependency, as it recognises the needs and rights of the citizen as caregiver. The right to time to care is an important condition for informal caregiving, at least when it is not perceived as a moral claim and when it is not frustrating caregivers' right to make an autonomous choice not to give care. The right to time to care may be more crucial for men than for women, insofar that it can help them to legitimise taking care of their children and dependent others.

The right to give care and the right to receive care are not the only ways in which welfare states care. In order to get the full picture, it is necessary to include all care policies, including those that downplay certain aspects of citizenship and have ambivalent consequences. There are other care interventions, such as indirect 'rights' to give care. These measures give citizens the right to participate in caring without granting income. Two policy programs are crucial. First, unpaid leave and statutory regulations for part-time work. These measures make it possible to participate in care, but award no income. They are favourable towards time to care and therefore contribute to the caring dimension of citizenship. At the same time, citizens – mainly women – have to solve the dilemma of care and work at their own expense, as they do not get financial compensation.

A second set of derived 'rights' are benefits mediated via a male partner, such as male breadwinner bonuses in taxation and benefits. They allow for caregiving but do not offer direct income to carers, and often lower women's employment participation. Again, social citizenship rights are per definition individual rights. If compensation is given to male breadwinners, it may even disempower women as they become dependent on men. These indirect 'rights' should consequently be placed between quotation marks, as they do not really contribute to full citizenship.

Hobson (1994) expresses worries that in the practice of welfare states it is impossible to develop participation in both work and caregiving. Social policy tends to value one route over the other. This is an important empirical issue. To what extent are both the right to give care and the right to receive care in place in the various welfare states?

Duties

'If citizenship is invoked in the defence of rights, the corresponding duties of citizenship cannot be ignored,' writes Marshall (1976: 117). He defines the duty to pay taxes and insurance contributions. Education and military service are also compulsory. The other duties are vague, he says: 'They are included in the general obligation to live the life of a good citizen, giving such services as one can promote the welfare of the community' (ibid.). But in the liberal tradition of citizenship duties are not a condition for citizenship, argues the philosopher Dahrendorf (1988). Indeed, as Marshall (1976: 111) stresses: 'Rights are not a proper matter of bargaining.'

Many politicians and scholars have argued for some time that too much emphasis has been placed on citizenship rights instead of on obligations and duties (e.g., Mead 1986; Wolfe 1989). Others argue that today's problem is not that women feel obliged to care, but that men withdraw from their caring duties. Too often, men exercise the right NOT to care. Their right to not be engaged in unpaid work has already been exercised (Orloff 1997). Cass (1994) therefore argues that care (as work) should be a condition for citizenship. One cannot be a citizen without the willingness to participate in caregiving. People have to first fulfil their responsibilities for caregiving work. Rather than developing rights, she argues, the duty to care should be extended particularly to men.

Such an approach conflicts with the Marshallian interpretation presented in this chapter. One of the aims of proposing care rights is to give people – women, but also men – some freedom from moral pressures. People should not be captured by what Land and Rose (1983) have called 'compulsory altruism'. Besides, forced care is not positive for the caring process either, as it hinders the relationship between the caregiver and care receiver. Nobody wants to receive care that has been given under pressure, portrayed as a duty. This argument is often expressed within the disability movement: better a good professional than an informal carer who does not want to care, but feels obliged to do so (Morris 1991). Stressing the duty to care, finally, also reinforces the Cinderella image that care is a burden, one which has to be spread equally between the sexes. Presenting care as a problem of redistribution will not seduce men to care.

Some argue that Scandinavian welfare states indeed force fathers to care. For instance, in 1993 Norway was the first country to introduce a father's quota or a daddy's month as part of the national leave scheme, followed by Sweden. The scheme is set up so that if men do not take up some part of the parental leave, the family will lose this time (Bergqvist 1999; Leira 2002). These 'seduction policies' should not be seen as a duty to care though, they are a right to give care but with a specific closure. In fact, the fathers also see it as a right (Brandt and Kvande 2001).

Duties are nevertheless an important feature of citizenship, but in a very specific, contractual way. Rights should never be made conditional on vague descriptions of moral behaviour: specific duties always need to be connected to specific rights. In other words, duties should be in place, but only as a derivation of rights. In practice this can mean that if a person claims unemployment benefit, she has the duty to apply for paid work. If a citizen receives money when ill, he is obliged to do all he can to become healthy again. If a citizen uses the right to give care, for instance via parental leave, he has to give that care. Rights and duties should be linked clearly and contractually. This also means that the act of caregiving can not be a condition for the citizenship rights to vote or to receive healthcare. It is only a condition to give care when a citizen receives financial compensation for it. The duty to give care can only exist when it is linked to the right to give care.

Conclusion: Including Care in Citizenship

Those who study the outcomes of welfare states cannot refrain from developing a yardstick by which policy effects can be measured. Some scholars choose redistribution of income between families, others the position of people vis-à-vis the labour market, or the level of protection from poverty. These yardsticks are always normative: they capture what researchers believe to be crucial. In order to understand gendered relations, this chapter shows how to include care in citizenship. Care is not only crucial towards understanding women's position in society, it is also an essential activity in society – past, present, and future. Especially when looking at Marshall's legacy – with his focus on participation in the community – it is not difficult to modernise his conception of citizenship and include care.

A new yardstick has been proposed in this chapter: that of inclusive citizenship, defined as the possibility of men and women to participate in employment and care relations and to receive income at the same time. This ads to other citizenship interpretations that care rights also have to be studied (as part of social rights): the right to give care and to receive care. The right to give care, such as paid parental leave, entails participation in caring while receiving income. The right to receive care, such as state-subsidised childcare services, means the right to work, which also produces income. In addition to these rights, it is important to study the whole assortment of care policies. Important are derived 'rights' to give care, such as unpaid leave or the male breadwinner bonus in taxation or social security. These 'rights' allow citizens to participate in caregiving but without having an individual income. As a result, they may reduce rather than improve women's citizenship status as this makes women more dependent on a male breadwinner.

This book studies the caring rights of four European welfare states. To what extent can they explain gendered participation in work, care, and income across Europe? Although few studies have focused on caring states and participation in care, a long tradition exists in studying welfare states and women's work. The next chapter outlays two strands of theory that aim to explain the diversity of women's work patterns across Europe: the comparative welfare regime approach and the cultural approach. In addition, an alternative approach is presented which combines the best of both worlds and is based on the practice of caring: the ideals of care approach.

Explanations of
change & continuity.
 - socio-cultural
 - economic
 - political-legal.
Explaining -
    continuity.

3　Policy or Culture? Explaining Women's Employment Differences in Europe

Why do Danish mothers work more than their Dutch counterparts? And the Belgian more than the British? What explains gender diversity across Europe? And why are female employment rates changing? Fingers often point to welfare state policies. Their design can result in high or low female activity rates. The key question raised in this book is whether this is true, and if it is true, *how* can social policy influence women's decision-making with respect to work. More recently, a cultural approach has gained ground. It stresses that the impact of social policies should not be overestimated, as they only play a modest role in women's lives. Instead, this approach suggests that diversity of work patterns among European women can best be explained by women's own wishes, values, and preferences.

This chapter is devoted to a discussion of these two approaches. How do comparative welfare regime theories as well as cultural theories explain European diversity in women's work patterns? Important issues in describing these theories are: what is the role of the state and what are the mechanisms that make women act? Which (micro)theories of human behaviour are used to understand how or if welfare states affect women's decision to work. Another issue is how care is portrayed. Do these approaches acknowledge the importance of care in women's lives? In the last section, a new approach is presented, borrowing the best of the two theories above and derived from the empirical practice of caring. In this approach the concept of ideals of care is centrally placed. To put it shortly: the different ideals of care that are embedded in welfare states can help to explain the differences in women's citizenship in Europe.

Welfare States Matter Most: The State as a Catalyst

The first approach to try to understand women's employment patterns in Europe are comparative welfare regime theories, theories that are often inspired by the tradition of political economy. Stressing distinctive coun-

45

try-specific employment patterns in Europe, these theories argue that diversity in work and care can be explained to a large degree by the design of welfare states. People's behaviour is shaped by the constraints *and* opportunities of specific social policies.

Comparative welfare theories often study women's employment patterns as a consequence of social policy. They acknowledge that first women started to work and then welfare states acted upon care-related demands, and that some welfare states were more responsive then others (Esping-Andersen 2002; Lewis 1992a). For instance: in a cross-national study of Norway, Spain, and Italy, Leira et al. (2005) show that the mass entry of mothers into the labour market preceded generous public support for childcare. When women entered the labour market, they used informal care sources and then pushed the state to take over some of their caring responsibilities. Women's entry into the labour market started social policy reform, but at a subsequent stage, state intervention facilitated the employment of latter generations of mothers. In other words, the state is not seen as an initiator but as a catalyst for women's employment.

Comparative welfare state regimes theories stress that diversity of employment patterns is shaped by diversity of welfare states. This dates back to Esping-Andersen's groundbreaking work *The Three Worlds of Welfare Capitalism* (1990, see also 1999, 2002), in which the world is split in three: the conservative corporatist, the liberal, and the social democratic welfare regime. These are clustered along three lines: *welfare regime*, the configuration of state, market, and family (which in its empirical part has been reduced to state-market relations); *stratification*, which by and large equals class inequality (rather than age, ethnicity, or gender); and *social rights*, which was translated into the concept of de-commodification, meaning independence from the (labour) market. The latter 'occurs when a service is rendered as a matter of right, and when a person can maintain a livelihood without reliance on the market' (Esping-Andersen 1990: 22). This comes straight from T.H. Marshall's (1976 or 1950) interpretation of citizenship in which citizenship is seen as a status vis-à-vis the market. In his *The Social Foundations of Postindustrial Economies* a fourth dimension is added to stress the state-family relationship: *de-familialisation*, meaning 'policies that lessen individuals' reliance on the family, maximising individuals' command of economic resources independently of familial or conjugal reciprocities' (Esping-Andersen 1999: 44).

The main claim is that each welfare regime, which has its own consistencies, produces specific gendered employment and income trajectories. Before *The Three Worlds of Welfare Capitalism* was published, it was acknowledged that different models of welfare states existed, which even resemble the ones of Esping-Andersen (Titmuss 1974). It was also acknowledged that welfare states had an impact on women's work and economic dependence. *Women and the Welfare State* by Wilson (1977) was one of the first to 'dismantle' the British welfare state, arguing that social policy – to sustain capitalism – maintained the institution of the family and within it the motherhood ideology. Welfare policies, she wrote, come wrapped in ideology. It was also acknowledged that in this respect the Scandinavian welfare state was different, and for women even preferable to the British or the Italian. In *Women and the State* (Showstack Sassoon 1987: 19), the differences between welfare states were shown with a focus on the 'differentiated analysis of different national and historical contexts'. In the *Three Worlds of Welfare Capitalism* these insights came together and showed that welfare states can be clustered along analytical and explanatory lines, creating specific and predictable outcomes for women's employment careers.

Many scholars have added a fourth and fifth model to Esping-Andersen's three worlds, renamed one or two, or incorporated a new dimension (e.g., Leibfried 1991; Siaroff 1994; Ferrera 1996; Bonoli 1997), but a huge overlap remains with the original regime typology (see also Arts and Gelissen 2002). The three worlds remain of important heuristic and descriptive value and this is how they will function in this book. Therefore, I will give a short description of the three welfare state models and how women fare in them. I will not only copy Esping-Andersen's description but also add what other scholars have contributed since then (and before).

In social democratic welfare states, citizens are independent of the (labour) market; the welfare state protects them. This interpretation of citizenship can be ascribed to the social democratic movement, which strived to protect employees against the vagaries of the market as much as possible. The benefits are therefore generous – high-income replacements rather than residual social assistance – and universal. This model is very women-friendly. As Sainsbury (1996: 45) argues, 'entitlements based on citizenship neutralize the influence of marriage on social rights'. The social democratic model is the only one that gives citizens individual rights and produces independence from family ties (de-familialisation). It takes responsibility from family life and has extended the service state. Because of childcare and other services, women can engage in paid labour. In addition, a major commitment exists to the right to work, which has equal status to the right of income protection. Sweden and Denmark are archetypical social democratic regimes (Esping-Andersen 1990, 1999). Norway seems to be a different model, also in terms of 'women-friendliness' (Leira 1992).

The social democratic model has often been praised for what Hernes (1984-1987) terms being 'women-friendly'. The Danish scholars Borchorst and Siim (1987) even speak about a 'new partnership' between the state and the family. The same scholars also reveal the backside of the model, arguing that the social democratic welfare state institutionalises women's double burden. While the welfare state was built on women's employment, it offered no solution for inequalities at home. While women are busy at work, men have not shouldered responsibilities at home. Just as in the US – as Hochschild (1989) has shown – Danish women are also doing a second shift at home (Borchorst and Siim 1987). Others argue that the social democratic model is not more than a shift from 'private patriarchy to public patriarchy', with women still doing the less-valued caring work. The only difference is that they now do it in the public care sector. This results in high gender segregation in the labour market as well as low wages for women and few women in top positions (Borchorst and Siim 1987; Langan and Ostner 1991; Orloff 2006). Finally, women may have become less dependent on their husbands, but they are now dependent on the state. Hernes (1987) even writes about women's triple dependence on the state as workers, citizens, and clients of welfare services (Hernes 1987). Therefore Leira (1993: 25) argues that 'if the welfare state established a "partnership" with women, women would be their junior partners'.

Whether social democracy is the cause of this so-called women-friendliness of these welfare states remains a question. Does this ideology produce social policies per se that are 'good' for women? Siim (2000) shows that particularly in the pre-war years Danish social democracy had its fair share of patriarchy. The emphasis on social equality and equity in the political culture was combined with a belief in the sexual differences between women and men. This passion for (class) equality while maintaining women's inequality was also visible in the other European countries central to this study (Bussemaker 1993; Lewis 1992a).

The second regime is the Christian democratic, labelled as conservative corporatist by Esping-Andersen (1990). In such a welfare state, citizens' independence from the market is moderate. With churches playing a pivotal role and continually warning against unbridled capitalism, the state has indeed intervened in the society, but only to the extent that formulations of social rights do not ignore the 'natural order' or turn it upside down. Van Kersbergen (1995) speaks of social capitalism being at the core of this model. The Christian democratic regime preserves status, class, and gender differentials. The underlying idea is that differences as well as inequality are natural and ultimately unproblematic because men are bound together by ties of love, charity, and recognition of their mutual needs. Only the extremes of inequality must be eliminated (Daly 1999). In practice, this means that benefits are based on employment record; that benefits and taxation encourage full-time motherhood; and that social insurance is based on dependency relations within the family – that is, women are presumed to be financially dependent on their partners. As a result, few women work. This is also a cause and effect of the lack of care facilities. In the Christian democratic model, the family is the most important social foundation, not only for income but also for services. In the family people should have their natural roles, the man as breadwinner and head of the family, the mother as homemaker and wife. This fits an organic societal image in which societal spheres or subsystems are homogeneous and the autonomy of market, families, and state are presumed (van Kersbergen 1995).

The Catholic principle of subsidiarity is considered crucial for understanding both the reluctance of state intervention and the fact that states do intervene (Esping-Andersen 1990; van Kersbergen 1995; Daly 1999). The state only gets involved when the family's resources are exhausted, but also to make sure that the sphere can do what it ought to do itself. Or more precisely: 'Subsidiarity is the state's function to guarantee and facilitate the steady and orderly proficiency of the lower social organs up to a point where these components can operate independently of political arbitration' (van Kersbergen 1995: 181). In that sense, subsidiarity is open-ended and the actual likelihood and boundaries of politicisation are historically contingent.

Consequently, the Christian democratic cluster is very broad and which countries fall into this category is up for discussion. According to Esping-Andersen's first regime study (1990), countries such as Germany, Austria, and France are part of this cluster, while Belgium and the Netherlands fit into the social democratic model. In 1999, he argued that France's and Belgium's membership in the conservative cluster was problematic in that familialism is less dominant (following Gornick et al. 1997). Native researchers however emphasise that countries like Belgium and the Netherlands are part of the Christian democratic cluster, particularly because of their strong family dimension in social policy (van der Veen 1994; Knijn 1994; Knijn and Kremer 1997; Andries 1997; Cantillon 1999; Bussemaker and van Kersbergen 1994, 1999).

The question is whether so many different countries can be lumped together. Belgium, France, Germany, and the Netherlands have always showed significant variety in women's employment rates (Pott-Buter 1996). More recently, the Netherlands has experienced a revolutionary increase in mothers' employment (Eurostat 2005, see chapter 4). What is the analytical benefit of all of continental Europe ascribing to the same welfare state logic? Van Kersbergen (1995) argues that Christian democratic forces or, more precisely, Catholic forces have lead to a distinct type of welfare state. Their core is a religiously inspired politics of mediation in which social adjustability and the integration of social interests are crucial. These 'politics of mediation' help explain the diversity within the cluster. Daly (1999) argues, along similar lines, that the differences between Catholic countries – she herself studied Ireland and Germany – relate to which social forces and pressures Catholic forces have to battle, such as a powerful socialist labour movement or a rival Protestant Church.

Finally, in the liberal regime people are very dependent on the market. They are commodified and thus forced to work, regardless of age, health, and family situation. Therefore, women have high activity rates. If welfare state services are in place, they are lean and exclusively for the most needy. The ideological point is that the free market produces the best results in terms of social emancipation and economic efficiency. Only when the market and the family are short can the state be the last resort. The consequences of such a regime are huge differences between those who are and those who aren't dependent on stigmatising welfare (Esping-Andersen 1990). On the other hand, since benefits are low for everyone – men and women alike – liberal welfare states do reach gender-equality, but on a very low level. Women and men are just as likely to become poor, so gender differences may not be as strong as class differences. There is an implicit claim that class-related dimensions determine the gendered outcomes (O'Connor et al. 1999; Daly 2000). The US and Canada are part of this cluster, while the UK tends towards it: it is one of the few countries in Europe that can apply for the liberal label.

Empirical analysis of the liberal regime shows that in practice it is not exclusively based on class: gender matters too (Lewis 1992a; Sainsbury 1996; Daly and Rake 2003). A liberal model is based on a sharp split between the public and the private, the individual being the primary policy object. But in practice, social benefits are seldom built on the individual but on the family, and liberal regimes do have male-breadwinner arrangements. In a country like the UK protective rights exist for carers, such as benefits for lone mothers and informal carers. O' Connor et al., comparing four liberal countries, concluded that Esping-Andersen was wrong when he argued that in liberal regimes the sanctity of the market is more important than gender concerns. In fact, 'the sanctity of motherhood has shielded women from the sanctity of the market' (1999: 154).

To conclude, the three worlds of welfare have had a crucial impact on analysing gender diversity in policy and practice across Europe. The models have an important heuristic value, even though each regime offers new questions: is social democracy per se connected to women-friendliness? Is liberalism blind to gender and care? Does the Christian democratic model have enough analytical power to understand gender diversity in Europe? And importantly: can these welfare regimes explain the recent changes in women's work patterns? How can the dynamics at play in women's lives be understood?

It's a Man's World: Care and Gender Models

In recent work of Esping-Andersen et al. (2002), gender has become a crucial concept. *Why We Need a New Welfare State* argues that gender equality is not only a women's affair but a social one. Working women contribute to the economy, offer the best protection against (child) poverty, and support the welfare state financially. Therefore, an important policy objective should be the harmonisation of the dual aims of career and motherhood. Childcare policy and parental leave are the crucial policy instruments to increase the possibilities for mothers to work. The other objective is to aim at full gender neutrality in the allocation of opportunities, life chances, and welfare outcomes. For Esping-Andersen a new welfare state is built on women's economic participation. In 1999 Esping-Andersen also included the concept of de-familialisation as a fourth dimension in his analytical framework of welfare regimes, in addition to the three he already outlined in 1990. Citizenship not only means being independent from the market, but also being independent from the family.

Esping-Andersen included gender in his three worlds of welfare, but many scholars argued that he did not do it well. The first criticism was that in analysing social rights he fused families and individuals. This is quite visible in his definition of de-commodification: 'the degree to which individuals or families can uphold a socially acceptable standard of living independently of market' (1990: 173). But what is good for the family may not be good for women. Families may receive sufficient benefits, but when these benefits are given to the male breadwinner that does not necessarily mean that women will fare well financially. Women are often financially dependent on a male breadwinner, even though they have recently gained much more economic power. In other words, equality between families can be high even when equality within families is low (Hobson 1990; Lister 1991, 1997; Sainsbury 1996). McLaughlin and Glendinning (1996), as well as Lister (1994), subsequently proposed to include the concept of de-familialisation. The latter defines the concept as the degree to which individual adults can uphold a socially acceptable standard of living, independently of family relationships, either through paid work or social security provisions.

The second criticism was that in the regime approach women's caring responsibilities in the home are hidden. Citizenship is primarily conceptualised as a status related to the labour market, as in Marshall's original approach. Women only appear when they enter the labour market. But in fact, many women in Europe have to be commodified first, before being decommodified. And after that they will be re-commodified, to use Pierson's term (2001). The right to work may be just as important as being independent from the labour market, or at least a necessary condition for achieving such independence (Taylor-Gooby 1991; Lewis 1992a; Orloff 1993). Alber (1995) also points out that the concept of decommodification does not say anything about the citizenship status of care receivers such as the frail elderly and children. Their first concern is not being independent from the labour market but the organisation of care.

It is doubtful whether the notion of de-familialisation includes caring well in the comparative welfare regime approach. The previous chapter showed that for women the organisation of care is important to understand their citizenship status. The way children and the elderly are cared for also reveals the conditions under which many women live. For caregivers (and care receivers) it does not matter per se in which domain care is provided – the state, the market, the family – but who provides care and under which conditions it is provided. In that sense, notions that start with 'de', such as de-commodification or de-familialisation – articulating independence from one domain – are inadequate.

Moreover, the concept of de-familialisation seem to suggests 'no family at all', even though the scholars wanted to capture the terms and conditions under which people engage in familial or caring arrangements. It is unlikely that all care can be taken over by the state, not only because care is more than work or an activity – it also has a moral dimension (Lewis 2001). And even in Scandinavian welfare states families still have responsibilities (Leira 2002). O'Connor et al. (1999: 32) criticise the concept of de-familialisation because 'it conjures up exactly the sort of illusions about individuals capacities to operate without interdependencies.' The concept and practice of care reminds us that we should not depart from the image of completely independent individualised people without ties. They prefer to include 'the capacity to form an autonomous household', or the shorter 'autonomy'. In other words: are women – like most men – in the position of being able to choose freely whether or not to enter marital or other relationships, and to some extent have a voice in their character? (Orloff 1993) This book stresses the more active notion of participation in work and care, while also sharing in income. This citizenship interpretation stresses the importance of care.

The notion of de-familialisation is also a missed opportunity to integrate family sociology into the study of the welfare state. Also, the right to an autonomous household is too narrow a concept to study care and dependencies within families, including generations. Welfare state analyses have always had a strong emphasis on women as wives and as mothers (e.g., Wilson 1977; Leira 1992; Silva 1996; Sainsbury 1996). This however highlights only two categories of caring women and two types of caring relationships. Looking through the lens of care can also help deconstruct gendered relations within the family: care not only highlights horizontal dependency relations, but also vertical (generational) dependencies (see Millar and Warman 1996; Knijn and Komter 2004).

Moreover, the concept of de-familialisation reveals a Cinderella image of care. In the *Social Foundations of Postindustrial Economies* (Esping-Andersen 1999), the concept of de-familialisation is empirically translated as the right to receive care, rather than the right to give care. It includes child allowances and day care provision only, and no possibilities for caring at home, such as would be facilitated by parental leave. Welfare states are doing well when they take over 'the costs of familyhood', meaning that the state has to provide services. In *Why We Need a New Welfare State* (Esping-Andersen et al. 2002), paid leave is considered to be a crucial policy instrument, but only to increase mothers' employment rate. Between the lines, citizenship is again translated as the right to work. Care policy is only instrumental to get mothers to work, not so much to provide good care for children. The previous chapter argued that citizenship cannot stand on one leg, it staggers without the recognition of care.

Breadwinner Models

Other scholars like Lewis (1992, 1997) and Daly and Rake (2003) argue that it is impossible to simply attach women to a framework that is completely built upon a male norm. Lewis therefore developed new gender models rather than integrated gender dimensions into the existing welfare regime framework. These gender models should not only diminish problem one – individualisation – but also get rid of problem two, the invisibility of unpaid work. The models are based on the variation in policy support of the male breadwinner norm and the gendered division of labour. In other words: Lewis stresses that unpaid and paid work are not divided equally in the various welfare states. The first is the *strong male breadwinner model*, visible in the UK (and probably in the Netherlands), which is based on married women being excluded from the right to work, subordinated to their husbands for purposes of social security and taxes, and expected to undertake the caring work within the home. The second is the *modified male breadwinner model*, seen in France (and probably Belgium), in which a parallel strategy is observable: women claim rights as workers and as mothers. Third, the *weak male breadwinner model*, as seen in Sweden (and probably Denmark), where mothers' employment is supported by generous childcare services. Lewis focuses most clearly on the way welfare states have reproduced and contested gender inequality. Her typology 'serves as an indicator of the way in which women have been treated in social security systems, of the level of service provision particularly in regard to childcare; and the nature of married women's position in the labour market' (1992: 163).

While also using these insights, Sainsbury (1996, 1999) criticises the models. She argues that the weak male breadwinner category is particularly problematic, as 'it seems to indicate what a country's policies are not, rather than what they are' (Sainsbury 1996:43). Hence she re-labels the weak breadwinner model as the individual model and contrasts it with the male breadwinner model. The difference between those two models can be deduced from 10 (!) separate dimensions, which are from a very different order, such as the basis of entitlement to social security, caring work, taxation, and family ideology. Sainsbury's model has the advantage that it gives a name to the weak breadwinner model, namely the individual model.

Unpaid work has been a crucial concept in these gender models. The problem is that the notion of unpaid work may reinforce the idea that welfare states are primarily about 'work' and 'workers'. This is however inadequate, as in practice much of the care work, also within the home, has been paid for (often collectively) via taxation or social security. The notion of care as described in the previous chapter includes caregivers at home as well as those who are paid via the state or the market. This is helpful as it goes beyond (nationwide) politically-decided boundaries: caring can be done privately as well as through the market and the state. Sometimes it is paid for, sometimes it is not. Again, unpaid work refers too much to the Cinderella notion of caregiving. Care resembles labour, and it is unfair that it is not paid for well.

Later on, Lewis (1997a) herself was one of the first to focus on caring regimes to capture the gender dimension of welfare states. She argues that it is important to study under which conditions caring for dependants has been undertaken. This indicates women's position in society. Bettio and Plantenga studied these care regimes cross-nationally and also conclude that 'care regimes also act as independent incentive structures that impinge on patterns of women's labour market participation and fertility' (2004: 85). This book, as chapter 2 shows, attempts to contribute to such an approach by linking the concept of care to the study of gender citizenship and social policies (see also Anttonen and Sipilä 1996; Knijn and Kremer 1997; Daly and Lewis 1998; Jenson and Sineau 2001; Daly 2002; Daly and Rake 2003; Anttonen et al. 2003).

Still, the male breadwinner models have important heuristic value as they tried to catch three distinctive cross-national logics. As with Esping-Andersen's typologies, only the Scandinavian countries will probably fit into the ideal of the weak male breadwinner model or the individual model. What is valuable about Lewis' models is that while nearly all of continental Europe fits into the Christian democratic/conservative cluster, there may be distinctions within continental Europe based along the lines of a moderate or strong breadwinner model. Lewis' models are especially useful as ideal types. To what extent can we understand the differences between countries and the recent changes by using these models?

It is problematic that in both Sainsbury's and Lewis' models cause and effect are not clear (Hobson 1994). In Esping-Andersen's welfare regime theory, as we will elaborate upon in the next section, a specific ideology led to a specific regime, which led to specific outcomes. By proposing new models, the theory's explanatory power is lost. What is actually the driving force behind a strong male breadwinner model or the individual model? The importance of class differences is also lost. Gender has replaced class differentials, while the (class) differences among women are not theorised. In other words, differences between women are not studied within the gender models. Orloff (1993) and O'Connor et al. (1999) therefore argue that Lewis' and Sainsbury's models are descriptive rather than theoretical. Orloff (1993) especially makes a case for integrating gender into the male stream models because the explanatory notion of power resources can then be used. The next section will deal with this topic.

Origins of Welfare States

The strength of Esping-Andersen's approach is that welfare states are not only studied as independent variables but also as dependent variables. This approach offers explanations of the outcomes of welfare states and studies welfare states' origins. The main claim is that social policy is shaped by the ideologies that have been struggled for by power resources, mainly working class, trade unions, and other social democratic sources (e.g., Korpi 1983). Different welfare regimes are then shaped by different class coalitions, but within the context of inherited institutions. History not only defines the past, but also the present.[2]

Rather than class-based power resources, scholars have claimed that women's power resources are crucial. A long tradition exists of studying women's representation: the extent to which women are present and powerful in political movements and corporate channels (e.g., Bergqvist 1999). While some scholars claim that women's presence in the political domain explains the woman-friendliness of the Scandinavian welfare state (Ruggie 1984), others argue that women are still lesser citizens exactly because they are not as well-represented as men in the crucial corporatist institutions of welfare (Hernes 1984, 1987).

Another strand focuses on the achievements of the women's movement (e.g., Bock and Thane 1991; Koven and Michel 1993) and especially on how collective actors make claims in what Fraser (1990) has labelled as the 'politics of needs interpretation' (e.g., Bertone 2003; Naumann 2005). When studying liberal regimes, O'Connor et al. (1999) made an important analytical difference between the way women put forward their political claims: is it through claiming gender-sameness or gender-difference? For the UK they found a weak women's movement with a strong 'difference' approach and thus a strong adherence to the traditional male breadwinner-female household model.

Finally, women's agency has been stressed, which in the broadest sense means a conscious capacity to choose and act on a personal and political level (see Lister 1997; Siim 2000). What binds these three approaches is that women should not be simply seen as objects of a particular type of political ideology: they are actors of social policy.

Neo-institutionalists link power resources to institutional settings, claiming that these resources are themselves partly the result of institutional variables such as the rules of electoral competition, the relationship between the legislative and executive branches, the role of the courts, the place of subnational governments, and the administrative body in politics. Since these institutions are part of a stable historical legacy, the notion of path dependency is central to this school of thought. While the power-resource school can be summarised as 'politics matter', the neo-institutionalism's credo is 'governance matters'.

Skocpol (1992) made a crucial bridge between power-resource approaches and the increasingly influential school of neo-institutionalism. Why, she asks in *Protecting Soldiers and Mothers*, in the early nineteenth century in a country with few welfare policies and no vote for women, did women have social rights, as evidence by the provision of 'mothers pensions'? She argues that gender – as well as identity, agency, and relationships – has to be brought into the analysis, but this does not explain everything. Crucial is the fit between politicised social identities and group political orientations and capacities within governmental institutions, political party systems, and the rules of the game. In other words, the overall structure of political institutions provides access and leverage to some groups and alliances, thus encouraging and rewarding their efforts to shape government policies. Others are denied access and leverage. Skocpol also found that, once enacted, policies restructure subsequent political processes. This feedback has two routes: new policies structure the administrative arrangements or affect the social identities, goals, and capabilities of action groups. As Skocpol (1992: 58) puts it: 'As politics create policies, policies also remake politics'.

Neo-institutionalists have more recently argued that power resources may explain the origins of welfare states but cannot explain the new politics of welfare states – politics of popular entrenchment (Pierson 1994, 2001; see also Green-Pedersen and Haverland 2002). The emergence of powerful groups surrounding social programs may make the welfare state less dependent on the political parties, social movements, and labour organisations that expanded social programs in the first place. Pierson (1994: 29-30; see also 2001) therefore argues that 'the analysis of the welfare state's supporters must shift from organised labour to the more varied constituencies of individual programs. Interest groups linked to particular social policies are now prominent political actors'.

At the same time, in this approach changes are hard to understand: there is no impetus or struggle as in the power resource theory. Path dependency and historical stability are crucial; what is explained is continuity rather than change. Hence its scholars advocate the notion of policy learning, often seen as 'puzzling and powering'. Social learning does take place when policy fails, anomalies occur, or new insights of policy effects arise (March and Olsen 1989; Visser and Hemerijck 1997).

More recently, culture is increasingly being studied as the foundation of welfare states (van Oorschot 2003; Bonoli; 2000; Gelissen 2002; Arts and Gelissen 2002). In this approach, culture helps to explain the design of value systems like the welfare state. In other words, social policy is seen as the sediment of culture; welfare states are solidified values. Power resources alone cannot explain welfare regimes, people's values are also important. What is problematic however is that by looking at surveys there is no clear relation between value orientations of people in different nations and the type of welfare regime they live in. In most European welfare states, public support for welfare states is high, yet systems are very diverse. Even in a country like the UK, which had strong retrenchment politics in the 1980s and in the 1990s, support for the welfare state is strong. Culture may thus help explain different welfare regimes, but how exactly is unclear.

Finally, the question is whether these theories are still valid when we study caring states rather than welfare states. When T.H. Marshall (1976) wrote his essay 'Citizenship and Social Class', his argument was very much 'power resource-like': social rights empower the poor, and the development of these anti-market rights has been achieved through conflicts between social institutions and social groups. In a later essay, 'The right to welfare', when he was more concerned about care, he wrote: 'It cannot be said that society needs happy old people in the same way that it needs a healthy and educated population. Nor would it suffer any great loss if the mentally handicapped were not assisted (at considerable cost in time and money) to make the most of their limited capacities. The motive that inspires the services rendered to these people is compassion rather than interest' (Marshall, 1981, or 1965: 91-92). Marshall thus felt that care rights should be otherwise explained. One of the questions this book takes up is whether this is true. Can the development of caring rights be explained by power resources (class-or gender-based) and institutional factors?

Homo Economicus in Welfare States

So far, I have discussed theories of how different sets of social policies are supposed to create specific gendered employment and income patterns. The question is, what are the mechanisms of social policy, and why do they affect the actions of people? How do welfare states effectively 'work'? Most welfare regime theory is not explicit about the mechanisms driving human behaviour. Implicit however is a focus on the financial incentive structures. Therefore, Duncan and Edwards (1999; see also Duncan et al. 2004) argue that when (female) labour market patterns are explained, the image of the *homo economicus* is often implicit. Women's actions seem motivated by economic gains and constraints. This is the more surprising as cultural notions are crucial in describing welfare state models as well as their origins (e.g., Esping Andersen 1990, 1999; Anttonen and Sipilä 1996; Sainsbury 1996, 1999; Gornick et al. 1997; O'Connor et al. 1999).

Comparative studies often see the relationship between employment and social policy as follows: if breadwinner arrangements are rewarded by tax policy and social security, women stay at home. If childcare is cheap and available, women will go to work. Women enter the labour market when the state takes over the 'costs of familyhood', but stay at home when they are compensated for caregiving. Hidden in many such studies is also a normative assumption that women should and want to enter the labour market as they would then be accorded full citizenship. The assumption is often that people make rational decisions on the basis of financial costs and benefit analysis. In understanding the outcomes of social policy, an economic logic prevails.

When the political economist Esping-Andersen describes the 'three worlds of welfare', cultural notions are prevalent. These three worlds are distinctive historical categories and the way they are described stresses distinctive ideologies. Inherently cultural notions like 'Folkhemmet', the 'people's home' – a place for everyone, based on equality and mutual understanding – help understand the social democratic regime, while the 'family as the cornerstone of society' is a cultural notion indicative of the Christian democratic regime. At the same time, Esping-Andersen is most explicit in using a Beckerian theory to understand gendered employment. Nobel prizewinner Becker (1981) argues that when decisions are made within the family, people behave altruistically and aim at the best financial profits for the family as a whole. This decision-making process within households is different from market processes. In families, people's actions are not based on straightforward individual calculations as in the marketplace: household behavioural rules are altruistic. Consequently, the gendered division of labour is based on the idea that the household's aim is to maximise economic gains. The person with the highest productivity in the household will specialise in household tasks (women), the other person will enter the labour force (men). This explains why women and men sometimes act contrary to their individual economic self-interest, as they are thinking about the economic profits of the family as a whole.[3]

In his *Social Foundations*, Esping-Andersen argues that in most European families it is less financially beneficial when men perform more unpaid work, as it is more profitable to bring a child to day care. Only when the gender pay gap is small, as in Sweden, are men more likely to take up unpaid work. 'Lamentable as it may be, it is perfectly consistent with a standard neo-classical joint-decision model of household behaviour', he claims (1999; 58). In *Why Do We Need a New Welfare State* he writes that women's labour is guided by two kinds of 'opportunity costs': 'One following straight from Becker's (1991) model, has to do with prospective earnings, relative to their husbands. A second has to do with the implicit tax on mothers' earnings that childcare incurs' (2002: 80).

Other welfare state studies do regard women not as family members but as individuals, and nevertheless base themselves on economic logic. Concepts like 'opportunity costs' and 'financial incentives or disincentives' or 'traps' are used to describe the mechanisms that determine women's behaviour. Economic cost-benefit analyses are made to understand gendered patterns. Tax and benefit schemes have been sifted through to find financial (dis)incentives. Childcare costs are seen as a hindrance to women's labour market participation. The recent OECD study 'Babies and Bosses' (2002) that compares several welfare states is a good example of such an approach. It tries to show that childcare costs and male breadwinner arrangements in tax and benefit structures result in low female employment rates. In welfare state analyses, as Pfau-Effinger (1998: 147) argues, 'women are treated as rational individuals who orient their behaviour according to financial incentives'.

Scholars who study gender in social policy often refer to cultural notions. In fact, gender itself is a cultural concept. It can be defined as the social, cultural, and historical construction of 'women' and 'men' with an explicit focus on power relations. It follows that those who work with the concept of gender study the cultural dimension of welfare states. But few of them do so explicitly, based on a clear theory and methodology (e.g., Lewis 1992a, 1993, 2001; Leira 1993, 2002; Langan and Ostner 1991; Knijn

1994; O'Connor et al. 1999; Daly and Rake 2003; Knijn and Komter 2004). At the same time, financial cost-benefit analysis also prevails in gender studies. Examples can be found for instance in Sainsbury's (1999) collection *Gender and Welfare State Regimes*. Bussemaker and van Kersbergen (1999) argue that means-tested pensions create a disincentive for employment. In the same collection, Meyers, Gornick, and Ross (1999) link childcare to mothers' employment by positing that the cost of childcare can be viewed as a 'tax' on mothers' wages. Even when gender is used as a central concept, it seems difficult not to describe women as being locked up in financial traps.

When analysing which image of human behaviour is used to understand welfare state policies, an ambivalence is thus revealed. Most welfare state scholars, including those quoted above, implicitly stress the cultural dimension of welfare state regimes. They reject the image of humans as motivated purely and exclusively by economic gains for themselves or their families. They do not see people as financial dupes only. Esping-Andersen for instance argues that the welfare state's 'institutions, incentive systems and inscribed norms of proper conduct' shape behaviour in different countries (1999: 172). The OECD study 'Babies and Bosses' (2002) stresses that social norms are a crucial factor in understanding women's employment. And Lewis (2001; also with Giullari 2005) emphasises the importance of social norms and notions of 'the proper thing to do'. Yet neither theoretically nor empirically is an alternative model of human behaviour used. The underlying, often implicit logic of human behaviour in comparative welfare regime theories is often purely economic; people strive for economic gains, either for themselves or for their families.

Culture Matters More: The Modest Role of the State

A second approach stresses that to understand the gender differences in work, culture matters the most. Women's values and gendered arrangements are more important than financial cost-benefit analyses. In contrast to the comparative welfare regime approach, diversity and inconsistencies are emphasised and so is the potential for social change. While social policy studies tend to stress deeply grounded structures, cultural theories are more concerned with how to understand changes such as women's revolutionary move into the economy. The role of the welfare state is considered to be modest, although its impact is not denied.

Given the dominance of the comparative welfare regime approach, cultural approaches on this issue are thinly sawn and often problematic. The first problem is that culture has no consistent, productive definition. It is often summarised with a few nouns such as values, beliefs, norms, traditions, and practices (Freeman and Rustin 1999). Culture is often said to be the force at work which makes human behaviour apparent and distinctive. It embraces what goes on in people's heads and hearts, and relates to practices. Perhaps a nice way of defining culture is to see it as 'the noise of a society's conversation' (Inglis 2004), but it is probably more useful to define culture as shared values legitimating different patterns of social practices (Freeman and Rustin 1999; Inglis 2004). A second problem with culture is that it is often a rest category: if nothing else can explain human behaviour – economics, demography, social facts – it must be culture (Chamerlayne 1999; Clarke 2004). If social policy cannot explain specific patterns, a cultural explanation is presented. Social policy and culture are then seen as two separate variables, they are considered each other's opponents.

Given the dominance of the comparative welfare regime approach, few cultural approaches exist. This section focuses on two of them, by Pfau-Effinger (1998, 1999) and Hakim (2000, 2003), which are not ad hoc explanations. Rather than seeing culture as a rest category, they focus on the independent power of gendered norms and practices (Pfau-Effinger), concrete values, or work-life preferences (Hakim). Although in a very different way, they locate culture primarily as a source of power from 'below'. Both consider themselves as critics of the comparative welfare regime approach, but they also differ: Pfau-Effinger uses a 'thicker' notion of culture which is nationally and historically grounded, whereas Hakim uses a 'thin' notion in which values and preferences change fairly easily. Pfau-Effinger stresses social norms and values, whereas Hakim emphasises individual preferences.

Gender Culture, Order, and Arrangement

The German sociologist Pfau-Effinger in an important advocate of a cultural approach (1998, 1999; also Duncan and Pfau-Effinger 2000). She argues that in understanding European diversity in women's work scholars have placed too much attention on the explanatory power of welfare states. Social policies cannot explain the rapid changes in women's lives, she argues. How to understand the increased numbers of working mothers in the Netherlands? And why did German mothers not enter the economy *en masse*? The reason why social policies cannot explain these changes is that 'the assumptions about the impact of state policies on the behaviour of individuals are too deterministic' (1998: 150).

'There is no doubt that institutional conditions such as the amount of public childcare, or the tax/benefit system, are of substantial importance for the employment behaviour of women', she writes, but due to the focus on the welfare state and its policies, 'the relationship between culture and structure has not been theorised well' (1998: 150).

To understand women's employment patterns, Pfau-Effinger argues that the interplay of three dimensions is important. The first is *gender culture*, which she defines as norms and values towards spheres of work, women and men, childhood and childcare, and power relations and dependencies between women and men. Gender culture can be relatively autonomous but does influence the *gender order*, which is the second dimension and includes the labour market as well as the welfare state (among many other things). Both gender order and gender culture produce the *gender arrangement* – the division of labour within families. Gender arrangements are also important in themselves as the practice within households also changes the gender culture and the gender order. As Pfau-Effinger (1998: 160) puts it: 'It is not the institutions [referring to social policies] per se that create employment behaviour. Rather it is the interplay of gender culture, gender order and the behaviour of women within the framework of gender arrangements which influences this behaviour'. This theory lacks a clear causal chain : institutions, gender practices, and gender culture can lag behind or come first. This is both a weakness of the theory and one of its strengths.

Pfau-Effinger also presents ideal types: the family economic gender model (as in family business), the male breadwinner/female childcare provider model, the dual breadwinner/state childcare provider model and the dual breadwinner/dual childcare provider model. These models refer to specific cultural practices and are nationally determined. She describes the 'modernisation paths', as she calls it, of three countries: Finland, the Netherlands, and Germany. While Finland is moving from a family economic gender model to a dual breadwinner model, Germany and the Netherlands have moved from a traditional male breadwinner model to a male breadwinner/female part-time carer model. The Netherlands, however, has gone one step further and is now a dual breadwinner/dual carer model.

What distinguishes this approach from the previous is the stress on the possibility of cultural change as well as the importance of people's practices. People can influence both value systems and institutions. Following Archer (1996), Pfau-Effinger stresses four basic assumptions about culture and cultural change. The first is that societies have long-lasting cultural traditions that have an impact on behaviour. The second is that although there is usually a set of dominant cultural values and ideals, there is no cultural coherence in society, as alternative and competing cultural systems may exist. Third, cultural change depends on the way social actors deal with contradictions and alternatives in value systems. And finally, cultural change is connected to structural change but it can also be autonomous.

Such stress on alternative and sub-cultures and the space for change differs from structural approaches like the comparative welfare regime approach, but also from cultural-structural approaches as represented for instance by Douglas (1986), the anthropologist. In *How Institutions Think*, Douglas argues that an 'institution works as such when it acquires ... support from the harnessed moral energy of its members' (1986: 63). At the same time, she argues that 'people have no other way to make big decisions except within the scope of institutions they built' (1986: 128). Cultural change is then hard to imagine. Today, however, we witness major cultural shifts with regard to gender norms and arrangements. Women have entered the labour market *en masse*, a practice that was 'not done' in many European countries after the Second World War. Hochschild (1989) describes this as the biggest cultural revolution of our time. Pfau-Effinger thus argues that women and men can make a change. People are not 'cultural dupes': they are able to change institutions, even though it takes a lot of energy and it is a slow process.

State policies and collective actors, on the other hand, cannot always change culture. If the gap between policies, gender order, and gender culture is too big, little will change. But if the gap is small, state policies are especially important to understand the degree and speed of actual changes. This is how Pfau-Effinger tries to explain why the Netherlands has moved towards a dual breadwinner/dual carer model while Germany has not. In the Netherlands, women, social policy, and the labour market were supportive of part-time work. This indicates that the theory should not be positioned too far from the comparative welfare approach. Especially the empirical analysis stresses the state and its social policies as a catalyst for the gendered division of labour.

Two issues remain unanswered or at least less theorised. It is unclear how economics fits into Pfau-Effinger's approach. Are material consequences subordinate to culture? Or are financial structures part of the gender order? Secondly, how does Pfau-Effinger take care into account?

To her, care is no crucial concept. Care is only explicitly dealt with in the first dimension: the gender culture. This gender culture has two related sides: attitudes towards mothers' employment (work preferences) and ideals of childhood. According to Pfau-Effinger, attitude studies show that especially in the Netherlands the employment of mothers today is much more accepted than in Germany. At the same time, the traditional ideal of childhood, according to which it is best for children to be cared for in the private household, is still dominant (see Knijn 1994; Plantenga 1993, 1998). Hence the supremacy of part-time work in the Netherlands. For Pfau-Effinger, care is especially located at the cultural level and conceptualised as the opposite of paid work.

It Is a Woman's Choice: Work-life Preferences

A second approach, which can arguably be labelled as cultural, is presented by Hakim (1999, 2000, 2003a, 2003b). According to her, women's changing employment in Europe can be explained only by women's diverse values or work-life preferences. In Europe, women and men now have 'genuine choices for the first time in history' (1999: 33). They can follow their own life preferences, their individual life goals. This follows Giddens (1991), who wrote the preface to one of Hakim's books, as well as Beck and Beck Gernsheim (2002). They argue that in modern times people have no option but to choose how to be and how to act. In this 'thin' definition of culture, in contrast to Pfau-Effinger, preferences can change rapidly. The main claim of Hakim's theory is that personal preferences and goals now determine women's fertility as well as their employment patterns.

This new scenario, in which women are no longer constrained, is a result of two revolutions and three changes: the contraceptives revolution, the equal-opportunities revolution, the expansion of white-collar occupations (which are more attractive to women than blue-collar jobs), the creation of jobs for secondary earners (part-time work) and the increasing importance of attitudes, values, and preferences in lifestyle choices. Only in countries in which these conditions are fulfilled are women really free to choose.

If these conditions are fulfilled in a country, women will hold three divergent work-lifestyle preferences, which can be summarised in three different models of the ideal family (table 3.1). Some women's preferences are work-centred – family life is fitted around their work and motherhood is not their main priority. These women are the minority (about 20 percent of women in Europe). The second group, women with an adaptive work-lifestyle preference, who try to combine work and care, is the majority (60 percent). These are the ones that enter the labour market but may not be actively seeking work during recessions. Part-time workers also belong in this group. The third, smaller group is home-centred women (20 percent), who prefer to give priority to private and family life. Thus these preferences focus around how women want to deal with work and motherhood. Care is not a crucial concept, work-life preferences are.

Table 3.1   Hakim's (2000) classification of women's work-life preferences in the twenty-first century

Home-centred	Adaptive	Work-centred
20% of women Varies 10-30%	60% of women Varies 40-80%	20% of women Varies 10 to 30%
Children and family are the main priorities throughout life.	This group is most diverse and includes women who want to combine work and family, plus 'drifters' and unplanned careers.	Childless women are concentrated here. Main priority in life is employment or equivalent activities such as politics, sport, arts.
Prefer not to work.	Want to work but are not totally committed to career.	Committed to work or equivalent activities.
Qualifications obtained for intellectual dowry.	Qualifications obtained with the intention of working.	Large investment in qualifications for employment or other activities.
Number of children is affected by e.g., government social policy, family, wealth.	This group is very responsive to government social policy, employment policy, equal opportunities policy/propaganda, economic cycle/regression/growth.	Responsive to e.g.. economic opportunity, political opportunity, artistic opportunity.
Not responsive to employment policy.	Such as: income tax and social welfare benefits, educational policies, school timetables, childcare services, public attitude towards working women.	Not responsive to social/family policy.

Women's values or work-life preferences are different from the way Pfau-Effinger (and many others) have tried to capture gender culture, mainly by using national attitude studies. According to Hakim (2003b), national cultures are completely ambivalent about the appropriateness or necessity of working women. No relation exists between general social attitudes – those that indicate public morality – and behaviour. As in Pfau-Effinger's article, Hakim uses the example of the Netherlands, however she draws the opposite conclusion. While in national attitudes studies Dutch women and men report that they are in favour of gender equality and accept women's work, their behaviour is different. For a long time the Netherlands has had one of the lowest female employment rates in Europe (see Halman 1999/2000; Knijn and van Wel 2004). Consequently, writes Hakim, only personal goals and personal concrete preferences have a causal relation to individual behaviour. When people say that they are in favour of gender equality, this does not mean they practice this belief. Hakim argues that the crux lies in the difference between choice and approval. Dutch people may approve of other mothers working, but for a long time it was not their choice. Work-life preferences are therefore able to explain work-and-care differences, general value studies cannot.

Hakim seems to argue, more in line with Pfau-Effinger's approach, that welfare policies are only effective when they fit women's work-lifestyle preferences. In fact, her theory can be seen as a revision and strengthening of welfare state theories that sometimes have difficulty taking into account the differences between women. The table above (3.1) indicates which categories of women are adaptive to specific welfare state policy and which are not. Home-centred women are not sensitive to employment policy, but they are susceptible to welfare policies in deciding how many children they want. Work-centred women will not change their behaviour due to policy aimed at keeping them at home, but are susceptible to equal-opportunity policies. The critical majority of women (60 percent), however, are of the adaptive type. They are very responsive to social policy as well as to labour market opportunities. The majority of European women are thus receptive to tax and benefit structures as well as to the existence of childcare services. This however is at odds with the main claim of Hakim's theory that in the new European scenario women have few constraints and follow their own preferences.

Additionally, in contrast to all the previous theories presented in this chapter, Hakim tries to show that there are no longer nationally distinctive gender patterns. Diversity across Europe as a whole is bigger than between countries, she suggests; there are no nation-specific patterns.

In other words, variation *within* each European country is greater than *between* countries. Most countries, she shows – although the focus is primarily on the UK, the US, and Spain – have a mixture of home-centred, work-centred, and adaptive women. These countries also see a growing polarisation between home-centred, adaptive, and work-centred women: women within the countries have different preference sets. European societies are therefore not converging into any single dominant model of the family, and certainly not towards what is often seen as the final stage of modernisation: Scandinavia. Hakim emphasises that in contrast to the assumptions of the comparative regime approach, not all women want to work: some of them (around 20 percent) are home-centred and will always be. Hakim highlights that some women prioritise caregiving.

While comparative welfare state theories tend to show that preferences are shaped by social policy, Hakim argues that public policy *has to* follow the preferences of women and develop structures that support all three family models. She criticises the European Commission (and thus also the Lisbon agreement), as it aims at high employment for all women. With this normative statement she stresses the importance of 'the right to give care'. Her justification however differs substantially from the care approach presented in the previous chapter, in which the right to give care is not primarily justified because women want it. Other reasons are more crucial: it increases gender equality, decreases the care gap (which is especially important in light of the greying of society), and contributes to the possibility to participate in society as a human being. Additionally, the right to give care in combination with the right to receive care should ensure that women (and men) are not imprisoned by caregiving duties. The latter does not worry Hakim, probably because she believes women are free to choose anyway.

Human Behaviour

Finally, in contrast to the (Beckerian) *homo economicus* that often underlies the comparative welfare regime approach, Hakim's theory is explicitly based on the micro-notion of preference, a concept borrowed in fact from economics rather than from cultural theories.

Hakim challenges (mainstream) economic logics. Micro-economics in general do not matter much, she suggests, and certainly not to every woman to the same extent. In Europe, she tries to show, families are generally rich enough to support women to stay at home. Earning sufficient income is no longer a reason to work, according to Hakim, women's preferences are. In addition, economic human capital theories, which claim that the more highly educated women are the more they want to put their knowledge and skills into practice, also fail to explain women's employment patterns. Even when educational levels rise, some women still want to stay at home and indeed will do so. Cross-national surveys show that more highly educated women in the UK, the US, and Spain do not necessarily want to work. In short, economic factors are not determinant when it comes to explaining employment patterns.

Hakim argues that in modern societies preferences are not simply a post-hoc rationalisation of prior decisions but a motivational force. They are a cause, not a consequence of behaviour. British and Dutch women, for instance, work part-time because they prefer it. But the question is whether people have not changed their preferences (or concrete values) according to what is possible or what they are used to do. In Pfau-Effinger's theory, the gender arrangement influences both gender culture (norms) and the gender order. People's own behaviour in work and care affect their attitudes. This is supported by research on the basis of the European Value Study (Kalmijn 2003). It may thus well be that British and Dutch women prefer part-time work because they work part time (Fagan 2001; Visser 2002).

A final remark is that Hakim's theory is incomplete. What it lacks is an explanation of the origins of preferences. Why are some women home-centred, while others are adaptive or work-centred? And why do women have different lifestyle choices than men, who play no role at all in this theory? Hakim's answers to these questions are not very convincing. In her 289-page book, four pages are devoted to this issue. While trying to debunk socialisation theories that stress the importance of upbringing to women's preferences, she devotes some attention to the different psychological backgrounds of women. She argues roughly that work-centred women have more self- esteem. Ironically, this can just as well be used to challenge her belief that home-centred women are genuinely free to choose: if they just had more self-esteem, they would do something else besides home-keeping (Hakim 2000).

The image of the 'preference person' and the *homo economicus* have been heavily discussed in sociological, anthropological, and economic debates (e.g., Sen 1977; Gardiner 1996; Douglas and Ney 1998; Nussbaum 2000; McRea 2003). Scholars also developed alternative concepts such as 'bounded rationality' (Simon 1957), 'purposeful choice' (Folbre 1994), and even four new 'whole persons': the 'person robust', 'person unpredictable', 'person needs structure', and 'person under duress' (Douglas and Ney 1998:

109). Rather than going into this theoretical and philosophical debate, my approach – see the next section – is more empirical and inductive. What kind of image of human behaviour resembles most women's decision-making? How do people with care responsibilities decide how to live?

To conclude: the comparative regime approach has produced important heuristic frames to understand the relationships between social policy and women's employment. Women's *differences* in Europe can be explained by different (economic) incentive structures. The cultural approach adds that the recent *changes* in Europe cannot be explained by welfare states, not in the least because economic mechanisms do not affect women. Women's individual preferences (Hakim) or the interplay between gender and culture (Pfau-Effinger) can explain the recent changes and increased diversity in Europe.

Yet, both theories do not satisfy because of empirical (see also chapter 4) and theoretical reasons: neither the image of human behaviour nor the image of the state are helpful. If we turn to the practices of caring and welfare states, a new approach will come to the fore, which combines the cultural approach and the welfare regime approach. A cultural approach to welfare states in which the best of both are combined seems more appropriate, locating culture within welfare states and not outside them. The next section is therefore devoted to the cultural dimension of welfare states, or more precisely the culturally shaped moral notion of 'ideals of care' which are also embedded in welfare state policy. These ideals of care – which are expressed in social policy – do have consequences for women's employment behaviour.

Ideals of Care: Culture within Policy

When mothers wanted to work moral debates took place in many European welfare states. Who was going to care for the children? By working, some said, mothers harmed their own children. They were 'bad mothers', egoistic, careless. They placed their own lives, their wishes, and demands, before their children's. In many social and political arenas, children's interests were played off against women's interests: the debate took place in moral absolutes (Bussemaker 1993, Somers and Peters 1991, Bertone 2000). When mothers wanted to work, they had to overcome this debate. In every welfare state such a debate has taken place and in every welfare state country-specific solutions were made to resolve the moral clash between motherhood and women's employment. When the full-time motherhood model became outdated in practice what new moral ideal of care was put forward? What new ideals of care have arisen, or have old ones been revived? And what have been the consequences – especially for women's work – of these new care norms? To understand gender *differences* and gender *changes* it is crucial to study which new ideal of care has been put forward in social policy and by whom, and what has been the impact of these new cultural care norms on women's citizenship. Ideals of care are thus an instrument to understand the culturally defined, moral impact of welfare states.

What are Ideals of Care?

A care ideal 'implies a definition of care, an idea about who gives it, and how much of what kind of care is "good enough"' (Hochschild 1995: 333; see also 2003).[4] More specifically, it implies something about *where* care should be provided: the child's home, the carer's home, or a day care centre; by *whom* it should be provided: who is trustworthy and well-equipped for the 'job'; and in what way care contributes to the upbringing of children: are children supposed to be socialised with other children, educated individually, cherished, or simply 'looked after'? In my definition, care ideals identify what is 'appropriate care'. Care ideals are the answer to the moral predicament of working and caring that many parents – often mothers – feel they face.

Care ideals are existing practices, but they are more than that: they contain a specific normative legitimation, a logic of appropriateness (March and Olsen 1989). Care ideals are highly gendered, they are part of a gender culture: their legitimation is framed in terms of whether they are better, worse, or just different from mother care; motherhood is a vital frame of reference. Ideals of care are not rigid moral rules: they can be negotiated, are diffuse, and imply some form of negotiation and change. Ideals of care are not hegemonic or mutually exclusive. The moral predicament of work versus care is likely to be solved through a pick-n-mix strategy, it's a cultural toolkit allowing for a bricolage of ideals. At the same time, it is hard to make some ideals compatible with others. While countries are not culturally coherent, some ideals are more dominant then others (see Pfau-Effinger 1998; Archer 1996; Swidler 2001).

When the four caring states are unravelled, five ideals of care arise: full-time mother care, parental sharing, intergenerational care, surrogate mother care, and professional care. Of course, other ideals can be found too, but these five cover most images of good care. The five ideals listed below are more precise about caring practices as well as policies than the gender models developed elsewhere (Lewis 1992a; Leira 1992, 2002; Pfau-Effinger 1998, 1999) or work-life models (Hakim 2000). They are also much more precise than the six items that measure attitudes towards work and care in the European Value Study (see also Halman 1999/2000; Kalmijn 2003). Examples are: a pre-school child is likely to suffer if his mother works. A working mother can establish just as warm and secure a relationship as a non-working mother. No questions are asked about the proper solution for childcare. Care ideals not only deal with the (rudentimentary) question of whether women should work or stay at home, but focus on what are perceived as appropriate care solutions when mothers are at work at a given time, in a given country.

The ideals are exaggerations of realities and are thus constructed for analytical purposes, but they are not constructed as Weberian ideal types. Ideal types in the Weberian sense are built inductively. The purpose is to confront these ideal types with reality and search for deviation. This gives insight into causal relations (see Ritzer 2000; Zijderveld 1988). It is the way models such as those of Esping-Andersen and Lewis are used in this book. Ideals of care, on the other hand, came into being deductively: they arise out of the study of the four countries as well as cross-national studies of care (e.g., Millar and Warman 1996; Rostgaard and Fridberg 1998; Lewis 1997b, 1998). Moreover, in this book care ideals are not used as ideal types: they are real types. They tell a story about welfare states and are not used as confrontational strategies.

Table 3.2	Gendered ideals of care		
	Gendered by definition	*Gender-contested*	*Gendered in practice*
Informal	full-time mother	parental sharing	intergenerational
Formal	surrogate mother	professional care	

The first ideal is obviously that of full-time mother care. In this ideal, continuous mother care performed at home is seen as the best way of bringing up children. It is the ideal of Madonna and child. In the wake of the Second World War this ideal became hegemonic in every welfare state, although it quickly disappeared in some Scandinavian countries after the 1950s. The ideal of full-time mother care was strongly reinforced by psychologists, paediatricians, and other children's professionals who stressed the importance of a strong mother-child bond as a necessary condition for the development of a child. The work of the psychologist Bowlby was important for this theory, which was made popular by Dr. Spock. Bowlby is the founding father of attachment theory. Using subhuman primates, he showed in numerous studies that the natural social formation is the mother and her children rather than the family, including the father. The father is of no direct importance to the young child, only as an indirect value as an economic support and in his emotional support of the mother. These theories of Bowlby and Spock enjoyed their prime in the 1950s and 1960s but their legacy has lived on (Singer 1989, Soomers and Peters 1991, Lewis 1992b). The ideal of full-time mother care is increasingly outdated and has been replaced by others (and sometimes these have been replaced again).

The second ideal is that of parental sharing. This model is based on the assumption that men are able to care for children just as well as women. Advocates for this model sometimes go as far as to argue that an increase in fathers' care would be better for children (Lamb 2004 or 1981), who then would have another role model in addition to the more feminine one. Another line of reasoning suggests that parental sharing contributes to gender equality; at a time when women work outside the home men must also take up a share of the caring duties. Good examples of efforts to increase parental sharing include a 1998 intervention by the Dutch government, which ran a campaign entitled: 'Who is that man that comes to our home every Sunday to cut the meat?' and the Norwegian and Swedish laws on 'daddy leave', parental leave with special rules for fathers. In the ideal of parental sharing, caring is just as important as working. Therefore, men should exchange time at work for time at home, whereas mothers should do the opposite. Parental sharing is thus built on two legs: not only should fathers be involved, it also assumes that both partners in a couple are allowed to work on a part-time basis. The ideal of parental sharing is subversive because it degenders caregiving. In this model, good childcare is still presented as home-based.

The ideal of intergenerational care is also home-based. The basic idea is that the first generation (grandmothers) cares for the third generation (children). In return, the second generation (the daughters who are now mothers) will care for the grandparents when they become frail (Millar and Warman 1996; Leira et al. 2005). This is not just a calculated system of family exchange. It also guarantees good childcare, because who could care better than the mother's mother? She is not only experienced and can be trusted more than anyone else, she will also love the children the most. The ideal of intergenerational care is not gendered in theory, but is in practice. Grandmothers, daughters, daughters-in-law, and grand-daughters are the ones most likely to provide care. The system is generally matrilineal. The ties that bind are familial, and the extended family is regarded as a haven that protects its members from having to seek care in the outside world, from the market or the state. Care is best performed at home, either the grandmother's or the daughter's. Taking your parents into your home, rather than 'putting them' in an old-age home, is also an important expression of the ideal of intergenerational care. This is the way to pay back all the care work they did for you when you were young and when you needed help while raising your children.

The ideal of professional care strongly contests the ideal of full-time motherhood because it maintains that professionals provide a different kind of care than that performed by mothers, but offer something extra that should still be part of the upbringing of every child. Professional care often takes place in childcare centres or is part of the educational system, and its purpose is defined in various ways: improving children's welfare, enhancing their development, socialising them, and preparing them for school or for the labour market. Crucial to the ideal of professional care is that carers are educated and are accountable in a professional way. In fact, all welfare states implement the ideal of professional care for children aged five, six, and seven – this varies per country – through schools.

The ideal of professional care for younger children (0-3) is mainly manifest in a country like Denmark, which has the best-trained childcare workers in Europe (Siim 2000; Borchorst 2002). As we already saw in the previous chapter, the Danes believe that childcare improves children's welfare. Day care can give children the 'social pedagogical' attention that is not available at home. In the UK, education rather than welfare seems to be the most important rationale for professional childcare at the moment. This is a fairly recent development. Professional care in the UK used to be only for problem families, just as in the United States. There are thus already three different meanings for the ideal of professional care for children: welfare (for the needy), social-pedagogical, and education.

The last ideal is that of the surrogate mother. According to this model, good-enough caring is still done best by *a* mother, even if it is not *the* mother of the children (Gregson and Lowe 1994; Nievers 2003). Care is done by a childminder, babysitter, or family provider, usually for little pay, and because it is offered at the provider's home it most closely resembles home-based care. 'It may not help, but it can't do any harm either' is the way this type of care is legitimised. The purpose of such care is to 'look after' or 'keep an eye on' the child when the mother is at work. Surrogate mothers are not supposed to change or influence children's upbringing. They do not give something 'extra' to the child. In contrast, professionals have different qualities and qualifications than parents, but surrogate mothers are considered to have the same kind of qualities mothers have – motherly warmth, attention, patience – even though they remain surrogate. In this model it is still better if motherly warmth and attention is given by the real mother.

A Caring Image of Human Behaviour

The ideals-of-care approach is based on an image of human behaviour other than that of *homo economicus* or the preference person. For mothers, being a full-time carer is no longer obvious, but their decisions about work are always made in the context of care. To understand gendered patterns of work, care is therefore crucial. When women make decisions about work, the question is: how am I making sure that my children are cared for properly? And can I find a solution for care that fits my ideal of good caring? (Finch and Mason 1990, 1993; Morée 1992; Hays 1996; Brannen and Moss 1999; Duncan and Edwards 1999; Knijn and van Wel 1999, Hochschild 1989, 2003).

A second characteristic of decision-making is that it is not based on economic logic alone. Who cares is shaped and framed – although never exclusively determined – by gendered *normative* guidelines (Finch and Mason 1993), gendered *moral* rationalities (Duncan and Edwards 1999), or *feeling* rules (Hochschild 2003). In other words: 'to work or to care' is not exclusively a question of economics but a moral predicament, and morality is often linked to gender identity. This is nicely put forward in Duncan and Edwards' (1999) study on lone mothers. They were puzzled by the question of why British lone mothers make the choice to care full time and postpone a working career that would lift them out of poverty. They concluded that lone mothers' decisions are led by gendered moral rationalities that are constructed, negotiated, and sustained socially in particular contexts. According to Duncan and Edwards, lone mothers try to behave in line with their identity, their socially constructed 'self'. Only when the identities of worker and good mother are reconciled do lone mothers take up paid employment.

The importance of morality as well as gender identity is also visible in two-parent families. In Hochschild's (1989, 1997) studies on couples' juggling work and care, economic rationality often conflicts with morality. In *The Second Shift* (1989) she questions why men have not taken part in the cultural revolution and taken over some of women's responsibilities at home. With money in their pockets, women's kitchen-table power should increase much more. But some working women, she found out, did not even *ask* their husbands to do a little more. And men did not do it themselves. Hochschild seeks the explanation not in economic theories but in the moral accounting systems within marriage and the importance of gender identity for both men and women.

Studies on working and caring also show that decisions about working and caring are rational and purposeful; we no longer live in an era in which habits are the compass in life, although no human being lives without the weight of the past and the values he is brought up with. Caring is no longer an unconscious habit, a routine passed from mother to daughter. Caring has been modernised, it has lost its self-evidence, as Sevenhuysen (2000) puts it. It is no longer a cultural given (Hays 1996). In that sense, Hakim (2000) – following Giddens (1991) and Beck and Beck-Gersheim (2002) – is right in stressing that people *must* make decisions about their life, whether they want to or not. Normative guidelines are no longer clear-cut. For that reason, Finch and Mason (1993) called their book on caring for next of kin *Negotiating Family Responsibilities*. Family responsibilities are still in place but they are debatable.

They also show that people use their brains when they negotiate who will care for their frail parents, people are involved in rational processes. This is also the case for mothers (Hays 1996), including lone mothers (Duncan and Edwards 1999). For them it is a *rational* decision not to follow their wallet but their values. People in couples can also behave very calculative. Hochschild (1989) shows they use gender *strategies* – a strategy of action – to push what they want.

Action is not only rational but also relational and done in context. Or, as Finch and Mason argue (1990: 356), 'There is a sense of interwovenness between decisions being made by different members of the family'. The concept of individual, autonomous choice, they argue, is not the right word for the process of decision-making about caring. Caring as also described in chapter 2 reveals various interdependencies. For this reason, the concept of individual preferences as put forward by Hakim (2000) is inadequate to understand women's (and men's) lives. Even in Hochshild's studies, where households resemble battlefields, an ongoing (power) struggle coincides with the fact that partners make decisions in the continuous knowledge of dependence. This may be for love or because in modern times real efforts have to be made to keep marriages together. Hence rather than describing dependence within households as an altruistic haven, as Becker does, households are better presented as an 'arena of cooperative conflict', as Sen puts it (in Gardiner 1997).

Ideals of care are thus culturally shaped moral rules that are followed by rational people who make their decisions in relation to others. People do not follow these guidelines blindly nor will they always make the most appropriate moral decision (Wolfe 1989), simply because they cannot or because of conflicting moralities. As a woman in one of Hochschild's books (1997: 219) says, 'I do not put my time were my values are'. Human action is not decided by ideals of care, it is only shaped and framed by them. Ideals of care do not simply affect the strategic calculations of individuals or prescribe what one should do, but what one can imagine oneself doing in a given context. They are filters for interpretation, and in that way guide human action. Care ideals offer scripts on what to do. And these scripts are still gendered – not only for women, for men too.

Economics vs. Morality?

Ideals of care offer us a more adequate understanding of work-and-care decision-making in families, much more than for instance the individualistic preference person or the *homo economicus*. Still, the caring rationality should not be placed completely outside economic logics. For Finch (1989), economic factors are just part of the context of decision-making. Duncan and Edwards (1999) argue that individual economic calculations are placed in the framework of gendered moral rationalities, while Hochshild (1989, 2003) presents a cultural alternative to economic cost and benefit analyses. Financial structures are not simply context though: they are more important than that. In some countries more than in others – the UK in this book – decisions around work and care can lead to poverty. In addition, culturally defined morality itself can be shaped by material circumstances: financial structures often indicate the proper moral hierarchy in behaviour.

In many welfare state studies, financial conditions and social norms are too often seen as two separate causes of employment patterns. *Homo economicus* is put against *homo morales*. Researchers test which variable is more important (e.g., Fagan 2001; OECD 2002, O'Reilly and Fagan 1998, Esping-Andersen 2002). But it is more important not to separate them cruelly (Knijn and van Wel 1999; Wheelock and Jones 2002). Financial measures have a normative meaning too. In the 1990s Dutch and British social assistance laws exempted lone mothers from the obligation to work. These women were in fact paid to stay at home. Such financial arrangements shape what is considered to be proper. Not all financial measures and structures have similar important consequences. For example, the male breadwinner bonus in the Danish tax system has not had the effect that women or men stayed at home to care for children (chapter 5).

The crucial condition for being effective is that financial incentives must fit the dominant normative guidelines, moral rationalities, or feeling rules which I have labelled as ideals of care. Economic incentives can become extremely powerful when they fit these norms, but they have little power when morally isolated. Affordable, state-subsidised childcare services are therefore probably only effective when they fit smoothly into a broader moral context and fit the dominant ideal of care. In other words, financial incentives should be examined within the context of a larger moral framework. This reveals whether they are powerful or not.

Cultural Institutionalism

Decision-making within this ideal of care approach is described most adequately by what March and Olsen (1989) have labelled as the logic of appropriateness. They argue that behaviour (beliefs as well as actions) is intentional but not wilful. For them, action stems from a conception of necessity rather than preference. Within the logic of appropriateness a sane person is one who is 'in touch with identity' in the sense of maintaining consistency between behaviour and a conception of self in a social role. Ambiguity or conflict in rules are typically resolved not by shifting to rational calculation but by trying to clarify the rules, make distinctions, determine what the situation is, and what definition 'fits'.

March and Olsen's theory fits into what Hall and Taylor (1996) have labelled as 'cultural institutionalism'. They argue that institutions indeed provide strategically useful information, but also affect the very identities, self-images, and preferences of actors. In this approach institutions not only includes formal rules, procedures, or norms, but also the symbol systems, cognitive scripts, and moral templates that provide the frames of meaning guiding human action. Such a definition breaks through the conceptual divide between 'institution' and 'culture' (see also Zijderveld 1988). What is particularly valuable about March and Olsen's approach is that the logic of appropriateness is open to change: it can be a result of historical experience (including socialisation and education) but also the destabilising of older sets of rules and norms. As one logic of appropriateness is destabilised, for instance because of a war but also due to inconsistencies with practice, space opens up for deliberation over specific norms and values. Ideals of care are in fact a logic of appropriateness: they can be seen as an 'institution' or a 'culture' that is open to change. In one period a specific ideal of care is dominant while in a different period another.

Understanding Policy Change

The shift in ideals of care from full-time motherhood to another ideal has some logic to it. In most cases, the state changed its policy only when quite a number of women were already in the labour force. Most of the time, women started to work first and later welfare states acted upon their demands for child care (implicit or explicit), although some welfare states were more responsive then others (Lewis 1992). For instance in a cross-national study of Norway, Spain, and Italy, for example, Leira et al. (2005) show that the mass entry of mothers into the labour market preceded generous public support for child care. This was also the case in Flanders and Denmark – as we will see later – which had higher employment rates for women prior to state provision (Pott-Buter 1990).

In other cases, the state intervened out of economic necessity, although economic necessity takes different shapes. An important catalyst for the early and strong development of childcare provision in Denmark, for instance, was the huge demand for women in the labour market in the 1960s (in addition to women's desire to work, since they regarded earning their own income as crucial to the emancipation process). While other countries engaged immigrants to fill in gaps in the work force, Denmark recruited women. Ironically, the large influx of women as employees was reinforced by the subsequent development of state services, especially in the 1970s, which also needed female workers (Borchorst and Siim 1987). In Flanders and Belgium, childcare provision was also motivated by an economic factor: micro-economics. Childcare was regarded as a necessary evil to protect families from poverty. And in the Netherlands macro-economic factors – saving the welfare-state – have been an important factor to move away from the full-time motherhood model. Thus both women's need and desire to work as well as a sense of economic necessity could serve as necessary preconditions for initial state intervention into the realm of childcare. But this does not explain the extent to which states became engaged in policy, or which ideal of care came to be promoted as an alternative to the full-time mother-care model.

How can we explain why a certain ideal of care became dominant in one country? As we will see in chapter 5 and chapter 6, the classic class-based power resource theory of Korpi (1983) and Esping-Andersen

(1990) is inadequate to the task of explaining the promotion of specific ideals of care. The assumption of a clear relationship between ideological movements and the extent of women-friendliness in European welfare states cannot hold. Social democratic forces, for one, have not resulted in women-friendly welfare states per se. In each country, social democratic movements struggled with the question, 'which is more important, class or gender?' and gender often lost (Lewis 1992a; Siim 2000; Bussemaker 1993). Moreover, party ideologies have different meanings and consequences in different countries: Dutch Christian democracy is not the same as Belgian Christian democracy, so outcomes also differ. The Christian democratic regime has invested much more in childcare in Belgium than has its counterpart in the Netherlands (Daly 1999). Political groups other than the social democrats have also been important for caring policy. For example, liberals, seldom considered women-friendly in welfare state theory, fought for the individualisation of taxation in Denmark and the Netherlands (chapter 5). Thus power resource theory can indicate some but not all of the power relations in each country.

What could be an alternative explanation? In many ways, the transformation of one ideal into another resembles a paradigm shift in science as described by Kuhn (2003, 1962). The old paradigm – the male breadwinner-female caretaker model – is criticised, dismantled, and reconstructed by various politicians, the women's movement, and the media. At the same time, people themselves, acting as primary agents, begin to develop new practices. Problems (anomalies) with the dominant care ideal, or paradigm, become visible. This period of 'crisis' is followed by a competition between pre-paradigmatic schools; some ideals develop in contrast to others. As Billig (1991) points out, our argumentation and actions are part of a wider social context of controversy; what we think and how we act refer not just to our own position or practice but also to other positions in a public argument that we oppose. We not only express our own position, we seek to criticise and thereby negate the counter-position. In other words, in the moral and cultural arena. There is a struggle over what type of care is most appropriate when mothers are at work. Some groups advocate the ideal of professional care while others push for fathers' involvement. Meanwhile, some parents simply embark on new caring practices.

In Kuhn's view, one paradigm grows in strength because of powerful arguments and the number of advocates, while the other pre-paradigmatic schools and the previous paradigm fade. This is also the case with ideals of care: when alternative ideals of care become stronger, the traditional model disappears. Thus, in Europe, the ideal of full-time mother care has been nearly eradicated by now. Finally, according to Kuhn, the reason one paradigm wins over another has nothing to do with its inherent 'quality' but with whether proponents of such a paradigm have good networks and alliances. In other words, paradigm shifts are a matter of politics.

The crucial condition for explaining why some ideals 'win' over others is thus the strength of a powerful alliance built by actors united around similar beliefs. This has been stressed by Jenkins-Smith and Sabatier (1994), who propose the concept of the 'advocacy coalition framework.' These scholars regard public policy in the same manner as belief systems, i.e., sets of value priorities and causal assumptions about how to realise them. The systems involve value priorities, perceptions of important causal relationships, and perceptions of the state of the world, which are core values. Advocacy coalitions are based not on common interests but on common beliefs. These beliefs are hard to change, so advocacy coalitions are rather stable over time. They argue that to understand policy change, it is important to focus on policy subsystems or domains. This includes a variety of actors, not only regular interests groups, but also journalists and researchers. Pierson (1994, 2001) also shows that powerful new groups may have emerged, surrounding social programs; he argues that 'the analysis of the welfare state's supporters must shift from organised labour to the more varied constituencies of individual' (1994: 29-30; see also 2001).

Building on Jenkins and Sabatier, one would assume that ideals of care are always constructed as positive notions. One cannot imagine people – even politicians – just fighting for spending money per se. Actors fight for something they more or less believe in, what they consider as appropriate in a given context (March and Olsen 1989). In other words, ideals of care are something to be strived for; they can connect people who have similar notions about the good life. Actors cannot make good alliances with groups that do not fit their belief system. This approach is thus different from a rational choice perspective of actors (see Hall and Taylor 1996). Of course, actions are sometimes instrumental and strategic (this is especially how actors define their actions afterwards, argue March and Olsen 1989). But actors are not seen as purely strategic operators who are continuously trapped in a prisoner's dilemma – what will give me the best chance to win: cooperation or individual strategies – as rational choice academics see the world. They do not usually act against their belief systems.

But in order to explain policy change with regard to the care of children, two more factors must be added. One is parents' preferred ideal of care. Women's entry into the labour market and the 'dismantling' of the male breadwinner model has constituted a sea change – one of the most profound shifts of the last decades; a 'revolution', writes Hochschild (1989); a 'paradigm shift' in Kuhn's terms; 'deep core' change in the words of Jenkins-Smith and Sabatier. But such change can never be confined to the policy communities or the political elite; profound changes such as this must be supported by the principal agents – by people. Kuhn already stressed this when he drew a parallel between scientific revolutions and political revolutions; in the latter, he said, the 'masses' need to be persuaded. Thus the advocacy coalition framework must take into account the feelings and opinions of the broader community. Transformations of ideals, or paradigm shifts, engage not only those who are directly involved in policymaking but must also mobilise the support of a critical mass of the population. At the same time, the larger community can also be part of an advocacy coalition.

With regard to care, one advocacy group has been more important than all the others: the women's movement. This movement was key not only because of its presence or absence, but especially because of its orientations and alliances. Women, as groups or embedded in other organisations, do not, however, have a constant set of interests or ideals across countries (Naumann 2005). For O'Connor et al. (1999), the principal line of opposition or cleavage among women's movements was where they stood with regard to the question of 'sameness' or 'difference'. But this cleavage is not exhaustive; when it comes to care policy, the most important line of cleavage falls between ideals of care. In addition to the care orientation of a particular women's movement – in the broadest sense of the word movement – it is also important to look at whether women used opportunities to form alliances with other powerful groups, movements, or power resources such as trade unions, professional organisations, or the dominant political coalition, and whether they were able to mobilise parental opinions.

In short, what kind of new ideal has been promoted is a result of a battle in which the argument for one ideal is often developed against a counter-ideal, but the result is often proposed by a wider advocacy coalition in which (parts) of the women's movement are crucial – often supported by general opinions about care.

Conclusion: Women's Work, Welfare States, and Ideals of Care

Care ideals can be loosely translated as 'what is considered to be good-enough caring'. Ideals of care are an answer to the moral predicament of working and caring. Care ideals are an instrument to study caring states: they place caring in the centre, are more accurate than the usual welfare state models, and shake hands with the broad notion of culture. They help study the moral and cultural dimension of policy and practice. What's more, care ideals can be seen as part of an adaptation process on the level of individual mothers (sometimes fathers), and are also embedded in societal structures such as schools, enterprises, social service agencies, political parties, and social movements, and also in welfare state regulation. Ideals of care are country-specific. In different welfare states, different ideals of care have come into being, for different reasons, and with different consequences.

Ideals of care operate on two levels, and thus contribute to the theoretical framework of welfare states in two ways. First, ideals of care can help explain cross-national differences in the *development* of social policy in the last decades. Few welfare states, political parties, or social movements still embrace the ideal of full-time motherhood. To understand why and how various patterns of state intervention in childcare developed as they did, ideals of care offer an analytical framework to understand social policy. Care ideals account for why some policy choices can and have been made, and others have not or cannot be made. In other words, studying specific care ideals may shed new light on existing welfare state theories such as the power resource approach and (neo)institutionalism.

Second, ideals of care can help explain gender relations and citizenship (outcomes). They offer a precise instrument to analyse the cultural (and moral) consequences of welfare states. In other words, care ideals can contribute to an understanding of why employment rates have not increased everywhere as much as they could, given the high levels of childcare (Flanders), or why there are country-specific differences between categories of women (e.g., grandmothers, lower-class women, and care professionals). The notion of care ideals can be seen as a replacement of the micro-image of human behaviour underlying much comparative welfare regime research: the *homo economicus* as well as the notion of work-life preferences (Hakim 2000). Care ideals are perhaps better seen as a specification of Pfau-Effinger's (1998) notions of gender culture and arrangements. In the approach presented here, care ideals have an important moral and relational dimension, and are also institutionally and collectively shaped.

The usefulness of this approach will be shown in the following chapters. Women's changing and diverse patterns of employment and care in the four European countries are explained in the following chapter.

4   Citizenship in Practice: Work, Care, and Income

'Women's move into the economy ... is the basic social revolution of our time', writes the American sociologist Hochschild (1989: 249). This has not only changed the structure of labour markets but also the balance of power within the family. This present chapter demonstrates that all four countries have waved goodbye to the ideal of full-time motherhood, though this has happened during different decades and at different speeds and in different manners. Hochschild also signals a 'stalled revolution': while women moved out of the house, men did not move into the house: parental sharing is not a common practice. Men's behaviours changed little, although some European diversity of behaviour among European men in relation to childcare is visible. This chapter is thus not only concerned about women's employment and income patterns, it also tries to reveal what men did when women were having their revolution.

Central to this fact-finding chapter are three indicators of citizenship as described in a previous chapter: paid employment, caring, and income. This chapter shows that it is still possible to distinguish country-specific patterns and trajectories, but it is questionable whether the welfare regimes (Esping-Andersen 1990), the breadwinner models (Lewis 1992a or Sainsbury 1996), or Pfau-Effinger's cultural models (1998, 1999) are still relevant. Can they capture the radical changes between 1980 and 2000 and at the same time catch the subtle country differences? Or can we see a move towards a European division in Hakim's three categories (2000) – home-centred women (around 20 percent), work-centred women (around 20 percent), and the adaptive types (around 60 percent)?[5]

This chapter begins with a description of women's and men's employment patterns over the last decades in the four countries (section 4.1). Special attention is given to gendered difference in part-time work (section 4.2). Are there country-specific patterns? Can we see any convergence? And more importantly: are women 'forced' to work part time because of institutional barriers, or do women wish to work part time? Considering part-time work is crucial, not only because it is hardly addressed in welfare models but also because studying people's part-time preferences together with their labour patterns reveals whether women (and men) are indeed free to choose.

After discussing paid employment, the focus is on the 'care factor', and especially on caring for young children (section 4.3). What are the consequences for gendered working patterns when women have children? How will they spend their time: on paid work or on informal care? Lone mothers are of special interest. The next section (4.4) deals with men who care for children. What happens when men become fathers? Do they reduce working hours to care more, or work long hours precisely because they consider earning money as a way to show their caring nature? The final section (4.5) deals with the third indicator of citizenship: income. What are the gendered economic dependencies in the four countries?

Change and Diversity in Gendered Employment Rates

Denmark as a forerunner

As table 4.1 shows, women's employment rates in Europe still vary, although all countries show increasing employment rates and smaller gender gaps. Denmark is undoubtedly the archetypical Scandinavian example. More than in any other country, including Sweden, Danish women work outside

Table 4.1   Male and female employment rates (as a percentage of working age population), 1975-2000, four countries

		1975	1985	1990	1994	1998	2000	Gap 1975-2000
BE	women	37	37	41	45	48	52	+ 15
	men	81	69	68	66	67	70	− 11
	gender gap	44					18	
DK	women	61	69	72	69	73	72	+ 11
	men	84	85	84	80	84	81	− 4
	gender gap	24					9	
NL	women	33	40	47	51	57	63	+ 30
	men	89	76	77	75	80	82	− 7
	gender gap	56					19	
UK	women	54	55	63	62	64	65	+ 11
	men	88	77	82	76	79	78	− 10
	gender gap	34					13	

Source: EC (2000); Eurostat (2001)

the home. Their employment rates are nearly just as high as men's – and they work even more than men in some continental countries, such as Belgium. Only for a short period, around the 1950s, was being a housewife a common 'job' for married women when three-quarters of women stayed at home (Borchorst 2002). Employment rates were high by the 1970s, and in the mid-1980s employment rates had already surpassed what are now the current rates for Dutch, Belgian, and British women. The Danish gender gap – the difference between men's and women's employment rates – has also been the smallest of all four countries (see also Daly 2000b).

Danish women had thus already entered the labour market in the 1960s. This early access is often explained by two factors: a labour market shortage – employers desperately needed workers – and a strong women's movement which demanded women's employment and economic independence.

While other countries invited migrant workers, women filled the shortages in Denmark (Pott-Buter 1993; Borchorst 2002). The 1960s were followed by a period of welfare state expansion, and in the 1970s many women worked in the newly developed service state: they became social workers, nurses, and group leaders in childcare centres. The welfare state was a catalyst for women's employment, as it not only provided the services that enabled women to go out to work, it also provided jobs (Borchorst and Siim 1987; Daly 2000b).

In 1975, as table 4.1 above shows, Denmark had already broken away from the other countries. When the debate about women and work was at its height in countries like the Netherlands and the UK in the mid-1980s and 1990s, in Denmark the process of 'entrance' had nearly finished. Women's employment was more self-evident than anywhere in Europe, and the word *husmor* (housewife) was no longer part of people's daily vocabulary. By the mid-1990s, just 4 percent of women (between ages 25-59) could be called a housewife in Denmark. This is remarkably low compared to Belgium (23 percent), the UK (27 percent), and especially the Netherlands (36 percent) (Eurostat 1997).

The United Kingdom and its Liberal Features

The UK, at first sight, indeed resembles the liberal model. Historically, women's employment rates there have been much higher than in Belgium and the Netherlands. Already in the early 1960s, British women's employment rates were comparatively high, also compared to countries like France and Germany (Pott-Buter 1993). This was probably a result of the Second World War, when the government asked women to work in the war industry. After the war, women were no longer needed and childcare institutions, which had been quickly built up, were just as quickly closed down: 50 percent of the wartime nurseries were closed by 1955 (Lewis 1992b). The practice of being a housewife, which had always remained part of the British mindset, regained strength, and the entry of women into the labour market became a matter of incremental change.

Slowly, women's employment rates increased, but due to the relaxed pace the UK had lost its position as a forerunner in women's employment in Europe. The Netherlands came very close in 2000, although table 4.1 shows that the gender gap in the UK (13) is smaller than in Belgium (18) and the Netherlands (19).

Welfare state theory always points out that class differences in employment patterns are more crucial in the UK than anywhere else (Esping-Andersen 1990; Lewis 1992a; O'Connor et al. 1999). Class differences are mostly captured by the level of education. The assumption is often that lower educated women are more likely to work because of financial need. In the UK, wages are low and it is difficult to qualify for social security benefits. Consequently, less-educated women are 'forced' to work. Human capital theories, on the other hand, stress that the more highly educated women are, the more likely they are to enter the labour market (see Hakim 2000).

Table 4.2 shows that more highly educated women in all countries are indeed most likely to work: there is little variety across Europe, and the gender gap – the difference between men's and women's behaviour – is relatively small. In that sense, welfare regimes may not matter much for highly educated women. The employment behaviour of less-educated women however differs from men's, although this is least the case in Denmark. In Belgium, the Netherlands, and, indeed, the UK, women's employment rates are much lower for the less educated.

Do welfare states have more impact on less-educated women? Strikingly, it is not the UK but Belgium which has the lowest level of labour market participation for this category. Together with the Netherlands, the gender gap is much bigger (32 and 33 respectively). In the UK, both less-educated men and women are more likely to be out of work. The gender division in paid work is less pronounced than the class division in the UK, while in Belgium and the Netherlands less-educated women are much more likely to work less than their husbands. Thus, while Hakim (2000) argues that class or education no longer matter – women's preferences do – the level of education is still an important factor in three of the four countries. In fact, there are important cross-national differences in the employment of less-educated women.

Table 4.2   Female employment rates and the gender employment gap (between
            brackets) by educational attainment, ages 25 to 54, year 2000, four
            countries

	Total	Up to secondary	University/higher
BE	68 (20)	47 (32)	87 (9)
DK	81 (8)	68 (9)	89 (5)
NL	71 (21)	53 (33)	87 (9)
UK	73 (14)	50 (17)	86 (8)

Source: OECD (2002b)

Belgium as a Conservative Country

Belgium is a country that seems to fit the 'conservative corporatist' model
better than Lewis' 'modified male breadwinner' model. As we saw in table
4.1, employment rates are modest. While 37 percent of women worked in
the mid-1970s, this increased to 52 percent in 2000. Until the early 1980s,
Belgian women used to work more than in the Netherlands but they have
always worked less than in France and Germany (Pott-Buter 1993). Due
to slow, incremental change, Belgium has moved to the lower end of the
European employment league of Europe.

Two factors lower the Belgian female employment rate substantially.
First, employment rates of older women are very low. In 2000, just 15
percent of Belgian women aged 55-65 were employed. Rates in the Netherlands are also low: 26 percent of Dutch women in that age category
were employed in 2000. In Denmark and the UK this percentage is much
higher, at 46 and 41 percent, respectively. This is however in line with the
employment levels of older men in these countries: Dutch and Belgian
older men are much less likely to work than Danish and British men (Eurostat 2001).

In addition, unemployment rates of Belgian women are comparatively
high, as is the rate of long-term unemployment. Men are also more likely to be unemployed, but the gender difference is significant. This may
be related to the fact that the Belgian industry, which employed many
women, did not change rapidly enough into a service economy. The benefit system may also be important, as we will see in chapter 5. The UK is
the only country in which women are less likely to be unemployed than
men.

Table 4.3		Percentage of unemployed (m/f) as percentage of the labour force, 1990-2000, four countries		
		1990	*1995*	*2000*
BE	men	4	8	6
	women	10	13	9
DK	men	7	6	4
	women	8	8	5
NL	men	4	6	2
	women	9	8	4
UK	men	7	10	6
	women	6	7	5

Source: EC (2003)

Statistics on gender differences within different parts of Belgium are not readily available. The statistics that are available show higher female employment rates for Flemish women than for Walloon women (Brussels always had higher rates), but the difference is less than two percent. The pattern is similar for men, who have slightly higher employment rates in Flanders. Moreover, unemployment rates for women have been much higher in Walloon, heading towards 20 percent in the early 1990s, compared to about 12 percent in Flanders. Again, the same pattern is visible for men. Thus the differences between Flemish and Walloon women may be attributed to overall regional diversity (Steunpunt WAV 1995).

The Netherlands: A Booming Laggard

Until the late 1980s, labour market participation of Dutch women was extremely low. Together with Spain and Greece, in this respect the Netherlands could be grouped with the 'laggards' of Europe. This has puzzled many researchers. 'How come this otherwise "modern" country has such an "old fashioned" practice?' In trying to answer this question, Pott-Buter (1993) and Plantenga (1993, 1998) offer an overview of the 'usual suspects' used to explain this situation. The first suspect is late modernisation. Dutch society was still rural when other European countries moved into industrialisation and urbanisation. The birth rate also remained high, so labour market shortages were not common. There were enough labour resources. A second, very popular explanation is the 'typically Dutch' societal structure of 'pillarisation'. Social and political life was organised into four pillars: Catholic, Protestant, social democratic, and neutral. These pillars helped to keep the norm in place that women's only role is that of mother and homemaker. The system of pillarisation was extremely conducive to this end. The pillars offered channels for communicating attitudes from above, by imposing them forcefully on the whole population.

After comparing the Netherlands with Germany, Plantenga (1993, 1998) concludes that pillarisation is an important factor especially because there was a strong agreement between pillars. The system of pillarisation existed in many other countries as well (Switzerland, Germany, and Belgium), but nowhere was the ideal of mothers' staying at home expressed with such a powerful passion. It seems unlikely though that ideological passion alone would have sufficed. Wishes must also have at least some possibility for fulfilment. Most European countries such as Belgium and Germany, have similar values about women's proper place, but the Netherlands is the only country that was wealthy enough to afford this practice. Plantenga argues that, in the end, Dutch prosperity explains women's low employment rates. The economist Pott-Buter (1993) comes to a similar conclusion: there was no financial need to sidestep the Dutch cultural tradition of women as homemakers.

This theory helps to understand Dutch social history, but it may be less applicable to other countries or recent times. In Denmark, for instance, labour market rates rose in the 1960s, but not because the country was so poor and women needed to work. The women's movement, which played a crucial role, demanded employment – not because they wanted to support women who worked out of financial need but because work offers individual emancipation (Borchorst 2002).

Moreover, for European women in general, financial need is no longer the main reason to work. Belgian research from the mid-1970s already demonstrated this (Pauwels 1978). Women wanted to work because they could have contact with other people. Financial reasons came fifth in the ranking of motivations, although less-educated women indeed mention this motive more often. When married women in the Netherlands and Belgium were compared in the mid-1980s, Belgian women in the same financial circumstances as their Dutch peers were still more likely to work (Henkes et al. 1992). Economic motives seem to have lost power. Economic needs have also become less diverse in Europe. Since the late 1980s, countries like Belgium, the Netherlands, and Denmark have had similar wage structures and minimum wages (also in terms of purchasing power parity). The UK is a somewhat different story (OECD 1994).

This means that from the 1970s onwards Plantenga's (1993, 1998) and Pott-Buter's (1993) theory of economic needs can no longer sufficiently explain the differences between the four countries examined in this book. This is not only because economic necessity has acquired a different meaning, but also because values towards work have reversed: women are no longer pushed to work because of economic needs; women demand to work.

The crucial turning point in the Dutch history of women's employment occurred in the late 1980s and early 1990s. A report by the Scientific Council for Government Policy entitled 'A Working Perspective' (WRR 1990) summarised the problem, and in so doing marked a turning point, particularly for women. The report said that in the Netherlands a large amount of human capital was wasted because women were largely 'inactive', and for a sustainable welfare state, particularly in the light of the ageing of society, it is crucial to invest in female labour market participation. As table 4.1 shows, in 2000 the percentage of employed women had indeed risen to 63 percent, which means a huge increase compared to 39.5 percent in 1985. Today, Dutch women are more likely to work than their Belgian sisters. In none of the other countries has such rapid revolution taken place.

So far, the countries more or less fit the welfare regime models described by Esping-Andersen, and less the gender models as described by Lewis. The Netherlands as well as Belgium score relatively low on women's employment levels, although in the Netherlands a real revolution is taking place. British female employment rates are higher and class division is indeed more important there. As the archetypical example of the Scandinavian welfare state, Danish female employment rates have the top ranking, as Danish women already entered the labour market in the 1960s and 1970s. To understand gendered citizenship not only the level of participation is important, the number of hours is essential too. What do differences in part-time work reveal: are welfare regime theories still more adequate than cultural theories?

The Meaning of Part-time Work

Part-time work is a crown witness for testing the welfare state theories described in chapter 3. Comparative welfare regime theories stress institutional barriers and tend to regard part-time work as a negative result of the lack of childcare services or tax policies that penalise double-earners. Hakim (2000, 2003a) on the other hand stresses that women work part-time because they want to. The cultural approach of Pfau-Effinger (1998) adds that welfare states followed women's demands. Both stress that there will always be women who want to work part time and combine work and care. The incidence of part-time work is an important indicator of what Hakim has labelled the adaptive type of woman, which is supposed to make up 60 percent of European women.

In most European countries, women's work is part-time work and part-time work is women's work. Part-time work has expanded rapidly since the 1970s and especially since the 1980s. In many European countries, part-time work acted as a lever for women to enter the labour market. As they could now combine paid work with care, homemakers became attracted to paid employment. The part-time revolution also had a second impulse. In the 1980s in some European countries, especially the Netherlands and Belgium, part-time work became a measure to combat unemployment, as part of a larger program of redistributing labour (O'Reilly and Fagan 1998).

Table 4.4	Part-time employment of women and mothers with children under age 6 (as part of all women aged 25-55), year 2001, four countries	
Country	Women	Mothers
BE	33	45
DK	21	6
NL	58	69
UK	41	66

Source: OECD (2002b)

Two countries have a tradition of women working full time – Belgium and Denmark – and two countries have a tradition of women working part time – the Netherlands and the UK. While in most European countries part-time work increased, in Denmark part-time rates have fallen significantly. In the 1970s and 1980s, Danish women were also more likely to work part time than full time, but from the 1990s onwards Danish women increasingly turned to full-time employment. A dual full-time breadwinner model is now standard practice in Denmark.

A high level of part-time work is often considered as a transitional phase between the male breadwinner model and the equality model where both men and women are fully integrated into the labour market (OECD 2002a). This is not a standard trajectory though. Belgium, for instance, was also on the move towards female full-time employment, but things changed: women are leaving full-time jobs and part-time work has become the norm (Cantillon et al. 1999). The Belgian trajectories are very different from the Dutch and the British. Before women worked part time in Belgium they worked full time, but before women worked part time in the UK or the Netherlands they were housewives. Indeed, in these countries, the possibility of working part-time meant a mechanism for women to work (Plantenga 1996).

Today in the UK and the Netherlands, large numbers of women work part time. In the UK, full-time employment for women is growing: there has been a net increase of working hours since the 1990s (OECD 2004). The Netherlands however is different from the other countries – since the 1980s it has been moving towards the first part-time economy in the world. In the Netherlands, part-time work is not some transitional phase but standard practice (Visser 2002). In that sense the Netherlands is indeed moving to what Pfau-Effinger (1998) has labelled a dual breadwinner/dual carer model.

Force or Choice?

In comparative welfare state theory, part-time work is often seen as a pattern that is forced upon women. Due to a lack of child care services or disincentives in social security and taxation, women cannot work longer hours. Scholars like Pfau-Effinger (1998) or Hakim (2000) nonetheless argue that part-time work is what women wish for; it is their preference. One indication of whether women have a say in the hours they work is the difference between actual and preferred number of hours. On the one hand, the number of hours women want to work follows the same pattern as women's actual practice. In other words, Dutch women prefer to work fewer hours than Danish women. On the other hand, in all countries a gap exists between actual and preferred working hours: nowhere do people work the hours they want, but the gap is smaller in Belgium, Denmark, and the Netherlands than in the UK (in that order). This is shown by the Employment Option for the Future Survey of 1998 (Fagan 2001; Bielinski and Wagner 2004). In general, women are more satisfied with their working hours than men, and this is especially the case in the Netherlands.

Whether women want to work more or fewer hours often depends on the number of hours they work. In general, women with 'small jobs' (with few hours) want to work more, women with 'big jobs' (with many hours) want to work less. In the Netherlands, the average number of hours of work for women is 26, the lowest in Europe. The average is 31 in the UK, 34 in Belgium, and 34 in Denmark (Fagan 2001). In addition, a relatively large number of Dutch women work less than 20 hours (one-third), compared to one-fifth for the UK, and much less in Denmark (8 percent) and Belgium (11 percent). The many women with 'small jobs' in UK and the Netherlands are particularly dissatisfied, while women with relatively 'big' part-time jobs are very satisfied with the hours they work. In general, British and Dutch women with 'small jobs' would like to work more (Keuzenkamp and Oudhof 2000; Fagan 1996).

On the other side of the spectrum – Belgium and Denmark – women work comparatively long hours but they want to work less. In Belgium, this desire has indeed come into being, as women have moved towards part-time work. This is not the case in Denmark, where the increase in working hours does not coincide with people's wishes. In general, Danish women do not want to work full time on such a large scale. To sum it up: there is more convergence in dreams than in realities. Most women in the four countries want to work between 20-34 hours per week, but in reality they work more (in Denmark) or less (in the Netherlands) (Fagan 2001). As Bielinski and Wagner (2004: 160, 161) conclude, 'Working-time preferences in general, and those of men and women in particular, are more similar than actual working times, both within and across countries.'

Table 4.5   Perceived barriers to part-time work: all full-time employees, percentage of those who mentioned one or more of the following items (multiple responses), four countries

	It would not be possible to do my current job part time	My employer would not accept it	It would damage my career prospects	Part-timers have fewer employment rights	Could not afford to work part time
BE	55	50	50	29	37
DK	52	59	49	50	28
NL	47	55	51	25	32
UK	63	60	53	66	61

Source: Fagan (2001) on the basis of the Employment Options for the Future 1998 (EOF)

Why do people not work the number of hours they wish? Table 4.5 shows that in all countries workers perceive problems with their employer or in their careers. Only the last two columns show interesting cross-national differences. Dutch and Belgian employees do not believe part-timers have fewer employment rights, in contrast to the British and Danish. Except for the UK, money is hardly a reason to work full time. Common assumptions that Danish women (and men) have to work full time because of the needs of the family economy are thus untrue. It is only in the UK, known for its high incidence of low-paid jobs, that full-timers prefer not to work part-time because they cannot afford to do so. Only in that country do economic factors seem very important.

Men

The final question is whether men also work part time. In any country in Europe men are more likely to work full time, but in some countries men are more likely to work part time than in others. In 1998 Belgium had the lowest score (3.5 percent), followed by the UK (4.4), Denmark (10.9), and the Netherlands (18.1) (EC 2000). The UK is especially known for its extremely long working hours for men, 44.3 on average. In Belgium, the Netherlands, and Denmark men work shorter hours, on average 41.6, 41.1, and 39.8 a week, respectively. Thus in the country that is often reported to have such a strong work ethic, Denmark, men work the least hours (Fagan 2001).

Do British men really want to work such long hours? A 1996 survey showed that 10 percent of men working long hours would like to reduce hours, indicating that actually few men behave against their wishes. However, an even higher percentage (18) would want to work even more hours. The reason given is to increase their income. According to Fagan (1996), in the UK increased overtime has been stimulated by low wages (at the bottom side of the labour market) and shortages of skilled labour (at the upper side of the labour market). The above-mentioned survey on working time preferences (EOF) found that 28 percent of British men would prefer a job of less than 35 hours. Men in other countries have a slightly stronger desire to work parttime: 30 percent of Belgian men prefer to work less than 35 hours, 33 percent in Denmark, and 42 percent in the Netherlands (Fagan 2001). Thus, overall, quite a number of men want to work less than they actually do. But the more men prefer to work part time, the more they actually do.

If men also worked less than full time, this would degender part-time work. Moreover, if men worked part time they could take responsibility for caring. Part-time work could reduce women's second shift. So what do men do when they work part time? In the 1970s, the male chairman of the Danish trade unions (LO), Nielsen, was very much against part-time work because he was sure that 'men would just go fishing' (int. 59). Statistics show that despite national differences one thing is common: men are more likely to work part-time when they are very young (15-24) and when they are older (55+, and even more 65+), but not in the period when they have young children (25-40) (e.g., OECD 2001; EC 2003). The majority of part-time workers are mainly students who need the supplementary income and older men who are tired of their career. Perhaps there is only a loose connection between men working part time and participation in caring.

Part-time Work as the Crown Witness

Part-time work in some countries (Denmark, perhaps the UK) can be seen as a transitional phase: it acts as a mechanism for women to start working and eventually turn to full-time employment. In other countries, part-time employment is the next stage for working women full-time (Belgium), while in others it seems to be a stable standard practice (the Netherlands). As Pfau-Effinger (1998) stresses, many diverse modernisation trajectories exist. Comparative welfare theories and welfare state models such as those of Lewis (1992a) and Esping-Andersen (1990) neither correspond nor deal with part-time diversity in Europe. These models are not equipped to deal with the radical social change that has taken place.

Moreover, part-time work is indeed the wish of many women as well as men, as cultural theories stress. But a scholar who focuses on culture such as Hakim (2000) is not fully right either. There are country-specific patterns in employment behaviour, and not in every country (see Denmark) are the majority of women adaptive types. Besides, men and women do not exactly behave according to their wishes. Many men want to work fewer hours while many women want to work more hours (if they have 'small part-time jobs') or fewer hours (if they have 'big full-time jobs'). Work behaviour and work preferences have no one-to-one relationship. In addition, in the UK economic motives may still explain the difference between reality and dreams.

When Women Become Mothers

So far, we have examined women's and men's employment patterns, but what happens when men become fathers and women become mothers? Are employment patterns affected by having children? To what extent are mothers and fathers involved in caring at home? Clearly, the ideal of full-time motherhood is less practiced. Women are more likely than ever to continue working when they become mothers. In the twenty-first century, having children is less decisive for women's employment than it used to be. The age of the child is important, but it is becoming less so. The number of children also matters. With one child people feel they are 'a couple with a child', two or three children means 'a family'. The latter increasingly leads to a new lifestyle in which women are more likely to stay at home. But the extent to which motherhood matters varies per country.

Danish Mothers

In Denmark motherhood is hardly decisive for employment patterns. The phenomenon of working mothers was largely accepted there prior to the mid-1980s and the percentage of employed mothers was stable: around three-quarters had a paid job (table 4.6). This applies to mothers with one, two, or more children. The difference with men is negligible, although the gender gap increases when mothers have two or more children. The age of children does not matter much either: mothers with children under three are nearly as likely to be employed as those with older children (ECNC 1996; Eurostat 2005). Full-time rates for mothers are generally high (table 4.6) and educational attainment does not make a significant difference (Rubery et al. 1999). Denmark is indeed the archetypical Scandinavian country where women work just like men, and it hardly matters whether they have children, how old they are, or how many there are. Full-time motherhood is an ideal that disappeared long ago (see also Plantenga and Siegel 2004).

Table 4.6	Women's employment rates by presence of children (0-15), persons aged 25 to 54, percentage of persons working part time in total employment, 2000, four countries		
	No children	*One child*	*Two or more children*
BE	66	72	69
Part-time rates	29	35	46
DK	79	88	77
Part-time rates	19	13	16
NL	75	70	63
Part-time rates	38	73	83
UK	80	73	62
Part-time rates	47	63	39

Source: OECD (2002)

Belgian Mothers

Historically, Belgian mothers were more likely to work than the British and Dutch. This was especially the case in the 1980-1995 period. Belgium had higher employment rates for mothers (with children 0-10) in 1985 (51 percent of mothers were employed in Belgium, 23 percent in the Netherlands). This difference was still the case in 1993 (62 percent were employed in Belgium, 46 percent in the Netherlands) (ECNC 1996). At the same time, Belgian mothers were more likely to work full time than in the UK and especially the Netherlands (tables 4.6). Although in this period employment rates for Belgian mothers were relatively high, they could not reach the Danish rates. Belgium never reached 'Scandinavian' levels (table 4.6, 4.7; ECNC 1996; see also Plantenga and Siegel 2004).

More recently, mothers' employment rates have not grown rapidly. The most recent statistics from Eurostat (2005) show that the Belgian rates of working women with children under 12 is 68 percent. This is much lower compared to Denmark (80), and even lower than in the Netherlands (70). Only the UK has lower employment rates for mothers (62). This cross-national pattern is also visible in table 4.7. In addition, mothers increasingly participate in the workforce on a part-time basis, although the level is still comparatively low. While in 1985 only 14 percent of mothers (with a child aged 0-10) worked part time, this doubled to 27 percent in 2003 (ECNC 1996; Eurostat 2005). Highly educated mothers are more likely to work part time while less educated mothers are a little more likely to work full time (Rubery et al. 1999).

While the previous section showed low female employment rates in Belgium, this is less the case for mothers. In Belgium, mothers were always more likely to be in paid work than women in general and they also worked full-time. This challenges the idea that Belgium is a conservative corporatist country and instead shows it to be a modified male breadwinner model. More recently however, mothers' employment rates have been stagnating and were surpassed by the Netherlands. Mothers also tend to move from full-time employment to part-time work.

British Mothers

In the UK, employment rates of women in general are higher than those for mothers. In other words, having a child is crucial for women's employment, full-time motherhood is sometimes still an ideal. This emphasises the UK's male breadwinner dimension rather than its liberal sides. Especially since the 1990s, the UK has dropped to last place among the four countries in terms of mother's employment rates; it has even been surpassed by the Netherlands. More than in the other countries, motherhood matters (Plantenga and Siegel 2004; Eurostat 2005).

First, more than in Belgium, the number of children is important. Two children or more significantly reduces mothers' employment rates. Table 4.5 indicates that when women have one child they continue working but preferably on a part-time basis. When the second child arrives, women are more likely to quit altogether. Those who continue working do so on a full-time basis. According to Rubery et al. (1999), highly educated mothers are slightly more likely to work full time, while less educated women are more likely to work part time. This is the opposite of Belgium.

Secondly, the age of the child is crucial for mother's employment. Many mothers take their first steps back into the labour market when their child reaches the age of three, but most of them go back when the child reaches the age of six or seven and starts school (Rubery et al. 1999). In the early 1990s, 44 percent of mothers with a child aged 0-3 and 59 percent of mothers with a child aged 3-10 were employed. Also, more recent statistics indicate significant differences between mothers with younger and older children (Eurostat 2005). This is a typically British practice: mothers start to work when the children go to school (ECNC 1996).

Table 4.7	Employment rate (percentage) for women with a child under age three, 1992-2003, four countries		
	1992	*2000*	*2003*
BE	61	68	63
DK	70*	71*	72
NL	42	63	70
UK	40	53	52

Sources: Moss (2004) on the basis of the European Labour Force Survey, Eurostat (2005)
* Since Denmark was not included, the OECD Labour Force Survey (2002b) is used for 2000.

Dutch Mothers

Dutch mothers have always had very low employment rates, but a spectacular increase in working mothers has taken place. In the mid-1980s only a quarter of mothers worked. At that time, having one child meant the start of a career at home. Women returned to paid work when their child reached 12 to 14 (Rubery et al. 1999). These women even had a special name: *herintreders* (returners). But much more pronounced than in the UK, which also had low employment rates for mothers, a real social revolution took place in the Netherlands, away from full-time motherhood, which pushed the UK to the lowest ranking of the four countries. Table 4.6 shows that in 2000 much more than half of Dutch mothers with young children worked (63 percent). Recent statistics report that in 2003, 80 percent of mothers of children aged 0-12 were employed. At the moment in the Netherlands, the age of the child is not a very significant factor in whether or not the mother is employed (ECNC 1996; Eurostat 2005). However, the gender gap between mothers and fathers is still the biggest in Europe. Typical for the Dutch case is that if mothers work, they do so on a part-time basis, no matter what their educational background is. Part-time work is standard practice for mothers and full-time work hardly an option (table 4.6; Eurostat 2005).

When Mothers are Lone Mothers

So far, we have discussed the incidence, volume, and class dimension of women in general and mothers in particular. But a very important category of women is that of lone mothers, who are often seen as test cases. The way they fare reveals the citizenship status of women: are they workers or carers? Lone mothers are the litmus test of female citizenship (Hobson 1994; Knijn 1994; Lewis, 1997).

Although different studies show different levels of employment, the picture in the mid-1990s is nearly always the same: the Dutch and British employment rates of lone mothers with young children (ages 0-6) are the lowest of all four countries, even though we can see a steady increase in both countries, also since 1999 (see also Evans 2003; Knijn and van Berkel 2003). Still, lone mothers are less likely to work than mothers in two-parent families. Moreover, in the UK and the Netherlands part-time work is the most important option (table 4.8). In Belgium and Denmark employment rates for lone mothers are higher. In Denmark little difference exists between mothers: nearly all of them work full time, regardless of whether there is a father at home. In Belgium, employment rates of lone mothers have always been higher than those of married mothers, but since the mid-1990s they are nearly the same. In Belgium, most lone mothers work full time (Cantillon and Verbist 2003; Millar and Rowlingson 2001; Pedersen et al. 2000).

Table 4.8	Employment rates of lone mothers with a child under age six, 1984-1999, four countries			
	1984	*1989*	*1994*	*1999*
BE	47	35	43	46
DK	N.A.	65/83*	53/71*	51/70*
UK	19	24	26	34
NL	13	NA	26	38

Source: OECD (2001)

* The Danish rates are not included in OECD (2001). Danish rates are based on OECD (2002a). 1989 =1991, 1994 =1995. The left side of the slash refers to employment rates of single parents with children aged three or under, the right side refers to single parents with children aged 3-6.

Do mothers' employment patterns falsify the logic of welfare models? There are clear country-specific patterns, but they show more similarities with breadwinner models (Lewis 1992a) than with the three worlds of welfare (Esping-Andersen 1990). The employment rates of mothers show that mothers in the 'conservative corporatist' countries – Belgium and the Netherlands – are historically more likely to work than in the 'Liberal' welfare state of the UK. At the same time, a big difference exists between Belgium and the Netherlands when it comes to mothers: the Netherlands has always had lower employment rates, even for lone mothers. Belgium in this respect does resemble Lewis' (1992) modified model. Belgian mothers, whether lone or married, are much more likely to work than in the UK and the Netherlands, and they are also more likely to work full time. Nevertheless, there remains a distinction between Belgium and Denmark. In Denmark, motherhood hardly matters for employment patterns, and again Denmark fits into the models it is ascribed.

When Men Become Fathers

The previous section showed that when women become mothers they are likely to work fewer hours. But when men become fathers they are likely to work more, and fathers are the least likely of all men to be unemployed. Men still translate caring responsibilities into bringing home money. At the same time, a 'new man' arises who wishes to work part time and spend more time with his family. Parental sharing has become a new ideal that replaces the traditional full-time moderhood utopia. Contrary to mothers, men's employment patterns hardly vary across Europe, although in a few countries we can see signs of change. And in some countries, fathers work more hours than in others.

In the mid-1990s, Belgian, Dutch, and Danish fathers who were employed worked on average 40-41 hours per week. British fathers worked more hours: 48. Dutch fathers are most likely to work part-time (7 percent). This is much less in Belgium (1 percent) and Denmark and the UK (2 percent) (ECNC 1996). Table 4.9 shows that both male and female in a couple working part time is the most common in the Netherlands (Denmark is not included). The percentage is negligible though. In that sense, Pfau-Effinger's (1998) classification of the Netherlands being a dual breadwinner/dual carer model does not fit reality. Besides, in Belgium more fathers work part time while their wives work full time.

Table 4.9	Households with at least one working partner, with one child, in percentages, year 2000, three countries			
	Male part time Female part time	*Male part time Female full time*	*Male full time Female part time*	*Male full time Female full time*
BE	1.9	1.7	28.3	40.8
NL	2.3	1.3	52.9	10.8
UK	0.7	0.9	40	28.6

Source: Eurostat (2002), based on the European Labour Force Survey

A second question is, what do fathers do when they work part-time: are they indeed involved in caring, or do they go fishing? Time budget studies are the only source to find out how people spend their daily lives, but it is not a very trustworthy source. Definitions often vary across countries as to what caring is exactly; people may not report well on what they do, and their answers may be culturally shaped. Besides, comparing time budget reports shows contradictory results and none of the comparisons includes all four countries. Keeping this in mind, what can still be said about men's participation in care?

Table 4.10	Childcare among parents living as couple with children up to age six, hours and minutes a day, 1998-2000, three countries		
	Women	*Men*	*Gender gap*
BE	1.40	0.50	0.90
DK	1.44	0.57	0.87
UK	2.08	0.58	1.50

Source: European Commission (2004)

Most comparative studies show little cross-national differences in men's caring behaviour. Table 4.10 reports on European Commission research (2004). The difference between women in the three countries – the Netherlands is not included – is significant: the country with the highest part-time rate, the UK, shows the highest rates in time spent on care. The difference between men is rather insignificant. Cross-national research that includes the Netherlands shows that Dutch men are similar to those other countries (OECD 2002a; SCP 2000).

Gershuny and Sullivan (2003: 219) confront ideal typical welfare states with men's contributions to the household, and do not find many country-specific patterns in men's involvement in caring and domestic tasks either: 'Contrary to what we might have expected on the basis of the discussion concerning the relationship between regime type, gender, and the use of time, it appears that there is no clear pattern of differentiation in the division of unpaid work according to public policy regime type.' Instead, they find a differentiation according to level of education – higher educated men contribute more to the household – and a general trend over time towards a convergence of men's and women's time spent in unpaid work across countries. Thus men are slowly changing, but not according to a country-specific pattern.

In sum, time budget studies come to an ironic conclusion: men's time spent on childcare is similar in Europe and is not related to women's employment patterns. This is what Hochschild (1989) refers to as the 'stalled revolution'. When rapid industrialisation took men out of the home and placed them in the factory, shop, or office, an analogous revolution encouraged women to stay in the home. Now another revolution is taking place and women are moving out of the home, but men have not shared in the social revolution of women's move into the economy. In other words, while the ideal of full-time motherhood became outdated, the alternative ideal of parental sharing has not replaced it. At the same time, fathers and men do work less than before, and especially Danish and Dutch men work fewer hours and would like to work less. The question is whether they will also care more.

Money of Her Own: Gender and Income

So far, I have discussed women's and men's participation in work and care: two indicators of citizenship. The third indicator is income. Welfare state theory has a long history of studying poverty and income distribution. For a long time this has been the core of such analyses, but studying how income has been distributed within the family has a much shorter tradition.

A handful of researchers have done pioneering work to examine the interdependencies within the family and women's economic position (Hobson 1990; Bianci et al. 1996; Bonke 1999; Daly 2000; Sørensen 2001). Most appropriate for this study is the analysis done by Bonke (1999), because unlike other studies it covers all four countries taken up in this book and uses an innovative perspective. He shows that although women's economic position within households is never equal to men's, in Denmark their positions are the closest: women earn 42 percent of the household income, followed by Belgium (37 percent), the Netherlands (33 percent) and the UK (32 percent). This overall picture is supported by the other studies.

Table 4.11 also highlights which types of income distribution within couples are most common in the four countries. A distinction is made between women who earn less than 40 percent of the household income, women who earn about as much as men (between 40-59 percent of the income), and women who earn more than men (more than 59 percent). In half of the Danish cases, the partners have nearly the same wages. In other words, half of the couples are really 'interdependent', as Sørensen would have put it (see chapter 2). The other three countries lay far behind Denmark, including Belgium where only a quarter of couples show real 'interdependence'. The difference between the UK and the Netherlands is the fact that in the latter few women belonging to a couple have higher wages than men: 'role reversal' hardly exists. In the UK, more than in the other countries, high-earning women do exist, and they probably have more bargaining power at the kitchen table.

Table 4.11   Woman's share of income (personal net income) in couples, 1994, in percentages, four countries

	<40	40-59	>59
BE	66	27	7
DK	44	51	6
NL	78	19	3
UK	72	20	8

Source: Bonke (1999) on the basis of the 1994 ECHP

The outcomes of this analysis of economic independence are completely in line with labour market participation rates, as Bonke himself also stresses. Many more double-earners exist in Denmark than in Belgium, the UK, and the Netherlands. This could indicate that only employment activity matters. In the previous chapter I discussed that carers could also gain economic equality when they received direct payments for care, such as paid leave or benefits. Do the above statistics mean that the route taken by state payments for caregiving has no significant effect on economic equality within households?

Individual income is an important indicator of citizenship, but not all women (or men) seem to demand economic equality. A European barometer survey (1993) questioned whether women should have their own income. 'Yes', said nearly 80 percent of Danish women and men, and 40 percent of Dutch women and men. Sixty percent of Belgian women but only 50 percent of men said so, and for the UK 50 percent of women and 40 percent of men wanted women to have their own income. The Danish score highest and the Dutch lowest, while Belgian and British women take a middle position. (The latter may also have slightly more discussions and fights with their men because the gender gap is biggest.)

A similar pattern is shown in a more recent European Value Study, although the UK takes a different position (Halman 1999/2000). In response to the question of whether both the husband and wife should contribute to household income, 71 percent of the British agree, 68 percent of Danish, 74 percent of Belgians, and only 35 percent of the Dutch. Clearly, the British answers differ from the above results but the Dutch are always the least likely to want economic independence. Of course, the answers may have been adapted to reality. At the same time, it may well be that the meaning of economic dependence or independence varies across countries (Daly 2000), and that in the Netherlands it is valued the least. According to Morée (1990), who interviewed many women on this issue, Dutch women do not really want economic equality but value having some money in their pocket. They want the 'illusion of economic independence'.

So far, studying economic interdependencies is concerned with income distribution within families rather than between families. But this is also a one-sided picture – as if women were indeed better off when they are extremely poor but just as poor as men. The best way to reveal economic interdependencies is through the analysis of 'individual poverty' in the context of 'family poverty', or 'individual income' in the context of the 'family income'. Since to my knowledge such comparative studies do not exist, table 4.12 gives at least an impression of the cross-national differences in poverty among household types.

Table 4.12   Poverty rates for different household types, head of household of active age, mid-1990s, four countries

| | Single adult | | | Two adults | | |
	All	Earning	Non-earning	Dual earners	Single earner	No earner
BE	5.0	1.3	16.1	0.1	2.4	18.0
DK	6.1	8.6	20.1	0.4	2.0	7.9
NL	8.3	12.1	27.8	0.7	3.5	17.1
UK	17.5	7.0	57.7	1.0	12.7	52.3

Note: Poverty is <50 percent of the median equivalent disposable income
Source: Marx et al. (1999) on the basis of LIS

As expected, the UK shows the highest incidence of poverty (17.5 percent). Belgium scores the lowest (5 percent), but also Denmark (6.1 per cent) and the Netherlands (8.3 per cent) have reasonable poverty rates. The Dutch poverty rates are perhaps higher than expected, as there has been a strong increase since the 1980s. Poverty is also strongly linked to paid employment; earnings indeed give the best protection against poverty. But if one does not earn, the UK as a liberal regime indeed gives the least protection to single earners and non-earning families. Jobless citizens are best protected in Denmark, followed by Belgium and the Netherlands.

The working poor, associated with liberal welfare states, is not a typical British reality: it is a problem for many single earners living on their own. Strikingly, the incidence of poverty among single earners is even higher in the Netherlands than in the UK. Marx et al. (1999) go as far as to argue that low wages and the working poor should not be exaggerated, not even in the UK. But the picture changes when we look at families. Especially in the UK, two incomes may be necessary to fulfil the needs of the family (see Esping-Andersen et al. 2002). Nearly 13 percent of families with one income is poor. At the same time, the UK has a relatively low incidence of double-earner families. This is puzzling. Why aren't double-income families more common in the UK, as this offers the best protection against poverty? Danish single-earner families, compared to the Belgian and Dutch, are the least likely to be poor. Does this mean that in Denmark too one wage will suffice for the family income, or can only families that can afford it chose the single-earner model?

Interdependencies within the family (the gender gap) should be placed in the context of household poverty in general. Income equality increases women's citizenship status, but when the family as a whole can barely survive, women's citizenship is threatened. This dilemma is most pronounced in the UK. Another question revealing differences in women's European citizenship status is whether mothers can survive economically when they are on their own. How do lone mothers fare? Can they do financially without a husband?

Table 4.13   Lone parent poverty, mid-1990s, four countries

	Mother works	Mother inactive
BE	11	23
DK	10	34
NL	17	41
UK	26	69

Note: Poverty is <50 percent of the median equivalent disposable income
Source: Esping Andersen (2002) on the basis of LIS

In all countries, lone mothers are more likely to be poor than two-parent families. If they want to improve their income, they better find a husband or a job. If they are employed they are less likely to be poor. Hence Danish lone mothers are less likely to be poor than lone mothers in the other three countries , as many of them work on a full-time basis. But even when Danish lone mothers do not work, they are better protected than Dutch and notably British mothers. British mothers and less so Dutch mothers are more likely to be part of the working poor; one of the reasons is because they tend to be employed part time. Belgian lone mothers are doing comparatively well, regardless of whether they work (often full time) or not.

Conclusion: Cross-national Differences in Work, Care, and Income

First of all, distinct country-specific patterns and trajectories still exist (see also Daly 2000b). But especially when we look at caring and employment patterns, women's and men's lives can hardly be captured by Esping-Andersen's models. Denmark does fit the social democratic model perfectly, but other countries are more problematic. Belgian mothers are much more likely to work (also full time) than the Christian democratic welfare regime predicts. Until very recently, Belgian mothers worked much more than Dutch mothers, who resembled the British practice to a higher degree. Mothers' employment rates have been low in both countries, also for lone mothers. In that sense Lewis' models seem to be better suited.

At the same time, neither welfare state model is able to properly address the diverse composition in part-time work and the recent changes in women's employment, including the farewell to full-time motherhood. How can the incredible increase of mothers' (part-time) employment in the Netherlands be explained? Or the Belgian decrease in female full-time employment rates and increase in part-time rates? Moreover, the welfare models do not address the slight increase in the diversity of fathers' citizenship. In other words, perhaps Lewis' breadwinner models revealed the reality of the 1980s well, but European work-and-care patterns are modernising rapidly and what is happening after the male breadwinner/female caretaker epoch cannot be adequately expressed by the dominant theories.

This chapter also showed that there is no standard 'modernisation' trajectory in which women first work part time and then move en masse to full-time employment (OECD 2002). While Danish and perhaps British women have moved or are moving towards a full-time female economy, in Belgium women who used to work full time are now moving to part-time jobs while in the Netherlands part-time work is becoming standard practice. Hakim is thus both right and wrong. She is right because there are no signs that all European women will move towards full-time jobs or wish to do so. She is wrong because there are countries, notably Denmark, in which most women work full time: her classifications of adaptive, work-centred, and home-centred women do not make sense in this part of the world. The question that still remains to be answered is how to understand these 'part-time' and 'full-time' changes.

It is also true that part-time work is something that many women and men both wish for and demand. This reveals the importance of women as agents over their private lives (Pfau-Effinger 1998; Hakim 2000). At the same time, the study of part-time works shows a large gap between words and deeds. Only in the UK does the financial necessity to work full time seem important. The cultural approach gives few answers as to why people of both sexes abstain from following their wishes.

How to understand and explain the European differences and changing employment and care patterns is still a matter of research. The next two chapters will unravel social policy and study if, how, and to what extent the composition of welfare states can explain diversity in gendered citizenship. I start with an examination of the right to give care. Chapter 5 discusses taxation, social security, and leave schemes. Chapter 6 examines the right to receive care and raises the question of whether state-subsidised childcare has an impact on women's and men's citizenship.

5   The Right to Give Care: Tax, Social Security, and Leave

Can financial compensation for caregiving explain different and changing patterns of women's employment in Europe? Will women indeed work less when they receive money to provide care, such as a male-breadwinner bonus in taxation, or compensation via social security and leave schemes? This chapter confronts the existing welfare state typologies with women's participation patterns. Following welfare state theories such as those of Esping-Andersen (1990), Lewis (1992a), and Sainsbury (1996), we expect strong breadwinner bonuses in the Belgian and Dutch systems, work incentives in the Danish system, and a more diffuse picture in the United Kingdom. Is this indeed the case? And how to understand policy origins and policy change?

Fiscal Care

When Titmuss (1958) described the welfare state, he distinguished between three types of welfare provision. The first two, benefits and services, are well known, but the third is less obvious: he calls it 'fiscal welfare', benefits through tax deductions. He complained that this aspect of European welfare states has had too little coverage. Nearly half a century later, such studies are still in their infancy, although tax policy has received increased attention in the welfare state debate – not in the least because fiscal instruments gained popularity in the neo-liberal decades of the 1980s and 1990s. This chapter tries to unravel the impact of tax policy on citizenship. The topic is more specific than Titmuss' broad area of fiscal welfare: it is fiscal care. How does the tax system care?

Historically, man and wife were taxed together. This meant a huge work disincentive for second-earners because when the wife went to work, the household would fall into a higher tax bracket. After individualisation of taxation took place, mostly in the 1980s, some welfare states incorporated a transferable allowance, the 'male breadwinner bonus': a compensation for men who had a wife working at home. This gives women the opportunity to provide care, but it is a derived 'right', as it makes them dependent on their husbands (and they are only entitled to this right if they have a husband). The bonus is also seen as a major disincentive for working women. Many economic calculations have been made to prove its negative impact on female employment rates (e.g., Gustafsson and Bruyn-Hundt 1991; Grift 1998; OECD 2002a). The following paragraphs examine which welfare states have incorporated such derived 'rights' and what are the consequences of fiscal care for women's employment. And what are the origins of changes in taxation? Is it social democracy or the women's movement?

Individualisation and Transferable Allowances

First, it is important to consider when countries introduced an individual system of taxation in which women and men are seen as independent earners. Scandinavian countries (as well as Austria!) introduced individualisation early. The key period was the early 1970s. Denmark individualised tax on income in 1970, but on wealth only in the mid-1980s. The Scandinavian countries may well have taken this step because individualisation was seen as urgent due to high marginal tax rates; working was hardly worth it for a second earner (int. 43, 66, 67). Most continental countries introduced individualisation one or two decades later: the Netherlands in 1984 (although already in 1973 an individualised system existed which still discriminated against working women, as we will see in the next section), Belgium in 1989, and the UK in 1989 (Dingeldey 2001).

But even in individualised systems, the family can come in through the back door: individualisation can, and often does, go along with a bonus for single breadwinners: the transferable allowance. In most tax systems, people have either a set allowance of income for which no tax needs to be paid or for which they receive a tax credit. In some tax systems, this personal allowance can be transferred from a non-working (and non-tax-paying) person to the working partner. In other cases a special dependent spouse allowance is given. The tax systems of Belgium, the Netherlands, Denmark, Spain, Ireland, Italy, and Austria contain a substantial tax benefit for families with a single earner (Rubery et al. 1999).

At first glance, this tax benefit gives women the possibility to stay at home to care. In that sense, taxes can contribute to citizenship rights to care. On second thought, this benefit is generally given to the male worker rather than to the care-giving woman. Therefore, one cannot speak about an individual citizenship right, as it reduces women's economic independence as well as the urge to participate in the labour market. Feminists therefore refer to transferable allowances pejoratively as a 'male breadwinner bonus' (Lewis 1992a, Sainsbury 1999b). Such a bonus indicates the dominance of the ideal of full-time motherhood. Which countries have such a bonus?

Table 5.1   Single Breadwinner Bonus in Taxation for 100 percent APW per year, 1998, four countries

	BE	DK	NL	UK
Single breadwinner bonus in euros	2324	2537	1256	460
As percentage of the APW	8.4	7.1	7.3	1.6

Calculations on the basis of OECD (2000)
In cooperation with Hans Hansen, The Danish Institute for Social Research/SFI.

Calculated from OECD tax studies, table 5.1 shows the extent to which tax systems favour single-earner families. In many countries, notably Belgium and Denmark, having children also leads to tax deductions, but in the present chapter the effects of having children is left out as this book deals with rights to give care. Relative to the average production wage (APW), the Belgian tax system contains the highest bonus for single breadwinners, followed by the Dutch system. In that sense, both countries do fit the Christian democratic model as well as the male breadwinner model. The British system contains the lowest benefit for single earners. In fact, it is one of the few European countries that actually encourages women to work (Daly 2000b). While low tax rates already show its 'liberal' face, we can now also see its 'individual' face. The biggest surprise however is the Danish tax system. Theoretically, it should be as individualised as the British turns out to be. Instead, the Danish tax system contains a substantial bonus for single breadwinners and discriminates against double earners.

Many researchers have been surprised by the Danish system of fiscal care, particularly given the 'high rate of female labour force participation and settled recognition of the two-earner family as the norm for social behaviour and public policy' (Shaver and Bradshaw 1995: 22; see also Sainsbury 1999b; Montanari 2000; Dingeldey 2001). The British fiscal system does not correspond with employment patterns either. The UK has a very low number of double-earner couples and many mothers stay at home, much more than in the other countries. In addition, following the logic of the tax structure, married Belgian women should work less than Dutch, but they do not. The tax systems of the four countries thus bear many surprises: they neither fit the models nor correlate with women's employment patterns. How then to explain the outcomes and origins of fiscal care?

Understanding the Origins

Although welfare state theory as well as feminist theory stress the effects of social democracy on gender relations, the social democrats continuously stumble on the class-gender debate. Individualisation of taxation should thus not been seen as a trophy of social-democratic movements but of the women's movement, often in alliance with liberal forces and the women's movements.

In Belgium, the 1989 tax law replaced the joint system that heavily punished dual-earner families. The Flemish tax compromise had two components: individualisation (*decumul*) and the marriage quotient (*huwelijksquotient*). The latter is the name of the transferable allowance but it can be used exclusively by married couples, as in Denmark but unlike the Netherlands (Van Haegendoren and Moestermans 1996). This law is a compromise of two claims, typical for Belgium. Belgian policy, according to the Belgian sociologist Dumon, always had a strong family dimension as well as a sound history of women working outside the home (int. 11). On the one hand, feminists, often social democrats but also Christian democrats, were the most pronounced advocates of individualisation. The new law thus needed to comply with women's wishes to work outside the home as well as to honor marriage and caring responsibilities. On the other hand the strong christian democratic movement as well as the very influential Organisation for Large and Young Families (BGJG) which represents about 300,000 families, was against complete individualisation. The argument was that men and women should have a free choice to stay at home to provide care, and they also wanted to support marriage. A mostly male division of the social democratic movement was also in favour of the family rather than the individual as the crucial unit of the welfare state (int. 1, 11, 15, 23).

The objective of the 1989 tax law was to institutionalise free choice between working and providing care. Individualisation offers married women the choice to work, while the marriage quotient offers them the choice to stay at home (Marques-Pereira and Paye 2001). Demeester, the (female) Christian democratic (CVP) minister responsible for the policy, indeed argues that the marriage quotient is a compensation for caregiving. It should be seen as 'a direct compensation for the work done by the woman at home', she said (Vanistendael 1989). Indeed, the benefit is colloquially called an *opvoedersloon*, which literally means 'parenting wage'.

In the Netherlands, in the 1980s, nearly all Dutch political parties supported the penalty on double-earner families. In none of the countries has 'double earner' been such a swearword as in the Netherlands. The social democrats motivated their position by 'the strongest shoulder principle': since double earners are richer, they have to pay more. This principle was also advocated by the Christian democrats, but they emphasised a second reason: taxation policies should support the ties that bind a family, the cornerstone of society. Both parties, but mostly the social democrats, struggled with the gender and class dilemma, personified in 'Mrs. Philips', the imaginary wife of the director of the Dutch multinational of the same name. The dilemma presented itself as 'should we treat Mrs. Philips as an individual with independent rights and independent income, despite her rich husband?' or 'is Mrs. Philips "the wife of" and should the state refrain from supporting rich families?' During the period of high unemployment in the 1980s, Mrs. Philips was certainly seen as 'the wife of'. It was considered to be unjustified for a family to have double incomes while the number of no-income families increased. In both parliament and the media, unemployment in one family was played against double incomes in another family (TK 1980-1981).

Two 'parties' were in favour of dismantling the male breadwinner bonus, primarily to increase women's employment. Already in 1984, the Women's Alliance (1998) proposed a system of individual tax credits. The returns (19 billion guilders), which are spent on male breadwinner arrangements, should be invested to improve conditions for women's employment. As a party of higher-income members, such as businesspeople, the right-wing Liberal Party (VVD) was also not impressed by the 'Mrs. Philips' rhetoric , who at that time was indeed highly imaginary: only eight percent of all second earners had a substantial income, argued a VVD member of parliament.

A decade later, in the mid-1990s, the VVD proposed to dismantle the transferable allowance cohort-wise. At that time, consensus did exist on the necessity of women's independence and entry into the labour market, as described in chapter 4 (WRR 1990). However, all parties, including the VVD itself, voted against the proposal. Calculations showed that single-earner families earning a minimum wage would be hurt – a Dutch taboo. Dismantling the male breadwinner bonus could only occur if the treasury was rich enough to compensate single-earner low-income families and if the Christian democrats could not block such a plan. This was the case in the late 1990s, when the Dutch government included a liberal minister of finance (Zalm) who wanted to end the situation of money being given to 'the husband who was able to keep his wife at home' (NRC Handelsblad 1998) and a 'work-minded' social-democratic secretary of state (Vermeend). Together they were responsible for modernising the tax system.

Even in Denmark, a country which is considered to be social democratic it was not this movement that stressed women as individuals. Already in the 1940s and 1950s, the traditional Danish women's movement (DK) problematised the tax system. At that time, quite a number of women were already working and because of the high tax rate it was hardly worth it. For women, individualisation was a major topic. It was not until 1967 that the law on individualisation was passed. Still, it was one of the earliest in Europe (Ravn 2000). The social democrats, including the powerful trade unions, were no advocates of individualisation. Although welfare state theory as well as feminist theory stress the effects of social democracy on gender relations, the Danish social democrats continuously stumbled on the class-gender debate (Siim 2000; int. 63). Individualisation of tax, they argued, was only beneficial for bourgeois women, not for working-class families. Appearing on television in the mid-1960s, the social democratic finance minister claimed that individualisation was only a request of well-educated women (int. 60). Social democrats were not against working women, they were afraid of punishing lower-income single-earner families (int. 60, 63). Venstre, the right-wing bourgeois party, the party of farmers, was also against individualisation for farmer's wives, and promoted 'family values' more than social democrats.

It was a small radical liberal party of intellectuals, teachers, and enlightened farmers, Det Radikale Venstre, that pushed the case of individualisation of taxation – or more precisely, its female members. They were able to stimulate a female cross-parliamentary alliance as many female members of the Social Democratic party were in favour of individualisation. The traditional Danish Women's Society (Dansk Kvindesamfund) supported this alliance. Radikale pleaded for individualisation because they believed that women and men should have individual rights, not so much because they sought to stimulate women's employment, since women were already working. The Danish political scientist Birte Siim has argued that 'the driving force of the universal welfare project was the Social democratic party in alliance with the small radical liberal party'

(2000: 113). Individualisation in taxation, however, is thus much more a liberal trophy (int. 60, 66).

In Denmark, in contrast to the Netherlands and Belgium, the bread-winner allowance was never labelled as a male breadwinner bonus. Indicating that it was meant to support low-income single-earner families, the transferable allowance – in contrast to Belgium and the Netherlands – was nearly flat-rated and excludes higher incomes. In the 1982 tax reform, however, the possibility of transferability was broadened so that middle-income bracket families could profit too (Montanari 2000). The party responsible was the Kristeligt Folkeparti, arguing that married couples in the higher-income group should also be able to transfer the allowance as it stimulates marriage and offers people a choice to stay at home. Although the Christians now have very little support from Danish voters and have only a few seats in parliament, they were powerful at that time. Venstre and the conservative party needed them to form a government. 'This taxation policy should, however, perhaps rather be viewed as one part in alternative political packages which support specific forms of the gendered division of work in a society', argues Montanari (2000: 237).

The British tax scheme, finally, has indeed – as a typical liberal regime – always been favourable towards working women, even when it had a joint system (Daly 2000b). Not only because taxes have always been comparatively low in Britain: uniquely, working women received a financial bonus which significantly reduced the impact of the joint tax system (Cmnd. 8093, 1980). As early as 1918, the 'married man's allowance' was introduced 'to fulfil the obligations to support his wife': a single-earner married man was thought to need more money. This was soon considered unfair to men whose wives worked. Therefore a (lower) 'wife's earned income allowance' was introduced already in 1920. In 1942 this bonus was increased substantially to encourage married women to remain in employment during the Second World War. Unlike many other war measures, such as childcare, the income allowance was not cut back after the war. This was not only due to the administrative hassle but also because removing the incentive for women to work seemed inappropriate (Cmnd. 8093).

The pro-individual tax system is thus not a direct consequence of party beliefs but of a broader historical country-specific ideology. In fact, in the 1980s, the Conservative government led by Margaret Thatcher flirted with a male breadwinner bonus. At that time, high unemployment hit the UK, especially for men. As the tax system has always displayed incentives for working women. 'Isn't it about time now to support single-earner families?', argued the government in a Green Paper (Cmnd. 8093, 1980).

In 1986, a transferable allowance was proposed for married single-earner couples, as it would bring the UK in line with continental Europe. Ironically, the liberal non-discrimination argument was also put to the fore: 'The Government believes that the tax system should not discriminate against families where the wife wishes to remain at home to care for young children' (Cmnd. 9756, 1986: 15). To protect the proposals from attacks, the government used a strategy that Pierson (1994) has labelled as obfuscation: to downplay the salience of the consequences. The 1986 Green Paper pointed out that Denmark also had transferable allowances – which is true – and at the same time had the highest proportion of married women in the labour market of the European Community.

The proposal was never implemented. Although the conservative women's groups were very much in favour, the Green Paper received an unfriendly reception from a wide range of groups, including some of the government's traditional supporters. 'Sending women back to the kitchen' was the dominant accusation, and the massive administrative costs were also criticised. The main reason why the proposal was not implemented was because the Treasury ruled it out on expensive grounds: the reform would cost 4.5 billion pounds (Dilnot 1989; Parker, 1995). For a Conservative government that is attempting to retrench the state and cut down its expenses, investing a large sum of money in people who care at home would be at odds with the policy line. The financial aspects turned out to be more essential than ideology. The Conservative party did not want to pay for its conservative values.

The Impact of Tax

Two fiscal regimes do not seem in line with their employment rates for women: Denmark and Britain, while two seem more related: the Netherlands and Belgium. But on a closer look, this correlation also raises doubts.

British fiscal care is indeed in line with a liberal system, and has always encouraged married women to work. So, the question remains as to why British women do not work more. Dean and Shah (2000) argue that low-income British families are hardly aware of taxation. They are more knowledgeable about the benefit system. Perhaps financial measures other than tax incentives are more decisive for women's employment.

The Danish breadwinner bonus is an anomaly to the system, a holdover from the past, supported by only a few Danes, yet in practice the system is used quite substantially: 400,000 individuals transferred the allowance to their partner around the year 2000. The transfers are very modest, leading to discounts of around 400 euros a year, a negligible sum of money in the Danish economic context. This indicates that the users are likely to be students and people with very small part-time jobs (int. 54). Thus, although in theory the breadwinner bonus could be used to support the provision of care at home, it is not used as such. Denmark's early individualisation of taxation may thus be more crucial than the anachronism of the (male) breadwinner bonus. Dingeldey (2001) stresses that in Denmark, the official political and social model largely encourages egalitarian family patterns of labour market behaviour. Against this background, the tax concessions granted to sole earners are of no significance. They are not an incentive for a permanent pattern of labour market behaviour. What we can learn from the Danish case is that high financial incentives in theory can become petty in practice when they oppose a policy context in which working women have become a cultural given.

After comparing various tax regimes, Sainsbury concludes that 'In the Belgian case, the tax system provides an explanation for the puzzle of women's low rate of employment despite ambitious policies supporting women's employment' (1999: 195). The Belgian tax system indeed fits the Christian democratic model (and less the modified male breadwinner model) and Belgian mothers have moderate employment rates. Employment activity, however, is still higher than in the Netherlands and the UK. In fact, the relationship between employment and taxation is not clear cut.

First, the tax system set up in Belgium in 1989 is friendlier to working women than the previous joint system, but women's employment rates have increased only slightly since the 1990s. There has not been a massive move towards work (chapter 4). Second, the Belgian tax system disproportionately benefits single-earner families with high incomes, yet in Belgium highly educated women are much more likely to be employed than less educated women. Finally, research by Pittevils and Timmermans (1995) about the take-up of this fiscal care arrangements shows that the marriage quotient is not used as a parenting wage: half of those who make use of the allowance do not have (dependent) children; the majority are older, low-income couples. Therefore the researchers conclude that 'the marriage coefficient ... can in no way be considered as a payment for bringing up children, but as a payment for retired women at the hearth' (Pittevils and Timmermans 1995: 69; also Verbist 1999). The Belgian financial scheme offers the highest bonus for caregiving of all four countries. Strangely enough, this does not clearly relate to mothers' fairly high work rates. The tax system is not used as much by mothers as a wage for parenting.

Finally the Dutch scheme. Until 2001, the Dutch welfare state was completely in line with the Christian democratic model as well as with the strong male breadwinner model. The low employment rates of Dutch women seem to be in line with tax policy. But doubts are expressed about the correlation in the Netherlands too. The Dutch economists de Jonge and de Kam (2000), who composed table 5.2 about the history of marginal tax rates for a second earner, question a clear-cut relationship. Throughout history, the marginal tax rates have fluctuated substantially, while labour market participation of women continuously increased. Additionally, in the 1970s marginal tax rates were lower than in the 1990s, yet at that time fewer women worked. Even after the dual-earners law was introduced, which penalised second earners, women's employment rates rose. Therefore they conclude: 'Now that paid work for married women is widely accepted, things other than tax measures, such as the expansion of childcare, could be more important to mobilise the supply of (married) women than a fiscal trapeze act by policymakers' (2000: 842). They implicitly argue that now that the cultural battle has been won, financial measures are less important than facilities to make sure women can work.

Table 5.2	Marginal tax rates, as percentage of the gross wage, including social security contributions, of the average production worker, 1970-2001, the Netherlands						
	1970	1975	1980	1985	1990	1995	2001
Marginal tax pressure for the average production worker	36.0	43.4	51.0	58.5	43.1	42.6	49.5
Marginal tax pressure when a wife is employed	28.9	34.8	32.0	39.7	33.4	33.1	29.2

Source: De Jonge & de Kam (2000)

To Conclude

Tax studies, argues Sainsbury (1999b), estimate that a fiscal system tailored to dual-breadwinner couples can increase women's labour market participation by as much as 20 percent (see also Gustafsson and Bruyn-Hundt 1991; Grift 1998). This is an overstatement. The design of the tax system cannot sufficiently explain women's employment patterns. While the Danish tax system promotes single earners and the British system double earners, the realities are exactly the opposite. Although the Belgian and Dutch tax systems seem to coincide much more with women's employment patterns, correlations can also be questioned. First, due to the progressiveness of the systems high-income families benefit more from transferable allowances, but in fact low-income families are more likely to be single-earner families. Secondly, the historical pattern of employment does not coincide with the pattern of fiscal care. In the Netherlands, for instance, women's substantial increase in the labour market occurred right at the time that double earners were penalised the most. Thirdly, in Belgium the tax scheme has often been regarded as the explanation for moderate female employment levels, but in practice Belgian mothers hardly draw on this 'parenting wage'. In her cross-national study, Dingeldey (2001:653) comes to the same conclusion: 'In ten different European countries ... a clear shaping effect of tax systems can not be found.'

Fiscal care is thus neither a sufficient nor a necessary cause for women's employment and income patterns. Hakim is simply wrong when she writes that 'fiscal policy is one of the most effective tools of social engineering' (2000: 227). This chapter found that while tax incentives should fit into the broader design and objectives of caring states (Montanari 2000; Dingeldey 2001); perhaps services (De Jong and de Kam 2000) or social security arrangements (Dean and Shah 2002) are more important. The latter is the focus of the next section.

Rights to Care, Duties to Work: Social Security

What are the consequences of social security for women's citizenship? This section is concerned with the following hypothesis: If people have the right to give care, women are more likely to participate in caregiving *and* be more financially independent. The danger is that they may be captured in the sphere of caring and excluded from employment. Furthermore, if caring is compensated *indirectly*, via male breadwinner arrangements, this not only reduces women's labour market participation but also their economic independence: a 'derived right' to give care has negative effects on citizenship. This section tries to empirically sort out the relationship between social security and work, especially when care responsibilities come in. Besides: to what extent do social security schemes fit into the theoretical welfare state models? What is the (political) background as well as the direction of social security restructuring?

The focus is on rights but also on duties, as the latter is stressed less in academic research than in political debates in the period between 1980s and 2000. I will be focusing on unemployment insurance and income support because these schemes lie at the heart of the work-and-care dilemma. Special attention is given to two test cases of women's citizenship. The first is part-time work: does social security facilitate or obstruct part-time work? The second are lone mothers as they are the litmus test of female citizenship. Are they workers or caregivers? (Hobson 1994; Knijn 1994; Lewis, 1997).

Britain: Worker or Carer

The British social security scheme has strong liberal features but liberal ideology is not consistently put into practice. Work is not the only valued action: caregivers do receive protection (see also O'Connor et al. 1999 and Lewis 1992a). But one has to choose between being a worker or a carer. A worker has to comply with stringent rules.

First, the British unemployment scheme was comparatively care-friendly. Until 1988, no working record was needed to receive unemployment benefits – something unique for Europe. A person could receive credits – called 'home responsibility protection' – for caring for children under the age of 16, those seriously ill, or for invalids. Work, however, became increasingly important as a basis of entitlement. After the 1988 reform just receiving credits was no longer enough; the claimant should have worked in one of the two years before unemployment. Due to the introduction of the 1996 Job Seekers Allowance (which merged unemployment benefits with income support) compensation for caring for children disappeared altogether and only caring for the seriously ill or invalids had a right to compensation (CPAG 1996). Unemployment benefits moved from a care-friendly to a work-based system. It became 'more liberal'. Hence women's right to income decreased, as we see in the table below, at a time when more women were working.

The obligation to work also became more important. Moore, the secretary of state to the social security department under Thatcher, said: 'For more than a quarter of a century public focus has been on the citizens "rights' and it is now past time to redress the balance' (quoted in Lister 1990a: 7). At first glance, the discourse on duties addresses men only. The image of the unemployed was the idle scrounger, a man sitting on the couch in front of the television (during the day) with a bottle of beer, who after years of getting the dole has become lethargic and lazy. When Moore introduced the 1988 Actively Seeking Work test he said: 'Each and everyone of those vacancies is an opportunity for an unemployed person

Table 5.3	Men and women who receive unemployment benefits (UB) compared to the number of unemployed, November each year, Great Britain*		
	1986	*1991*	*1996*
Men receiving UB	578	626	398
Women receiving UB	346	462	275
Number of unemployed men	1817	1470	1525
Number of unemployed women	1214	891	796
Percentage of male claimants as a percentage of unemployed men	31.8	31.4	18.0
Percentage of female claimants as a percentage of unemployed women	28.5	18.4	15.5

* Statistics after 1996 are not comparable because of the merging of the income support and unemployment benefits programmes into the 'Jobs Seekers Allowance'.
Source: DSS (1996); DSS (1997); NS (1997)

to gain the self-respect and independence that comes from supporting themselves *and their families* by their own effort' (Hansard 1989: 714; emphasis added).

A closer look shows that married women are also deemed to be abusers 'because they are not unemployed but care at home', as a chief of a local employment service said (Kremer 1994). The 1981 Rayner report was the start of the toughening of duties. Although the factual difference between men and women was not that significant, the writers nonetheless concluded of women that 'many had small children and did not wish to work but had realised that claiming UB was an easy source of money for a year' (DE/DSS 1981: 29). Consequently, the availability test was made stricter and from then on married women applying for benefits were looked at with particular suspicion. They have to prove that they can have childcare within 24 hours. This '24-hour rule' rather than 'at once' is already seen as a nice gift from legislators. If an applicant cannot prove that they can accept employment within 24 hours, they do not qualify for unemployment benefits (Bryson and Jacobs 1992).

People receiving unemployment benefits have to fulfil all obligations as workers, even when they have care responsibilities. They have to live up to the worker model. The strong division between the citizen-care-giver and the citizen-worker is typically British: you are either a worker or a carer. This is especially problematic for those who want to combine both or want to work part time. Being available for a part-time job is only possible in the first period of unemployment (13 weeks). And a part-time job is often not sufficient to qualify one to receive benefits either: access to benefits is not directly based on an applicants record of employment but on the contributions they have paid, however such contributions can only be paid if one reaches a certain threshold, the lower earnings limit (LEL). In the mid-1990s, 2.2 million working women are estimated to be excluded from contributions because their income is too low, while this is the case for 0.8 million working men (Koopmans et al. 2003).

In contrast to liberal ideology, British unemployment benefits were also family-based. For a long time the unemployed received a supplement for an adult dependant as well as for children. This derived right to provide care dates back to 'Beveridge Married Women's Option'. Until 1978 women could pay reduced national insurance contributions, thereby renouncing benefits. Until 1988 the installed supplement was not equal for men and women, who received less. Feminists have always argued in favour of individualisation of benefits, but they have been concerned about the consequences of a simple abolishment of the supplements for wives and children because benefits are so low (Lister 1992). Since the introduction of the Job Seeker's Allowance, supplements have been cancelled and the UK now has an individualised system. However, since the allowance is very low, claimants with a partner at home often have to turn to family-based income support to top up the insurance.

While women with care responsibilities have difficulties in qualifying for unemployment benefit, lone mothers on social assistance in the UK are still allowed to be 'full-time mothers' until their youngest child reaches the age of 16. Until that time, they have no duty to work. This is quite unique in Europe and has been considered to be a telling anachronism to the liberal welfare model (Lewis, 1992; O'Connor et al. 1999; Millar and Rowlingson 2001). As a consequence by far the majority of lone mothers receive social assistance. This exemption of duties is, again, not linked to a specific party ideology. For a long time a political and social consensus has existed on lone mothers' right to provide care. Indeed, Conservatives were preoccupied with the amorality of lone mothers; they saw them as the epitome of the failure of the family, as irresponsible mothers whose motives and capability for motherhood were questionable (Millar 1996). Conservatives also saw them as the epitome of the failure of the welfare state, since these women 'choose' a life of benefit dependency, yet they never dared to force them to work: this was not in line with the idea that care is best provided inside the warm and homey haven of the family.

Instead of forcing lone mothers to work, Conservatives were mostly interested in getting dads to pay, as the primary Conservative policy objective was to reduce the costs of benefits (see Lister 1996; Millar and Rowlingson 2001).

The Labour government however has not changed the policy towards lone mothers drastically either, although a more active approach has been introduced (Lister 1996). The Labour government wants to move towards a citizen-worker model and tries to encourage all mothers, including those married to an unemployed man, to work. Policy towards lone mothers carried out via two routes. First, by 'making work pay' – via the improvement of the work benefit of Family Credit to the Working Families Tax Credit (WFTC) and the establishment of a (low) minimum wage. Secondly, by 'making work possible', by setting up a 'New Deal' for lone parents (Millar and Rowlingson 2001). But unlike other 'deals', the New Deal for lone parents (and partners of the unemployed) is voluntary.

As Table 5.4 shows, most British lone mothers indeed lived off of social assistance benefits. The problem is that this does not lead to a substantial income. British benefits have the lowest replacement rates of all four countries (table 6.7), hence 70 percent of British lone mothers on benefits are poor (chapter 4). However, compared to other categories of claimants in the UK – such as the disabled or the unemployed – they are just as poor. 'Equality on a poor level' seems to be the flagship of the British social security system. Gender differences – in line with the liberal model – indeed may not be as strong as class differences (see O'Connor et al. 1999; Daly 2000).

Table 5.4	Lone mothers: social benefits and employment status, in percentages, 1994, four countries		
	Social benefits main income source	Employed	Employed full time
BE	32.0	66.5	51.8
DK	32.1	77.6	70.8
NL	66.3	42.7	22.6
UK	65.6	37.6	18.4

Source: Pedersen et al. (2000), on the basis of the ECHP, 1994

The Netherlands

The Dutch social security scheme has never been social democratic for women: it most resembles the British scheme, since Dutch women have had little access to individual income unless they are lone mothers. But the latter is also changing.

While in the early Esping-Andersen study (1990) the Dutch unemployment scheme achieved the highest decommodification score, already at that time few women received unemployment benefits (see also Sainsbury 1996). Since then, women have nonetheless gained spectacular access to unemployment insurance, as table 5.5 shows, but this stagnated after the mid-1990s.

Table 5.5	Men and women who receive unemployment benefits compared to the number of unemployed, various years, the Netherlands*			
	1987	*1990*	*1995*	*2000*
Men receiving benefits	103,900	102,300	226,900	109,600
Unemployed men		168,000	234,000	99,000
% unemployed men receiving benefits		61	96	110
Women receiving benefits	56,400	74,600	168,300	84,000
Unemployed women		222,000	244,000	126,000
% unemployed women receiving benefits		33	69	66

* These statistics only give an impression as statistics on unemployment benefits and unemployment rates are collected in a different way (for instance year averages versus picking out one month in the year).
Sources: SVR (2001), European Commission (1997, 2003), based on European Labour Force Survey

The present system is built on the 1987 restructuring of social security. Because of the huge cost explosion of social security, the Christian democratic and liberal 'no-nonsense' government made reducing expenditures a priority. The architects of the restructuring were Christian democrats, but they received no fierce opposition from the social democrats (Bannink 1999). In addition to cutting the level of benefit, access to unemployment benefits was more closely connected to employment history. The connection to employment histories was again tightened in 1995, under the 'Purple Coalition'. In the Netherlands it is comparatively easy to receive a short-term benefit but it is now much harder to receive benefits for a longer period. No matter which political parties are in power, the Dutch reflex has been to strengthen the link between employment and access to benefits, so that hierarchies in the labour market are perpetuated.

Linking access to benefits to employment history is especially problematic for Dutch women because they have weak work histories. At the same time, the 'no nonsense' government also improved the system for women. Forced by the EU directive on equal treatment, the existing discrimination between men and women was abolished in 1985. Until then, only breadwinners could receive a prolonged benefit (at that time WWV) (Righter et al. 1995). Motivated by Dutch rather than European policy consensus, the 1987 reform also protected part-time work. Already in 1982 in the Wassenaar Regulations, the social partners (trade unions and representatives of employers) had agreed on the necessity of a flexible labour market to combat the economic crisis. 'A flexible labour force is fine', said the trade unions, 'but then part-time workers must be socially protected'. This deal – flexibility for employers and social security for flexible workers – not only resulted in the eight-hour rule, which means that eight hours of work per week is enough to claim unemployment benefits, but also resulted in the rule that one can apply for benefits (on top of wages) when their employer reduces their working hours by five or more hours per week (Righter et al. 1995; Teulings et al. 1997).

In addition, the *verzorgingsforfait* was introduced in 1987, a moderate compensation for providing care. Only in order to receive the prolonged unemployment benefits can caregiving be included in someone's 'work history', but only childcare qualifies. Providing care for children under the age of six counts as full-time work, while caring for children between ages six and 12 is only considered half-time work. The debate in parliament, in 1985-1986, was nearly a women-only debate and agreement was reached across political parties (Wentholt 1990).

In contrast to the UK, Dutch women covered by unemployment insurance have not been subjected to an intensification of requirements to seek work, on the contrary: women were hardly sanctioned for not applying for work. Males, unmarried and young, were, simply because for them sanctions were considered to be a real incentive (Teulings et al. 1997). The discussion of whether unemployment benefits should cover care activities was sorted out in 1987. When a claimant is partially available – for a certain number of hours per week – benefit will be paid in accordance with the number of hours (Wentholt 1990; Beckers and Verspagen 1991). This means that in the Netherlands a part-time duty to work is perfectly possible, unlike in the British case. The caveat is that if one is available for part-time work and one has worked full-time before becoming unemployed, the person herself must carry the financial loss. This citizenship right to give care thus reduces people's income.

Lone mothers have been the epitome of a real paradigm shift. From the 1970s onwards, lone mothers (and married mothers) receiving social assistance were informally and unintentionally exempted from the requirement to work until their children reached the ages of 12, 16, or 18 – the exact practice depended on the municipality. In the 1980s this became official policy, to the delight of lone mothers. The state-as-their-breadwinner offered them peace of mind (Stolk and Wouters 1982). But in 1996 the paradigm shifted drastically and the state turned out to be less trustworthy than lone mothers had hoped. Under the 'Purple' regime lone mothers of older children (over age five) 'gained' the obligation to work.

Unlike the British case, Dutch lone mothers are not morally stigmatised. They are just a case study of the larger paradigm shift from the male breadwinner/female caregiver model into a (part-time) double-earner model – a move away from the Christian democratic regime. The underlying idea is that the best way for women to be emancipated is to work and become financially independent. This will not only bring women self-development, autonomy, and self-esteem, it will also liberate them financially. Although they are better-off than the British, Dutch lone mothers are also relatively poor – not in the least due to the freezing of social assistance (chapter 4).

The changes are supported by all political parties and social organisations (including the women's movement). The discussions that took place are about the age limit of children and whether the requirement to work should be full-time or part-time. When the social democratic secretary of state (Wallage) proposed the new law, he wanted mothers of all children, no matter what the age of the children, to be obligated to work. Taken up by the small Christian orthodox party (GPV), most political parties agreed that there should be children's age limit, which was set at five. More recent debates showed that all parties and social organisations are against a univocal requirement for lone parents to work full time. In the new 2003 law municipalities are allowed to place work requirements on lone mothers of children up until the age of 12, but they have to take into account the wishes of lone mothers and make sure enough childcare is available.

Denmark

Belgium and Denmark show the opposite story. In these countries women have many more individual rights and greater financial autonomy. The right-wing Schluter government in Denmark had nearly 11 years to retrench, but Green-Pedersen (2002) shows that compared to the Netherlands cutbacks in rights and budgets were comparatively mild. If cutbacks took place it was after the 1993 election of a social democratic government. But with the introduction of its 1994 labour market reform eventually the right and the duty to work were installed.

Table 5.6 shows that Danish women are well covered by unemployment benefits. Unlike the British and Dutch security scheme, insurance rather than social assistance is the main benefit for all those unemployed. Why is women's access well guaranteed? Pure citizenship-based benefits, the dream of researchers like Daly (1996) and Sainsbury (1996), do not exist, not even in the Danish social democratic welfare state. Women do not have high access because of easy eligibility criteria either. In Denmark one year of employment (out of three) plus being a member of a fund is necessary for entitlement. Prior to 1997, when eligibility criteria were toughened, 26 weeks were sufficient. Moreover, compensation for providing care has no tradition in Denmark.

Table 5.6	Men and women who receive unemployment benefits compared to the number of unemployed, various years, Denmark*					
	1985	*1990*	*1995*	*1997*	*1998*	*1999*
Unemployed men	107,257	109,054	134,176	91,071	76,478	72,774
Unemployed women	127,955	124,858	144,677	102,601	92,513	85,416
Men on benefit				80,609	64,086	59,356
Women on benefit				105,061	87,321	74,532
% unemployed women on benefit				102	94	87
% unemployed men on benefit				89	84	82

* These statistics only give an impression as they are not fully comparable. Benefit statistics are year averages; unemployment statistics are compiled at the closing of the year.
Sources: DS (1999b) Ligestillingsrådet (1999) Ministry of Labour/Ministry of Economic Affairs (2000)

The Danish system is not friendly to part-time work either. It has become impossible – unlike in the Netherlands, and especially different from Belgium (next section) – to receive benefits when working part-time. In the 1970s, many part-time workers received a supplement but by 1979 the minister of labour demanded that part-time workers get a signed statement from their boss that they could immediately quit their job if offered full-time employment elsewhere. As a result, many women resigned: they were better off receiving full-time benefits than working at a mere part-time job (int. 50, 59). In 1983 a second discouragement was implemented: the rate for supplementary benefits was reduced and a time limit was set. A policymaker at the ministry of labour explains (int. 69): 'The government has always been afraid that companies would use the benefit as a wage supplement and people would continuously work part time. Part-time work is a short-term solution and women should not be locked into it'. Secondly, part-time insurance is less beneficial than full-time insurances: recipients of part-time insurance receive relatively lower benefits and those who work less than 15 hours cannot be insured. The trade unions wanted to place disadvantages on part-time work because they prefer to reduce working hours collectively and leave little opportunity for individual arrangements. (int. 59). Indeed, part-time insurance and part-time work are marginal and diminishing in Denmark. In 1998, only 2.3 percent of workers were insured part-time (DS 1999b).

One factor which helps to explain women's good access to the right to income is the trade union protection against marginal jobs, another the length of benefit. Until the mid-1990s, when the 1994 labour market reform was introduced, people could be on benefit for a very long time. The maximum was seven years but since temporary jobs were offered to renew the rights, benefits could be lifelong in practice. As a result, people would not fall out of the social insurance scheme. Hence Danish unemployed women are likely to be covered by individual benefits not so much because of lax eligibility criteria or care compensation but because they have full-time and long-term work histories, and benefits are comparatively long.

In Denmark, all people – including (lone) mothers and caregivers – are obligated to work but the state has to offer childcare as well as paid employment. If unemployed are unavailable to work, benefits are withdrawn. Typical of the Danish case are again the disadvantages for part-time workers: even if they have smaller part-time jobs, they have to be available for 30 hours a week. For a long time, however, the practice was much looser than the principles. The funds, which are connected to trade unions, did not monitor the claimant's availability and job-seeking activities: they protected the unemployed, who are union members (OECD 1993). A small-scale study in the mid-1990s shows that professionals who worked for the unemployment fund, A-kasser, often sided with the claimants. One fund employee said that childcare problems 'are none of our business', while another explained: 'We would rather not know whether people have childcare problems' (Kremer 1994). In 1993, for example, few unemployed people were refused benefits: just 117 men and 199 women (DFA 1993).

In fact, it was the former social democratic minister Bent Rold Andersen (1987) who started the debate about citizenship and strongly argued that duties should be reinstalled. Only after 1994, when the Social Democratic government started the move from a passive to an active system, was the right and duty to work really enforced. The 1994 labour market reform not only cuts unemployment benefits to a maximum of seven years but gives the unemployed the right and the duty to seek employment (Madsen et al. 2001). It is only because of the labour market reform that the Danish welfare state has really become 'social democratic'.

Belgium: Too Much Access for Women?

Perhaps surprising for a Christian democratic welfare regime, Belgian women are also well covered by unemployment insurance, which in the Belgian context is also far more important than social assistance. The Belgian unemployment insurance coverage level is the highest in Europe: the OECD (1994) calculated that as many as 150 percent (!) of the unemployed receive benefit (see also table 6.6). And of all people of an active age, one in four claims unemployment benefits (De Lathouwer 2003b). What makes the Belgian unemployment scheme so friendly – some would say too friendly – for the (female) unemployed?

One of the reasons is obviously women's high level of unemployment, but there is more to it. First, eligibility criteria are not too stringent and unlike any other welfare state, unemployment benefits in Belgium is in principle lifelong, a practice heavily criticised by the OECD. As in Denmark, strong trade unions have prevented the development of jobs that would not be covered by benefits, so marginal, short-term jobs were relatively absent in Belgium. Since 1985, when the Belgian leave scheme was introduced, there has been compensation for care.

In Belgium, unemployment benefits are not individualised. The system of 'derived rights' was introduced before the Second World War. As in the UK, women were directly discriminated against: they were entitled to lower benefits than men. In 1971, however, the 'neutral' terms of 'supplements' and 'head of the households' were introduced. A dependant can be a child, a wife, or even a live-in family member up to the third degree (only if they have no substantial income for themselves).

In Belgium, a fierce debate took place on the issue of derived rights. In 1991, the *Comité de Liason*, a French-speaking women's organisation, took the Belgian state to the European Court of Justice. The Belgian benefit system, they argued, was discriminatory and derived rights unjust and problematic for several reasons: marriages are unstable (what happens to married women who become lone parents?), the current system did not fairly give back to women what they had paid into the system (women who had worked should see their contributions back in the benefits they received, argued the Comite, but instead their benefits were lower), and, they charged, the importance of the right to work as derived rights reduce women's labour market participation. In response, the Belgian state presented unemployment benefits as a system of social assistance and argued that due to a limited budget, priority be given to protecting the weakest group: heads of households with a dependant wife and children. This ideology is very dominant in Christian democracy. The Belgian state won the case (Cantillon 1994; Peemans-Poullet 1995; int. 1,4, 24). In Belgium, individual rights are less important than rights that protect the family, concludes the law professor Van Buggenhout (1994) (int. 4).

Table 5.7   Men and women who receive full-time unemployment benefits compared to the number of unemployed, various years, Belgium*

	1980	1985	1990	1995	2000
Men receiving benefits	106,393	196,234	129,101	207,563	154,314
Percent men unemployed			134	111	109
Women receiving benefits	188,477	259,234	202,666	282,734	207,450
Percent unemployed			126	129	129
Percent women unemployed			126	129	129
Women as a percentage of all claimants	64	57	61	58	57
Total number of claimants	294,870	455,530	331,767	490,297	351,864

* Benefit and unemployment statistics are not fully comparable – as in Denmark and the Netherlands. They just give an impression.
Source: Ministerie van Tewerkstelling en Arbeid (2000), European Commission (2003)

While rights are easily accessed, duties are lax, as the OECD has warned. Claimants hardly have to prove their availability (OECD 2000) and the number of sanctions is very low compared to other countries, including the Netherlands and the UK (see OECD 2000; De Lathouwer 2003). Today, in Belgium, activation policy is hardly developed, and benefits are coupled with a lack of assistance in seeking employment (De Lathouwer 2003). Why is control and verification of job-seeking activities negligible? First, institutional factors are important. The organisation and responsibilities of activation and benefit delivery are spread between federal and regional organisations, which leads to communication problems and discussions about responsibilities (int. 17). Moreover, trade unions, which play an important role in the organisation of the system, protect their members against harsh sanctions. Moreover, unlike the British and Dutch schemes, Belgian women receiving unemployment benefits are allowed to provide care if they are 'unavailable because of social and familiar reasons' (which includes caring for relatives and children). A substantial number of women – as it is only women who take it – use this option. Nearly half of them (43 percent) are highly educated, indicating that the wish to be a full-time mother is not limited to the lower classes, as also Hakim (2000) has pointed out. The drawback is that an unemployed person only receives a very limited sum of money; caregivers are less valued than those classified as 'real unemployed'. It is thus financially safer to be silent about care responsibilities, as a huge number of women receiving unemployment benefits are.

In fact, it is fair to say that unemployment benefits are used as 'a wage for bringing up children' (int. 7, 8). A well-published study in the mid-1990s showed that a substantial number of married mothers receiving benefits did not apply for work at all (De Hooghe and Witte 1996). A cross-national study also shows that while by far the majority of Danish (84.4), Dutch (83.1), and British (76.2) unemployed women want to work – even more so than men – Belgian women show much less of a commitment, with only 56.6 percent committed to work (Gallie and Alm 2000).

Therefore the Christian Democratic, female minister Smet introduced in 1991 the infamous 'article 80', which is one of the few social security changes in a comparatively tranquil welfare state (De Lathouwer 1996; Kuipers 2004) This article requires that if claimants are unemployed for an abnormally long time – twice as long as the average period of unemployment – benefits can be withdrawn, except when one can prove that they are seeking work or when one's partner does not earn enough to prevent the family from falling into poverty. With this rule Smet wanted to protect single-breadwinner families, as in Belgium these families are most likely to be poor (as we saw in chapter 4). Feminists have labelled the changes as the re-instatement of the male breadwinner model. 'In the case of expenditure it is always working women and double-income families which are treated with a visit', write Van Haegendoren and Moestermans (1996: 97). Policy change often focuses on double-earner families, instead of on single-earner families. Representing the Belgian Christian democratic ideology, Smet is more concerned with family poverty than with individual rights. Although it seems reasonable to reduce the length of benefit, penalising double earners or protecting single earners is a Christian democratic reflex in times of budgetary restrictions.

What has also been typically Belgian is the huge number of part-time workers receiving benefits: the so-called 'involuntary part-time worker to escape unemployment'. Many social security schemes have had (Denmark) or still have (the Netherlands) such a measure, but the usage in Belgium breaks all records. In 1992, at the height of the rule, more than 200,000 part-time workers received extra benefits. By far the majority were women (Simoens and Put 1996). The rule was introduced in 1982 and fit the Cabinet's plan to redistribute employment – the Belgian answer to save the economy. Employers wanted to fire people or have them work part time, but labour laws in Belgium were very strict. The powerful trade unions however opposed what they saw as a 'normalisation of part-time work': part-time workers, they said, had many financial problems. The Christian democratic minister Hansenne (PSC) intervened and compensated workers for loss of income via unemployment benefits. Since there was little monitoring of whether part-time workers indeed applied for full-time work, the income guarantee became a great success for employers as well as the mostly female recipients.

Again, Minister Smet introduced a guarantee that was not as generous as the previous. Her intervention had an enormous impact on many women receiving benefits: they received substantially lower benefits. Her motivation was that research had shown that 30 to 40 percent of the women working part time who received these benefits did not want to work full time at all (Holderbeke 1991). She said that the rule was unfair towards women working part time who had never worked full time, as they did not receive benefits in addition to their wages. In contrast to the Dutch model, where part-time work is more of an individual choice, she nevertheless argued that compensation for part-time work was needed, although not as generous compensation as was available before (Standaard magazine 1995). The women's movement, in particular the women's committees of the trade unions, were furious. In their view part-time jobs were always marginal jobs. 'Smet', they said, 'recognised part-time jobs as appropriate work'. The rule means 'the end to the idea that everyone has the right to a decent, full-time job, and adequate wage' (int. 8, 15, 24, 29).

When female *and* married, in terms of social security, it is better to avoid Christian democratic countries, argue Esping-Andersen (1990), Langan and Ostner (1991), and Daly (1996). These countries' policies make you dependent on your husband. But the Belgian welfare state shows that a strong notion of familialism in which dependency within marriage is the starting point of social policy can go along with a huge number of women who used unemployment benefits as a wage for caregiving. They used it to practice the ideal of full-time motherhood. Reinforcing dependence thus goes hand in hand with implicit individual rights and financial autonomy. 'Moderate male breadwinner model' and 'Christian democratic model' are thus not adequate labels for this welfare regime, as also the Christian democratic movement stresses women's work as well as women's care responsibilities.

Questioning the relationship between social security and employment

So far we have seen that social security schemes do not fit the classic welfare regime labels when women's finances, care responsibilities, and part-time work are examined. Moreover, changes cannot be directly linked to specific (party) ideologies: they are often a result of a new cross-national consensus on the rights and duties of men and women. The next issue is whether the (changing) social security schemes as described above correlate with female employment patterns.

Low and Reduced Benefits

Economic logic, as expressed well by the OECD (1994a, 2002a), states that low benefits will increase employment whereas high benefits decrease people's need to find work (OECD 1994a, 2002a). Daly (1996), for instance, argues that for this reason the UK system may have more potential for gender equality than some continental systems. It encourages everyone, including women, to work. The question is whether this logic can be empirically confirmed. Table 5.8 shows the replacement rates of social security in the four countries. British replacements rates are the lowest, as are mothers' employment rates. No clear-cut relation is found in other countries either. Dutch replacement rates are by far the best, followed by Denmark, but female employment patterns in countries with high replacement rates show few similarities. Women apparently do not fall into the standard (OECD) thesis.

Table 5.8	Net replacement rates for four family types at 100 percent of APW, after tax and including unemployment benefits, family and housing benefits in the first month, around 2002, four countries			
	Single	Married	Married two children	Lone parent two children
BE	64	61	64	65
DK	63	63	73	78
NL	82	89	89	91
UK	46	46	49	49

Source: OECD (2002c)

This also comes to the fore when we look at policy changes in Belgium. What happened, for instance, when minister Smet introduced article 80? This has indeed had huge consequences for women. Between 1993 and 1995 nearly 10 percent of all female claimants lost their benefits. And over the 1990s, 200,000 people – most of them cohabiting women with children – lost their benefits (Steunpunt WAV 1996). But what happened? Most of them withdrew from the labour market altogether. This not only indicates that unemployment benefits have actually been used on a large scale as direct compensation for caregiving – as an implicit unintended right to provide care – but it also indicates that micro-economic theory does not hold. When financial compensation for care was withdrawn, women did not take up jobs. Instead they stayed at home without pay (De Lathouwer et al. 2003).

It is also not true that unemployment benefits were mainly used by less-educated women to stay at home. In fact, women with secondary and higher educational levels are overrepresented in the number of claimants who lost their benefit. One explanation is the fact that in Belgium women from the lower classes have a higher work ethos than women from higher-income families. They do not want to be unemployed and are slightly more likely to seek work. Higher-income women have a higher care ethos – they prefer the ideal of full-time motherhood – and are more likely to stay at home because their partner likes it (De Lathouwer et al. 2003). This contrasts with the notion that low educated women are more likely to work because they need to financially.

Another test case to understand the relationship between women's work and social security rights and duties is the change of law concerning part-time employment. For one decade – between 1981 and 1992 – Belgium had generous compensation for those working part-time and this was used in large numbers, mainly by women. After 1992 the compensation was significantly reduced. What did women do? If we look at the financial gains, we would expect fewer women to work part-time after 1992 and move towards full-time work. But the facts show that women moved to part-time jobs, they did not behave as a *homo economicus*. Perhaps the normative ideas underlying policy are more important. The rule before 1992 stressed that part-time jobs were inappropriate as people needed compensation. The new rule however stresses, to the anger of women's organisations, that part-time jobs are decent work. This may have attracted women to work part time.

Moreover, it is unclear why Belgian women used unemployment benefits as a wage for bringing up children and Danish women did not. They could have done so, at least before the 1994 labour market reform which effectively installed duties. But they did not on such a scale as occurred in Belgium. Danish studies show that women did want to work (Mogensen 1995) as also the previously mentioned study by Gallie and Alm (2000) shows: nearly 85 percent of Danish unemployed women are very committed to work, in contrast to the Belgian (56.6 percent). In Denmark, only a minority of women do not want a job (see also Finansministeriet 1995). The question is, then: while the Belgian and Danish social security schemes prior to 1994 are similar, why did Belgian women use unemployment benefits as a wage for bringing up children and Danish women did not?

Breadwinner Bonus – or Indirect Payments

Another issue is whether men on benefits receive a supplement for a non-working wife – a 'breadwinner bonus' or 'double unemployment bonus'. This indirect financial compensation to care, according to the theory, would not only make women dependent on their husbands, it also keeps them at home (Esping-Andersen 1990, Lewis 1992a; Sainsbury 1996; Daly 1996; Gallie and Paugam 2000). This is not an issue in Denmark nor, perhaps unexpectedly, in the Netherlands, as these systems are purely individually-based. This was not the case in the UK and Belgium. Such a (male) breadwinner bonus indeed undermines women's financial independence, but does it also reduce female employment rates? OECD (1996) calculations show that an unemployed Belgian men with a dependent wife receives around 70 percent of his previous wage. He sees his income reduced to 47 percent of his previous wage when his wife enters the labour market. In the UK this income is reduced from 75 to 44 percent. Why, then, should a wife of an unemployed man go to work? 'This additional money destroys the incentive to work for a dependent spouse, because finding a job would lead to losing the extra income' (De Graaf and Ultee 2000: 280).

The question is why in an individualised welfare state like Denmark do gendered unemployment patterns exist that are similar to those in the UK. Additionally, British researchers show that the disincentive for spouses to work is still smaller than the incentive to work. Marsh and McKay (1993) studied the employment behaviour in couples and calculated that due to the existence of in-work-benefits in the UK (such as 'family credit', now the Working Families Tax Credit), paid employment would always lead to a higher income. They also question whether people really do calculate as the researchers did, and whether they are knowledgeable of the specific financial rules. 'Out of work couples do not engage much in working out the relation between what they might earn in work and they might get in in-work benefits' (Marsh and McKay 1993: 121).

Lone Mothers

There must be a relation between the absence of the obligation to work and the high number of women on social assistance. In Belgium and Denmark lone mothers are not exempted from work obligations and their labour market participation is much higher (table 5.9; chapter 4). Yet it is unclear how the welfare state works. Why do lone mothers make the choice to care full-time and postpone a working career that would lift them out of poverty? Social policy analysts often argue that lone mothers are confronted with the 'poverty gap': once they enter the labour market specific benefits, like housing, are lost. In addition, another economic barrier to work arises, namely the costs of childcare. Lone mothers do want to work, but they are blocked (Lister 2001).

A substantial number of British studies however shows that also for lone parents, being employed gives the best protection against poverty, again because of in-work-benefits (Marsh and McKay 1993; Marsh 2001).

Table 5.9   Lone mothers: Social benefits and employment status, in percentages, 1994, four countries

	Social benefits main income source	Employed	Employed full time
BE	32.0	66.5	51.8
DK	32.1	77.6	70.8
NL	66.3	42.7	22.6
UK	65.6	37.6	18.4

Source: Pedersen et al. (2000), on the basis of the ECHP, 1994

Employed lone parents are less likely to be poor than those not doing paid work (Kilkey and Bradshaw 2001). Poverty-wise, lone mothers are thus better-off in the labour market than receiving social assistance. The question thus remains: 'Why don't they go to work?

In their study of British lone mothers, Duncan and Edwards (1999) look at this issue. They concluded that lone mothers' decisions are lead by gendered *moral* rationalities which are constructed, negotiated, and sustained socially in particular contexts. At an individual level it may be economically rational for a lone mother to take up paid employment, but it may be socially irrational, for instance because identities as a worker and good mother are difficult to balance and can be in conflict. Duncan and Edwards therefore argue that lone mothers try to behave in line with their socially constructed 'self'. Only when the identities as worker and good mother are reconciled do lone mothers take up paid employment. Rather than focusing on financial incentives – the underlying logic of comparative welfare regimes theories – they point to cultural explanations. In the terms of this book, lone mothers' behaviour is determined more by their ideal of care.

Examining the Dutch law is also a great opportunity to ascertain whether changes in benefits alter the employment behaviour of lone mothers. In fact, the duty to work has not lead to a massive shift of lone mothers into jobs: no more than 12 percent of lone mothers stopped receiving benefits into order to move into the paid workforce in recent years, as Knijn and van Wel show (1999). More recent statistics show that in a period of 14 months between 2001 and 2002, six percent stopped receiving social assistance because they entered employment (Knijn and van Berkel 2003). One of the reasons for such an incremental change in lone mothers' employment pattern is that local officials do not implement the law; 60 percent of mothers with children older than five were still (partly) exempted in the late 1990s. More recently, in line with the economic boom, activation offers increased (Knijn and van Berkel 2003). Although those working with social assistance claimants generally agree with the policy change, they reject the full-time work obligation for mothers who really want to care for for their children and are afraid to push them into jobs that do not increase their income.

The latter is also an important consideration for lone mothers themselves. As they often are less educated, they have to work a minimum of 32 hours a week to get off welfare, as the level of welfare is relatively high and wages for less educated women relatively low. This is not what many of them want. Many lone mothers receiving social assistance have a high care ethos, they agree that 'the best thing in life is to take care of one's children'. Knijn and van Wel (2001b: 244) therefore conclude that 'because of this combination of low education and a high care ethos, lone mothers on welfare have problems in making use of financial and care incentives that are meant to help them out of welfare'. In other words, financial benefits are not in line with lone mothers' moral considerations, or their 'ideal of care'.

To Conclude

This section shows that the labels of welfare state models are not always adequate, while most social security changes are not immediately linked to the ideology of the political powers in government. Right-wing parties in Denmark retrench less than in the UK or the Netherlands. Christian democracy is different in each country and many changes occur in consensus, such as the paradigm shift in the Netherlands – the shift away from full-time motherhood – and the Danish labour market reform.

This section also questions the connection between rights and duties in social security and women's employment behaviour. Several puzzles came to the fore. The level of benefit, in contrast to economic theory, is not connected to women's employment rates. Lone mothers in the UK and the Netherlands do not go to work, while receiving unemployment benefits makes them poor. Belgian women use unemployment insurance to facilitate a right to provide care while in Denmark they do not, even though prior to 1994 the welfare schemes resembled each other. But why did part-time work become popular in Belgium right at the moment financial compensation was lowered? And why did women whose benefits were withdrawn due to article 80 drop out of the labour market altogether? Micro-economic theory would expect them to take a job, because now they have lost their financial compensation for care.

The next section will focus on more recent financial arrangements"care leave.

Care Leave: For Women Only?

The expansion of care leave shows that the welfare state is not past perfect. Most European countries have now introduced the right to time for care, not in the least due to pressure from the European Commission, which in 1996 prescribed that all member states must implement a non-transferable right to parental leave (O'Connor et al. 1999). The right to time to care is groundbreaking. The Norwegian sociologist Leira even goes as far as terming leave as 'evidence of an interesting shift in the conceptualisation of "the worker", such that the demands of social production take priority over those of production' (1993: 333, also 2002). Leave schemes indeed value caregiving, but this is only temporary. In the end, citizens are supposed to work.

This section deals with the consequences of these new rights for gendered citizenship. On the one hand, care leave may have negative effects on women's citizenship because women may be seduced into staying at home, thus injuring their employment careers (Leira 2002; Morgan and Zippel 2003). They are also likely to receive less income than when employed: caring is usually less valued financially. On the other hand, especially in countries with low female employment, labour market participation may increase. Rather than quit employment altogether, women remain attached to the labour market (Bruning and Plantenga 1999). Moreover, instead of being dependent on a male breadwinner, the payment, however modest, can contribute to women's financial independence. Leave arrangements may finally be a way to attract men to care. If allowed to stop working for a short period they may be encouraged into providing care. Care leave is a tangible translation of the citizenship right to give care. It allows men and women to participate in caregiving.

This section consists of three parts. In the first, the conditions of parental leave will be compared. What welfare state has really implemented the right to time for care? I will then discuss the origins of leave schemes. Are they indeed a victory of conservative politics, which were dominant in the 1980s, as has been suggested by Morgan and Zippel (2003)? Finally, I will question the effects of leave on women's participation in care and paid employment. Does the leave scheme reinforce the gender division of labour? Do women go back to work afterwards?

Table 5.10   Rights to parental leave around 2000 in four countries

	Denmark	*Belgium*	*The Netherlands*	*UK*
Key arrang-ement	Parental leave	Voluntary career break Parental leave	Parental leave	Parental leave
Key year(s)	1994 2001	1985 1998	1990	1999
Maximum length	32 weeks per parent (1994) 32 weeks shared between parents (2001)	Five years (career break) 13 weeks (parental leave)	26 weeks	13 weeks
Conditions and rights	Individual right for parents of children aged 0-1 (excluding maternity) for 16 weeks, and 13 weeks for parents of children aged 1-8 (1994)	Parental leave became an individual right for 13 weeks in 1998	Individual right	Individual right
	Transferable (shared) leave scheme (2001)	The voluntary career break (up to five years) is an individual right for 1% of employees within a company		
	Leave can be negotiated with the employer for up to 52 weeks.	The break is part of all collective agreements but employer's permission is needed		
Payment	About 55% of an APW, public employees 100% of their previous wage	About 20% of an APW	None, except for public employees and those covered by collective agreements	None, except when individually negotiated.
Part-time possibilities	Since 2001 only possible after negotiating with employer	Made possible in various steps in the mid-1990s	Obligatory at the introduction. From 1997 onwards full-time leave is possible but part of just a few collective agreements	Yes

Of the four country schemes, the Danish is still the 'best'. In 1994, Danish parents received an uncontested individual right to childcare for a relativly long period (see table) and if parents could reach an agreement with their employer they could extend this leave up to one year, but on a full-time basis only (Fridberg and Rostgaard 1998; Rostgaard 2002). In 2001, under the liberal-conservative government the length of leave has been reduced as the period has to be shared between the parents but the scheme has also been made more flexible – if employers agree – and payment has been increased, even though Danish leave payments were already the highest of all four countries.

Denmark may have a relatively good leave scheme, but it was not the first of the four countries to institute parental leave: Belgium had the European debut. In 1981 a governmental agreement introduced the 'voluntary career break', which was legally enacted in 1985. This gave individual employees the possibility, not the right, to paid leave. An employee could take a pause from work for one year, five times in his (working) life – which is very considerable. The purpose of leave does not matter: one can use it for care, education, travelling, fishing, whatever. Reflecting the labour market rationale behind the scheme, the only condition is that a vacancy arising because of leave has to be fulfilled by a long-term unemployed person, a demand which can be problematic in practice. Gradually steps were set to establish rights, and to make it more flexible, as leave used to be full time (Deven and Nuelant 1999). In 2002, the career break system was transformed into a system of time credit for private employees – not public employees. The main differences are that it now is a right, but the length has been reduced to one year full time and five years part time, and eligibility criteria have been introduced: a person must have worked for one year (De Backer et al. 2004). Payments for leave are not very high in Belgium.

In the Netherlands, parental leave was introduced in 1991 and had a typical Dutch design: the leave could only be taken on a part-time basis and was exclusively aimed at those working more than 20 hours a week, excluding many women. While the Belgian and Danish schemes were at first not meant as part-time facilities, this was initially obligatory in the Netherlands. In 1997 the leave scheme was flexibilised and open to all employees, although taking up full-time leave is still problematic (Bruning and Plantenga 1999). Still, the leave was generally unpaid – about five percent of collective agreements have included paid leave, while state employees were compensated well (75 percent of their wage) (Portegijs et al. 2002). From 2006 onwards the Christian democratic/Liberal government introduced the individual arrangement 'saving for leave' (*verlofsparen*), which encapsulates parental leave, now an unconditional right and paid (50 percent of the minimum wage). In addition, people can save time by not taking holidays or working overtime, or paying in, in order to take time off. The criticism is that it has little use for caregivers because one has to predict and anticipate life, and people with care responsibilities have few possibilities to save time or money (Van Luijn and Keuzenkamp 2004).

The UK has only recently approved parental leave. The Labour government kept its election promise and implemented the EU directive on leave in 1999. Before a child reaches the age of six, parents can take unpaid part-time or full-time parental leave of up to 13 weeks (three months). However, payment is left to the individual employers' discretion. Before, British mothers – not fathers – could use a comparatively extensive maternity leave (maximum 40 weeks) which was poorly paid. But to be able to get this long maternity absence, the employee must have had two years of continuous employment: it was thus not a citizenship right but conditional on a person's employment record. Real parental leave, applicable also to fathers, became a right only in 1998.

The establishment of care leaves shows convergence: most countries nowadays have some kind of right to give care, albeit with different designs (payments and conditions) and timing of leaves. How are we to understand cross-national differences in the design of care leave?

Politics and the Design of Leave Schemes

After studying the leave schemes of Austria, Finland, France, Germany, and Norway, Morgan and Zippel (2003) conclude that care leave policies have an element of partisan power: centre and conservative parties have been the main advocates of childcare leave and the left has acceded either tacitly or actively to these policies. In their view, feminists have blasted care leave policies and called for an expansion of public care instead. It may be a coincidence, but in the four countries examined here, the development of care leave cannot be ascribed to a conservative or anti-feminist movement. In fact, in many of these countries, women's groups were in favour of care leave, although they were not always content with the specific end result – they often preferred better paid leave with better rights attached to them.

What's more, no specific political party – and certainly not the conservative parties – has been the main advocate of care leaves, as they were introduced by various political configurations. In three countries – the Netherlands, Belgium, and Denmark – leave schemes have been introduced with a strong consensus. In Denmark it was one of the crown jewels of the 1994 labour market reform, which was enacted by the social democratic government, agreed upon by various parties, including the trade unions, and already prepared when the right-wing government was still in office (Compston and Madsen 2001; Borchorst 1999). In Belgium, career breaks were strongly supported by the Christian democrats but generated a fair amount of consensus (Marques-Pereira and Paye 2001). In the Netherlands, eventually both social democratic and Christian democratic forces stressed the need for care leave.

The only country in which a specific political party introduced care leave is the UK. The social democrats implemented the scheme while in the Conservative period parental leave was consigned to the margins of the political debate. For the 'New Right' welfare policies undermined and endangered the family, and the working/caring predicament is part of the private choices that have to be solved in the family (Abbott and Wallace 1992). In addition, the Conservative government seemed more concerned about the economy than about the family. When the 1993 EU parental proposal was rejected, the British Minister Forsyth said that it would impose 'added burdens on employers without regard to their impact on jobs' (in O'Connor et al. 1999). State intervention would place a burden on employers, and for conservatives the wishes of employers are sacred – they are the ones seen to be building the country (Wilkinson 1998). Thus, except for the British case, party politics and party ideologies cannot explain the timing and composition of care leaves. What is more important is cross-party consensus on the issue.

What also helps to understand the leave schemes, particularly whether they are paid or not, is their objectives and framework. When leave is primarily considered to be a labour market measure aimed at fighting unemployment, it tends to be better paid. If leave is introduced for care reasons it is generally unpaid. In Denmark and Belgium, the leave scheme was introduced primarily as a labour market measure that can also support caregiving. In the early 1990s, when the economic crisis was at its peak, prime minister Rasmussen (Social democrats) wanted to do everything 'to break the curve of unemployment' (int. 55). Job rotation became the leading concept in Danish employment politics. While many young parents felt they had little time to care, particularly when their children were very young, many unemployed had the opposite problem: they had lots of time but no work (Kremer 1995). Full-time leave for sabbaticals, education, and parental care would connect the two categories. Trade unions and social democrats were mostly attracted to the concept as a solution to the employment problem, while more family-oriented groups – including the women in trade unions and the Christian People's Party – agreed with leave because they wanted to solve the care problem (Compston and Madsen 2001). Nevertheless, employment was the first rationale behind the new policy, the second being that parents would spend more time with their children (Borchorst 1999).

The Belgian career break scheme was also motivated by employment policy. The francophone minister Hansenne from the PSC, together with Prime Minister Deheane from CVP (both Christian democrats), introduced the career break system chiefly as a measure to redistribute labour. Belgium was facing a huge economic crisis, with one fifth of the population unemployed. But providing time for people to care was also an important motive. When Hansenne introduced the measure, he also stressed how wonderful the break could be for families as well as employers: 'On January the 25th, 1985, a somewhat unnoticed law will change the lives of the Belgians ... For six, nine, twelve months, it becomes possible to fully enjoy family life, to be with the children, to get a new diploma or, when you dream about it, to hitchhike around the world ... The career break scheme is a social measure that offers the possibility to hire new employees who have to replace the employees who have chosen leave' (Ministerie van Tewerkstelling en Arbeid 1997: 3).

In the Netherlands and the UK, time to give care has been an objective of the parental leave scheme, not of employment policy. Two reasons for this objective were important in the Netherlands: the redistribution of paid and unpaid labour and softening the problem of women returning to the workforce (Bruning and Plantenga 1999). With parental leave, mothers can remain connected to the labour market rather than choosing between all or nothing. At the same time, leave should attract fathers to care. In the UK, the Labour government also introduced parental leave as a measure to integrate work and care. Parental leave helps women who would otherwise have to quit their jobs remain connected to the labour market. These motivations support the argument that payment during leave is not necessary – that women on leave would otherwise stay at home without pay: paying them is a deadweight loss.

The lack of payment in the UK and the Netherlands also relates to the strong overall neo-liberal ideology, which is not linked to a specific political party: general politics in both countries have been influenced by liberalism, which assigns care to the private sphere. This has been described already for the British case, but is also true for the Netherlands: a liberal ideology is advocated by all parties, including the Christian democrats and social democrats. It is particularly visible in the notion of 'saving for leave', which has become a very popular political concept even though statistics show that citizens with care responsibilities hardly make use of such an option (Van Luyn and Keuzekamp 2004). Saving up for care leave can be seen as a typical liberal answer to the problems of combining work and care: the state does not take responsibility, at least not financially, but facilitates individual freedom, which still has to be bargained with the individual employer.

Finally, to what extent the right to leave has been established also depends on the dominant state-social partner regime of recent decades. In the 1990s in Belgium, the state developed binding laws on leave as it wanted to intervene in the relationship of the historically strong social partners (trade unions and employers); the government thought they were not progressing well on the issue of leave (Marques-Pereira and Paye 2001). In the Netherlands, by contrast, in the period in which leave became necessary, neo-corporatism was the main model. Due to the 'Dutch miracle' – the success of the partnership between the state and social partners to save the Dutch economy (Visser and Hemerijck 1997) – the Dutch government left many social arrangements, including childcare and leave, to unions and employers. The social partners were not only considered to be very successful in intervening in Dutch economic and social life: the government also believes workplace issues should be fixed at the level of employer-employee arrangements, which resonates with the subsidiarity principle (Kremer 2001). This practice has been highly debated in the Netherlands. To the disappointment of the Dutch Ministry of Social Affairs, research shows that only in about half of the collective agreements – and often those in female dominated sectors – include arrangements for leave (van Luijn and Keuzenkamp 2004). The problem with depending on the social partners is that they have little interest in bargaining about leave and other 'care business', critics like Schippers (2004) argue, especially when women are no longer needed in the labour market.

The British case also shows the importance of the state-employers-employees regime, albeit not in a neo-corporatist but in an individuated way. Although the new parental leave scheme is a real breakthrough it has not completely broken with the notion, articulated well by the Conservatives, that the work/family balance is part of the domain of industry and not of the state. 'Work and Parents: Competitiveness and Choice', the consultation paper launched by the secretary of state for trade and industry, clearly states that any measures to help parents to balance work and family life must be based on giving families reasonable choices taking the needs of business into account (Land 2001). When parental leave was introduced it was argued that the government is 'committed to help-ing parents achieve a better balance between their work and work lives, in ways which enhance competitiveness for business'. As a consequence, leave is still unpaid rather than paid.

Care leave is thus not an element of partisan politics or conservative party politics, at least not in the countries discussed here. More than party ideologies, the objective and framework of the care leave relates to whether leave is paid or not. Other important factors are the dominant ideologies regarding the relationship between the private and the pub-lic as well as between state and employers. They are important for the design of leave schemes. These ideologies are country specific, and are not directly related to the governing party. So far, I have discussed the composition and origins of care leave. The next question is: what are the consequences of the leave schemes?

The Gendered Consequences of Leave

According to Morgan and Zippel, who studied countries like Norway and Austria, the consequences of leave policies are undoubtedly women-un-friendly. Leave schemes are 'likely to reinforce the traditional division of care work in the home' and 'temporary homemaking is being institution-alised as the norm for many women, who face potentially negative conse-quences for their earning and long-term employment trajectories' (2003: 49). This implies that mothers are forced to practice the ideal of full-time motherhood. They report a substantial decline in women's employment rates, particularly for low-skilled women, and a re-entry of women into part-time, marginal, or temporary work. In the meantime, they argue, women have to rely on the income of a male breadwinner as payments are poor. Is this dark picture also visible in the four countries discussed here?

Table 5.11   Leave rates according to gender, 1995-2000, four countries

	DK 1995	DK 2000	NL 1995	NL 2000	BE 1995	BE 2000	UK
Number of people	51,000	20,000	-	57,000	50,000	30,000	n.a.
% of women who take leave	90	93	61	56	85	73	n.a.

Source: Own calculations on the basis of: Denis et al. (1995), Ministerie van Tewerkstelling en Arbeid (1997), AMS (DK) unpublished statistics, Grootscholte et al. (2000), Bruning and Plantenga (1998), www.rva.fgov.be

Indeed, leave is nearly 'for women only'. In Denmark, in its heydays in the mid 1990s, 50,000 people took leave, of which more than 90 percent were female, making it the least man-friendly scheme of the countries studied (table 5.10). In Belgium, 85 percent of leave takers were women, but this dropped to 75 percent in 2000. After the introduction of the time credit, the scheme became much more popular and was used by 150.000 people, only 61 percent of whom were women (Debacker et al. 2004). However, men have not always taken leave to give care. Women used the leave scheme primarily to take time off to care for children and spend time on housekeeping, but older men used it mostly as a form of semi-retirement. The time credit scheme does show that more younger men than previously take leave, also full-time (Denis et al 1995; Ministerie van Tewerkstelling en Arbeid 1997; Debacker et al. 2004).

Strikingly, Dutch fathers are much more likely to take leave than Belgian or Danish fathers. In the Netherlands, the female percentage was 61 percent in the 1993-1995 period, and even dropped to 56 percent in 1995-1998 (Grootscholte et al. 2000). What is important, however, is the fact that on average, people take about eight or nine hours of weekly leave, which means that the Dutch parental leave should be interpreted as a temporary payment to work part-time.

Few statistics are available for the British case yet. However commentators such as Rake (2001) have warned that the new parental leave arrangement will not change the cargiving patterns of fathers, which is one of the lowest in Europe (chapter 4). In the absence of payment, projections suggest that only two percent of men, compared to 35 percent of women, will make use of unpaid parental leave if they are entitled.

So, the biggest problem with leave schemes is not that women take so much leave but that so few men do. Why don't they go on leave more often? Why don't they practice parental sharing? And why are Dutch fathers doing better? The first factor is payment. A recent Eurobarometer survey (2004) shows that 42 percent of all men said they did not take leave because of insufficient financial compensation, and the more highly educated the more problematic the lack of payment seems to be. Research in both Denmark and the Netherlands shows that many men who did not use leave said they could not afford to (Madsen 1998; Grootscholte et al. 2000). However, the country with the highest payments (Denmark) has the lowest proportion of men taking leave. Why is that? Men are probably more likely to take leave if they are paid a substantial percentage of their wage as this allows them to maintain their living standard. In such a case not taking leave would give them the feeling that they have missed a very good opportunity: getting quite a lot of money for being at home (Grootscholte et al. 2000). Indeed, in the Netherlands, which has a high level of fathers taking leave, most fathers who do take leave (70 percent) are public employees and receive quite a high percentage of their wage (75 percent). Such high payments seem crucial to seduce men into care (Bruning and Plantenga 1999).

Men are also more afraid to be disconnected from the labour market (Eurobarometer 2004). Despite labour market shortages from the mid-1990s onwards, a Danish survey shows that nearly 30 percent said they fear losing their job if they take leave, cannot get permission to take leave, or are indispensable and therefore did not make use of the leave scheme. Women have hardly mentioned those arguments (Madsen 1998). The question is whether men's fears are justified. Ironically, a recent survey shows that only nine percent of Danes believed that the negative attitude of employers regarding leave was the reason so few fathers took leave from work (Rostgaard 2002). Nevertheless, introducing flexibility increases men's use. Especially in countries like Denmark and the UK, men say they would take leave if better part-time options existed (Eurobarometer 2004). In the Netherlands, leave is flexible and even obligatorily part time, and many fathers actually use it. In Belgium, rates of taking leave degendered as soon as part-time leave became an option. Hence when men do not feel confined in care settings, and remain connected to the labour market, they may indeed want to do more at home.

While it would be preferable that more men take leave, from the perspective of degendering citizenship the question remains of how bad it is for women to go on leave. In none of the countries do leave schemes send women 'back to the kitchen': it is only a temporary break. Most women in Belgium and Denmark continue working (Denis et al. 1995). In the Netherlands and in the UK, which were low-employment countries for women, leave is clearly used as a method to stay connected to the labour market. Dutch research shows that paradoxically, those who go on leave are very work-oriented. They take leave to remain in the labour market, although they often reduce the number of hours when they re-enter. In fact, the leave scheme prevents some women from quitting their job: 13 percent of women and two percent of men said they would quit their job if they could not take leave (Grootscholte et al. 2000; van Luijn and Keuzenkamp 2004). British research by Callendar et al. (1997) showed that women with extensive rights to the previous maternity leave scheme were more likely to return to work after childbirth, return to the same employer, and return sooner.

The fact that leave is taken only by women can lead to statistical discrimination: employers may be reluctant to recruit women with small children. One survey showed that half of private employers said that child-minding leave would imply that the firm will be more reluctant to recruit women with small children, while 90 percent of public employers said it does not make a difference (Madsen 1998). This may result in gender segregation in the labour market, as being a public employee is (even) more attractive for women. But a Belgian study showed that those who go back to the same employer do not experience negative consequences from their breaks: they get just as many chances for promotion and wage increases as those who do not take leave. Men and women who return to their jobs have nearly the same careers (Denis et al. 1995).

Although it is important to be alert to the consequences of leave schemes, there is not much evidence that it draws women back into their homes, at least not in these countries and in these economic contexts. On the contrary, in low-employment countries like the United Kingdom and the Netherlands leave schemes may stimulate women to remain attached to the labour market.

The final issue concerns differences between women. Is it true, as Morgan and Zippel argue, that low-skilled workers tend to make use of such leave, so they are the ones who will bear the long-term costs of these policies: they will feel the impact of leave policies more than others? In other words, is the right to give care used mainly by less-educated women? The problem with leave schemes is in fact the other way around: they are more likely to be used by more highly educated women. In Belgium, critics have always argued that leave is only for *madammen in een bontmantel* (ladies in a fur coat), and rates among those taking leave indeed show that more highly educated women are overrepresented (Denis et al. 1995). The picture is similar in the Netherlands. Taking leave is a practice of middle and highly educated women; less-educated women are less likely to use parental leave (only five percent do) than those with a secondary or higher education level (about one fifth to a quarter). In the UK, the pre-1994 arrangements were also a class-biased phenomenon. Women employed full-time, with higher educations often had good arrangements, while part-time women workers who were less-educated were worse off (Callender et al. 1997). Only in Denmark, were payment is higher, do all kinds of women take leave, although those in social service jobs are overrepresented and highly educated women tend to take only slightly more leave (Andersen et al. 1996; Wehner and Abrahamson 2003).

This indicates that also highly educated women, as Hakim (2000) rightly pointed out, want to stay at home to care for their children – but only for a certain length of time. And perhaps they are more able to afford it – as they are often married to highly educated men. Then again, we have to be critical about the financial argument: many less-educated women in these countries stay at home without extra payments (apart from tax relief). Also, taking parental leave in a low female employment countries can be a sign of a high work ethos as leave is taken up by women who want to remain connected to paid work. Less-educated women in these countries are still likely to quit work rather than take leave or work permanently part time. The question is thus not only whether the labour market position of low-skilled women is hurt by taking leave, but whether less-educated women also have the right to take time to provide care.

Lessons from Leave

Leave schemes are a major breakthrough in today's welfare states. They constitute attempts to develop new caring rights while connecting caregivers to the labour market. In that sense they go beyond Wollstonecraft's dilemma. The schemes were advocated by many groups: social democrats, Christian democrats, women's alliances, and were put in place under pressure of the European directive which even forced the UK to introduce parental leave. The structure of the schemes seems to depend less on the political party background of the government than on the objectives of the schemes, as well as the consensual ideology on the private-public and the state-employer axis.

When the leave schemes are indeed a right and are paid for, they contribute to women's citizenship. Such schemes should be long enough to ensure the possibility to give care but short enough to keep carers attached to the labour market. The Danish and Belgian leave schemes come closest to fulfilling these conditions. The payment for caring, however, is always substantially lower than that for paid work. The main problem with leave is that men hardly ever take it, although this is more true in Denmark and Belgium than in the Netherlands. Crucial for men is that leave schemes are flexible – they do not want to be trapped in long periods of providing care – and they want to be well-paid. Parental leave in practice is thus not per se woman-unfriendly, it depends on the design. In fact, leave schemes are supposed to maintain or even increase women's labour market participation, which is indeed the case in historically low female employment countries such as the Netherlands and the UK.

Conclusion: Financial Compensation for Caregiving

So far, we have studied the right to give care, or the financial care compensations in taxation, social security, and leave schemes. In the last decades these schemes have been changing rapidly. Although it is still possible to be a full-time mother while receiving income, especially in Belgium and the UK (if you are a lone mother), most arrangements no longer prefer to support the ideal of full-time motherhood: employment for mothers is the new credo.

Partly because it never has been correct, but also as a consequence of change, these financial systems do not – or no longer –completely fit the popular academic welfare models of Esping-Andersen (1990) and Lewis (1992). Indeed, there is no one-to-one relationship between ideology and caring regimes. That is to say: social democratic regimes do not always, at any time, in every country, produce individual gender-friendly schemes. In fact, there is a continuous struggle between what deserves most priority: class equality or gender equality. And while Christian democracy is not unfriendly per se towards working women liberal regimes may have caregiving arrangements. The design of compensation for caregiving is often a result of the efforts of (parts of the) women's movement and are strongly related to the dominant – country specific – consensual ideology towards work and care, although this ideology is changing everywhere.

Secondly, the right to care does not offer us a clear understanding of gendered employment patterns. To give a few examples: in a country such as Denmark, fiscal arrangements for caregiving have little effect on women's employment patterns. Lone mothers' labour market participation is indeed lower when social security offers time to provide care, as the Dutch and British case show, but at the same time, these lone mothers would be financially better off if they went to work. Mothers do not seem to respond to financial motives only. Finally, leave schemes do not necessarily lower mothers' rates employment – they may even connect mothers to the labour market.

Since financial compensation for caregiving cannot fully explain mothers' (changing) employment patterns in Europe, we now turn to the right to receive care. Is the availability, cost, and design of childcare services more decisive for mothers' employment behaviour?

6 The Right to Receive Care: The State of Childcare Services

Without childcare there are no working mothers; only when women have their hands free from caring duties can they enter the labour market. This is the dominant logic in welfare state studies. The Scandinavian countries – Sweden and Denmark (not Norway) – offer proof of this. Both have exceptionally high female employment rates. What sets them apart from the rest of Europe is the early development and universal coverage of state-funded childcare. Informal care can also relieve women, but if women want to work *en masse* for a substantial number of hours, publicly funded and organised childcare is a necessary condition (Borchorst 2002; Esping-Andersen 1990; Lewis 1992a; Sainsbury 1996). This is also the reason why in the follow up to the Lisbon Strategy (2002) the EU agreed that member states must provide childcare for 33 percent of children under age three, although what these provisions entail is unspecified (Plantenga and Siegel 2004).

The question central to this chapter is: how true is this logic? And would mothers in countries like the Netherlands and the UK indeed work *en masse* if plenty of childcare was available tomorrow? In other words: if the citizenship right to services were implemented tonight, would this change women's and men's decisions tomorrow? The question is also what comes first. Are childcare services a cause or a consequence of women's paid employment (Leira 1992; Leira et al. 2005). Some scholars (Mahon and Michel 2002) have also pointed to the headlines under which childcare has developed. The motives behind childcare services affect its design and eventually women's citizenship status. Is childcare implemented as a labour market instrument, serving an egalitarian goal, or is the main objective the welfare of children? Only universal childcare is thought to grant opportunities to all women. A final question is what exactly is the driving force behind childcare policy: ideologies presented by dominant political parties, the women's movement, or institutional factors?

This chapter examines the origins, development, and design of childcare services in the four countries. According to the regime typologies, the UK as a liberal regime will leave care to the market, the Netherlands and Belgium as

Christian democratic regimes leave it to the family, and Denmark as a social democratic welfare state will be the only one in which childcare is a state responsibility (Esping-Andersen 1990, 1999). Following the male breadwinner typology, however, Belgium should show moderate intervention in childcare (Lewis 1992a; Meyers et al. 1999). This chapter will give a country-by-country description of childcare policy. Since childcare is a regional responsibility in Belgium, the focus is on the region of Flanders. For the UK, the focus is on England because more information is available for this country.

The Right to Childcare: Denmark

Denmark holds the world record in state-subsidised childcare: most young Danish children spend part of their lives in day care. In Denmark the family goes public, as Wolfe (1989) argues, and parents have outsourced the moral obligation to care. More than half of the children younger than three go to public facilities and nearly all (90 percent) go when they reach the age of three (Rostgaard and Fridberg 1998). Denmark easily surpasses the Lisbon targets.

Table 6.1	State-subsidised childcare for children in percentages, age group 0-3, 1985-2000, four countries		
	around 1985-1990	*around 1995*	*around 2000*
BE	20	30	41*
DK	48	48	56
NL	2	8	19
UK	2	2	8**

* Flanders: age category 0-2,5. From 2.5 to 3 the percentage is 86 (Kind en Gezin 2001)
** This is an estimated guess. The number of children using facilities is 15 percent according to Bradshaw and Finch (2002) and 20 percent according to the OECD (2001), but these are not state services. By and large, the state only pays childcare for lone mothers (WFTC; chapter Five), in urban deprived areas, and for those who have a social need.
Sources: ECNC (1990), ECNC (1996), Bradshaw & Finch (2002)

In contrast to popular thinking, you will find few children (only 15 percent) younger than one in professional day care. Many Danish mothers nowadays take leave following childbirth, and when they resume work the child is often already one (Abrahamson and Wehner 2003). The majority of children under three are not likely to go to a crèche: most of them go to family day carers. This is not a private arrangement, as the state or, more precisely, the municipalities employ these caregivers, who care for children in the childminder's home (chapters 7 and 9). Table 6.2 shows that in the mid-1990s more than a quarter of very young children visit family day care, while 17 percent go to a day care centre – either a *vuggestue* (literally 'cradle') or an age-integrated centre. Little research exists on family day care. Older research shows that the actual choice of family day care is not related to class – both high-income and low-income families use family day care – but to geography: childcare centres are more available in Copenhagen than in the countryside (Bertelsen 1991).

Table 6.2	Children 0-2 cared for by state-subsidised care, 1996, Denmark			
	Family day care	*Childcare centre*	*Age-integrated*	*Total*
1982	21	12	2	45
1988	26	13	3	42
1993	29	10	6	45
1996	27	9	8	44

Source: Rostgaard & Fridberg (1998)

Childcare in Denmark is not only widely available but also quite affordable; parents are responsible for a small percentage of the actual payments, the state pays by far the most. A place in a day care centre costs the Danish state nearly as much as unemployment benefits for one person. As table 6.3 reveals, for parents the costs of childcare are relatively low. This means that childcare is indeed a service for all, regardless of financial means. As a consequence, rates of use of day care services show few differences between higher-educated and lower-educated parents. The difference between lone mothers and two-parent families is also negligible: especially in contrast to Flanders, lone mothers are even slightly more likely to use state-subsidised childcare (DS 2002). In Denmark, the use of state-subsidised childcare is indeed nearly a universal practice for children above age one.

The Danish childcare system is entirely built upon the assumption that both fathers and mothers work full time. Children go to childcare every day. It is even financially foolish to bring your child to day care on a part-time basis, because you have to pay the full price anyway (int. 57, 65). Since the 1970s the number of hours that children spend in childcare has dropped. In 1985 a child was at a crèche 7.2 hours a day, while in 1999 this went down to 6.9 or 6.2 hours (depending on the calculation). Although it is accepted and appreciated that children go to childcare every day, long hours are increasingly considered to be bad for a child. Consequently, even though parents work more hours combined than in the 1980s, they now probably have flexible working hours that allow them to coordinate their schedules in such a way that children spend less time at day care facilities (Abrahamson and Wehner 2003).

Table 6.3	Net costs of full-time childcare. Most prevalent type in each country, after direct and indirect subsidies and after taxes and benefits, PPP pounds per month, with one child younger than age three, around 2000, four countries			
	Lone parent, half average earnings	Lone parent, average female earnings	Couple, average male, half-average female	Couple, average male, average female
BE	68	83	128	147
DK	8	61	145	145
NL	8	8	375	375
UK	116	158	385	385

Source: Bradshaw & Finch (2002)

Origins and Highlights of Childcare Policy

How and when did this available and affordable childcare develop? Denmark has always been 'ahead' of other European countries. Already in the late 1950s, the level of state-subsidised childcare was higher than that of the UK and the Netherlands in the 1980s. In the 1950s, five percent of Danish children (between ages 0-3) went to a childcare centre, and with the expansion of the welfare state in the 1960s childcare expanded concomitantly. By 1964 a law was approved which gave municipalities the responsibility of securing adequate coverage of childcare services. This law, which was supported by all political parties – not only the Social Democratic – transformed childcare from a facility for working-class women to a universal service that should enable all women to work. Employment for women was no longer recognised as an economic necessity but as a universal desire. In addition, a pedagogic function was central to childcare; childcare was meant to increase the well-being of children (Borchorst 2002). In 1974 another development occurred: the first step was made towards an individual entitlement. The 1974 Social Services Law stipulated that municipalities were assigned the task of securing the 'necessary places' (par. 69).

An important catalyst for this early and forceful development of childcare was the huge demand for women in the labour market and women's desire to work. Work – and earning one's own income – was seen as crucial to the emancipation process. For Danish women it was natural to look toward the *state* to develop care services. Although the concept originates in Sweden, in Denmark the state is also seen as 'the people's home', so it should offer support to families. What has reinforced the development of state services was the large influx of women into state employment (Borchorst and Siim 1987). When public support for childcare was established in the 1970s, most families became deeply dependent on state services, not only because their children went there, but many mothers were employed as care workers (Hernes 1987).

Also contributing to the early development of childcare is the typical Danish political culture, described as 'bottom-up' rather than 'top-down', as in continental political models (Bergqvist 1999; Siim 2000). Danish political culture, stresses Siim (2000), is very integrative and directed towards conflict-solving. Defining and 'doing' politics is based on interactions of social movements and the state. This competence for democratic self-organisation came from the experiences of the folk high schools (*Grundtvig*) and the working class movement. In Denmark women were not as integrated in the political arena as in other Scandinavian countries: they had relatively low levels of political representation, fewer women in government, and were less represented in the corporate channel. But Danish women could raise gender issues from below (see also Bergqvist 1999). It was also important that women's groups were not fragmented and had opposing views (as in the Netherlands and the UK), and have a long tradition of political networks and successful alliances (Siim 1998).

Crucial too is that childcare has been organised and decided at the local level. The delivery of, subsidies for, and decision-making regarding childcare is in the hands of the *Kommune*, the municipalities (Kröger 1997). As Rold Andersen, a former Social Democratic minister in the 1970s and social scientist stressed:

> This ideology or process was promoted very much by the fact that the caregiving professions and services were placed with the local authorities and not the state. In the *Kommune* women meet the mayors and the councillors and other politicians every day in the supermarket, and there they tell them: "we need kindergartens, we need nursing homes

and we need home helpers and so on, please give us that'. So there was certainly a process at the bottom created by women. The huge expansion of care services could not have taken place if the services were placed with the state, and governed by the officials in the ministries or in the state institutions (int. 40).

Economic Crises and Boom

Danish childcare expansion was quickly confronted with economic crises. 'Necessary places', the key words of the 1974 law, became open to interpretation; waiting lists became a very common phenomenon, especially in the 1980s. At that time, the minister responsible for childcare, Bjerregaard (social democrats) argued that in a period of economic crises the universalistic principle should no longer guide childcare policy. She argued for a revaluation of the need principle (Bertone 2000). But even under Bjerregaard's regime childcare developed, although more incrementally: the number of places kept growing slowly. The right-wing minority governments, which were in office from 1982 to 1993 (see appendix I), did not introduce major changes either, although they hardly extended childcare despite long waiting lists. Therefore, Borchorst (2002) concludes that the Danish childcare system is characterised by stability and continuity, not by change. All political parties, from the 1960s up until today, have acknowledged the importance of childcare. Childcare is not an exclusive social democratic enterprise, in Denmark it has large cross-political support.

It was nevertheless the social democratic government which in the mid-1990s took the last step in recognising childcare services as an individual entitlement rather than as a human need. Childcare became a citizenship right for children. Generally more interested in services, the social democrats introduced the *Pasningsgaranti*: the promise that every child older than one has the right to use day care facilities. From the mid-1990s onwards childcare expanded rapidly. While 59,000 children were on the waiting lists in 1993, this number was brought back to 8,500 by the late 1990s. In the same period a total of 173,000 extra childcare places were created. By fall of 2000, 90 percent of all municipalities had implemented this guarantee (BUPL 1999; Abrahamson and Wehner 2003).

At the same time, both an increase and a decrease of professionalisation took place. To have as many places as possible, the quality standards in terms of staff ratios have been lowered. There are now fewer trained workers per child. For instance, in a *vuggestuer* (a day care centre for children aged 0-3) 5.88 children were cared for by one trained pedagogue (three years of higher education) in 1990, compared to 6.42 children in 1998 (BUPL 1999). One of the reasons is the development of a one-and-a-half year training program to become an assistant pedagogue. This slight decrease of professionalisation goes hand in hand with an important step, the legal formalisation of pedagogical objectives. The new 1997 Social Services Act states that childcare has three equally weighted objectives: minding, and social and pedagogical targets. The latter means that 'child care shall offer possibilities for experiences and activities which will stimulate the child's fantasy, creativity, and language development, and also provide the child with space to play and learn, being together, and the possibility to investigate the environment' (subsection 3). Childcare shall also 'offer the possibility to participate in decision-making and responsibility, and as part of it contribute to the development of the children's independence and ability to enter binding communities' (subsection 4).

The most recent changes in Danish childcare policy – the introduction of *frit valg* (free choice) may also undermine professionalisation of childcare because no requirements are set for the professional background of a childminder. Under pressure from the neo-liberal waves in Europe and the Danish right-wing party (Venstre), the new 1997 Social Services Act also makes it possible to undermine the monopoly of the municipality on childcare services. Parents can receive financial support if they arrange childcare themselves, although they cannot use it to stay at home – unlike in other Scandinavian welfare states, such as Finland. By the late 1990s not many people had used the option. If they did, they were often relatively better educated. In two-thirds of the cases they used the money to employ a maid so the child was cared for in its own home (Andersen 1998). Venstre also wants parents to be able to stay at home, but so far the social democrats have blocked this option. It would undermine the basis of the Danish childcare system and is at odds with the position that childcare is important for the well-being of children.

In Denmark, children's general and social development rather than preparation for education has informed pedagogy for pre-schoolchildren. Danish childcare services are based on social pedagogical ideas. Danish childcare policy is not only characterised by universalism but also by the transformation of human needs into individual entitlements. The right to childcare is not exclusively based on the right for working parents, it is a right for children to receive professional care. Although childcare policy is characterised by continuity, as Borchorst (2002) shows, the question is whether the latest introduction of free choice will bring more changes.

Flanders: From Necessary Evil to Approved Politics

Perhaps a surprise to some, Flanders comes in second in the childcare league. By 1988, 23 percent of children were cared for in state-subsidised day care, by 1993 this rose to 31 percent, and in 1999 more than 40 percent of Flemish children younger than three went to state-subsidised childcare, easily surpassing the Lisbon targets (table 6.1). The Flemish rates (as well as those for Belgium overall) are not only higher than in the Netherlands and in the UK, but also much higher than in the country often compared to Belgium, namely France (23 percent in 1995 and 39 percent in 2000). In fact, the Belgian level in general and the Flemish level in particular is just as high as in Sweden (ECNC 1996). As in Denmark, full-time care is most common (Vanpée et al. 2000) and childcare is affordable (see table 6.3). Indeed, a Christian democratic welfare regime can build just as comprehensive a childcare service as a social democratic welfare state.

How can this be explained? In Belgium and Flanders, Christian democratic coalitions were indeed vital for the development of the welfare state, and the Christian democrats have always held the (Flemish) cabinet seats for welfare, childcare, and family policy. How could state-subsidised childcare expand as much in a Christian democratic regime as in a social democratic regime? The following section discusses the motives behind the Flemish childcare policy (given that since 1980 care is a regional responsibility). Are they the same as in Denmark?

A Labour Market – Working Class Logic

While the level of childcare in Flanders is nearly as high as in Scandinavian countries, the rationale behind it is clearly Christian democratic: childcare services are supposed to benefit low-paid workers. The 1983 law of the Flemish region stipulates that 'priority should be given to children whose parents are not able to bring up their children themselves because of work, or to children who, because of social and/or pedagogical motives, are dependent on guidance and care outside the home, or children whose parents have the lowest income' (par 5, December 30, 1983).

Today, the practice is different. In Flanders, highly educated women use childcare more often than less-educated women, who, just as lone mothers, are more likely to use informal arrangements (such as the help of grandparents) (Storms 1995). This indicates what Merton (1968) has called 'the Matthew effect', after the passage in the Bible that states that those who have will receive more, and those who have nothing will have what little they have taken. Hence those who are well-off are more likely to use welfare state services, while those who actually need subsidised services are less likely to access them. This is not only in contrast to the universal practice in Denmark, it also is at odds with the objectives behind Flemish childcare policy.

Another contrast with Denmark is Flanders' firm roots in an anti-poverty labour market paradigm. In Belgium, childcare investments are seen as a necessary evil. The first state-funded childcare organisation was set up in 1918 because women had to work to keep their families out of poverty. The predecessor of the quasi-state organisation *Kind en Gezin* writes in 1940:

> The *kribbe* (day care) is just an actual necessity. Many mothers work
> outside the home, but we hope that this situation will improve and they
> will meet a future where they do not have to leave their homely hearth
> (Lambrechts and de Dewispelaere 1980: 38).

But the situation did not change. Subsidising childcare has increased continuously since the 1960s. In 1965 childcare facilities came under a legal framework: in order to be recognised and subsidised, they had to fulfil certain criteria. Still, public childcare was considered bad for children, though it was seen as acceptable for parents on a low income. By the late 1960s all crèches – 78 in total – were at least implicitly reserved for children of parents with low incomes, and were based in urban surroundings (Deven 1998).

An important economic investment was made in the mid-1970s. Because of rising wages and a growing pool of workers, the organisation that paid child benefit (drawn from insurance revenues) was well in the black: they had money to spend. What to do with this surplus? Social democrats, especially their women's organisations, gave priority to crèches. They argued that there were shortages, as parents could no longer turn to their own parents to provide care, because they were now also working in increasing numbers. Social democrats pointed out that Belgium lacked guaranteed and secure childcare solutions, and this was not good for the tranquillity of mothers and children. Social democrats also argued that investing in childcare centres would correct inequities; working mothers paid into the system but received no extra benefits.

The influential League for Large and Young Families (BGJG), however, preferred a more generous child benefit, just as the trade unions. The latter also wanted women to have a free choice and a lack of childcare would make this choice impossible, but they feared investing in childcare would only discriminate between families, because families with someone at home or those outside the urban areas could not make use these services. The women's organisation of the Christian democratic party argued that childcare would not be a good option as it would benefit the higher educated. In the Christian democratic view, the state only has to support the very poor. Eventually, the social democratic minister made the decision and spent one billion Belgian francs to increase the child benefit and 400 billion francs for public financing of childcare policy, which came into effect in 1974 (Marques-Pereira and Payne 2001).

This money helped to develop childcare, which increased incrementally. Due to the economic crisis, subsidies were frozen in the mid-1980s, but when shortages arose, investments increased again. As a result, real shortages of childcare were rare in Flanders. By 1983, 17 percent of children aged 0-3 were using state-subsidised childcare. In 1988 this rose to 23 percent, in 1993 to 31 percent, and in 2000 to 41 percent (Kind en Gezin 1997, 2001, table 6.1). In the Walloon region state-subsidised childcare is also substantial, although less developed than in Flanders: while in the mid-1990s 43,000 places for children under age three existed in Walloon, Flanders had 70,000 places (Jenson and Sineau 2001).

Since the 1980s, the bulk of Flemish state subsidies have gone to family day care: childcare within the home of a childminder. While in 1987 the state funded 10,000 places with day care mothers and 10,000 in childcare institutions, in the mid-1990s 12,000 places were available in day care institutions and more than 20,000 places were available with day care mothers (Kind en Gezin 1997). In French-speaking Belgium organised day care also exists and has grown substantially between 1988-1993, yet day care institutions are much more common than in Flanders. Jenson and Sineau (2001) calculated that for children under age three, more than 9,000 children use family day care and more than 10,000 children are in a day care centre. In the Flemish region more than 11,000 children are in day care centres and 19,000 in family day care: 35 percent of the children stay with day care mothers who are connected to a *dienst voor opvanggezinnen* (services for family day care), while 24 percent go to a public childcare centre (Vanpée et al. 2000; table 8.3). These services are subsidised and controlled along 'pillarised' lines, although most of them are Catholic. They organise the access and mediation between parents and childminders, and give professional advise and support as well as training. They also pay the childminders (from the money the parents pay the organisation). Unlike the Danish situation, municipalities are not involved.

The continued increase of state-subsidised childcare in the 1980s was a silent intervention; few political debates or arguments took place on the issue. In the 1990s a crucial shift occurred: childcare became a more positive choice. The defensive attitude towards childcare was transformed into an offensive attitude. Childcare in Flanders is nowadays no longer seen as a necessary evil but as a pedagogical tool for the development of a child, although the labour market paradigm is still in place. Childcare helps women to take on jobs. The Flemish government has choosen to fully invest in childcare and continues to improve the quality of care (Vanpée et al. 2000; Ministerie van de Vlaamse Gemeenschap 2000).

Subsidiarity or Free Choice

According to researchers like Esping-Andersen (1990), Christian democratic welfare states are based on the principle of subsidiarity, a concept that explains the reluctance towards state intervention. But subsidiarity, as also Daly (1999) and van Kersbergen (1995) argue, is a flexible concept: it indicates *when* the state has to intervene, so it can help explain why the Belgian state has intervened in childcare. Salamink (1991), a Flemish theologian, points out that many Catholic politicians and thinkers have argued that upon carefully reading the Pope's encyclical *Quadragesimo anno* (1932) they believe the state has the *duty* to support families. The original meaning of the Latin word subsidy means 'help'. This duty of the state is nevertheless rather different from the social democratic concept of universal social rights of citizens: within Belgian Christian democratic ideology, childcare is not seen as a citizen's right but as a measure to protect low-income families.

Subsidiarity in Flanders means that the state has a duty to support low-income families to protect them from poverty. Childcare was regarded as a necessary evil that could solve the financial problems of the family. The microeconomics within households forced the state to intervene. The politicians responsible thought this would be a temporary measure and working women could return to their homes when the economy improved, but mothers' employment rates continuously increased. In the late 1960s and the 1970s, women's employment was less an issue of financial necessity than of emancipation. Employed women as well as feminists defined work as such: working became a way to express oneself, meet other people, and have power in the public arena. In the late 1970s financial necessity became less crucial as a motive for working, although this was truer for more highly educated women, since less-educated women were less likely to have well-paid work (Pauwels 1978). Women's employment became a crucial issue of the women's movement, which was broad and certainly not exclusively social democratic; Catholic Working Women (KVA) for instance was a large and influential organisation with strong links to the Christian democratic Party. There was a consensus among all political parties that women's labour should be facilitated. So economic necessity at a family level (until 1970) was transformed into women's push for employment as a path towards emancipation (in the 1970s). At that time, the Belgian government could not excuse itself from a responsibility already taken. In this case path dependency, or Pierson's (1994) term policy feedback, is applicable. Families became dependent on the state and adapted their work and family life accordingly.

The question remains as to whether the notion of subsidiarity has really been that crucial. In the debates around women and work, as well as those regarding the role of the state, the concept of free choice is much more decisive, as we already saw in the chapter on taxation (see also Kremer 2002; Marques-Pereira and Paye 2001). The Belgian interpretation of free choice contributes to our understanding of the development of childcare policy in a Christian democratic regime, much more than the subsidiarity principle. Free choice has been used in childcare policies on two levels: first, people (read: mothers) must have a free choice between paid employment and providing care. Secondly, if mothers do decide to work, they must have a free choice as to which type of care they use for their children.

On the first level the Christian democratic view on working and caring holds that it is not up to the state to decide whether women should work or provide care, but unlike the liberal perspective the state does have to facilitate this free choice. Incentives to both work and care should be embedded in social policies. On the one hand, financial structures should be in place to ensure that mothers can stay at home if they wish. This is also seen in the motivation of the Belgian tax system, with its marriage quotient. On the other hand, free choice has also been the key concept to advocate childcare services. When facilities are available and affordable for all families, people really have a free choice. This was one of the arguments the Christian unions used when debating what to do with their surplus of funds (described above).

The quasi-state organisation Kind en Gezin, responsible for childcare in Flanders, has firmly based itself upon the free-choice principle. Guaranteeing free choice is the way this organisation defines its responsibility and task. Its 1988 white paper 'Childcare: A Growing Choice for Parents' emphasised that it was not their aim to influence the decision of families, though it was the duty of the state to enable families to make the choice. When parents opt for childcare on a large scale, Kind en Gezin has to acknowledge that choice and supply the necessary services. The increase in childcare thus reflects parental preferences since then, according to the organisation. The state is therefore obliged to follow the demands of the parents (Kind en Gezin 1988). This is in line with a Christian democratic ideology that the state is at the service of citizens and their needs, and should not have a prescriptive role.

Today the notion of free choice is readily associated with liberalism, but it is also a Christian democratic concept in a pillarised and conflictive society. The Christian democratic emphasis on free choice has two meanings. Daly (1999) argues that ideology is shaped by competing influences and rival models of social policy. She argues that the differences between Catholic countries – she herself studied Ireland and Germany – relate to the social forces and pressures Catholic politics have to battle, such as a powerful socialist labour movement or a rival Protestant Church. In Belgium and Flanders a strong fight took place starting in the late 1960s between the Christian democratic values of the family – which nevertheless accorded women's need for autonomy – and a socialist claim, expressed more forcefully by women's organisations, that mothers should be enabled to work in the labour force, this being the key to their economic and personal autonomy. Social democrats not only argued in favour of reducing inequalities in the workplace but also called for infrastructure of services. The notion of free choice expresses not only the social democratic right to work but also demands appreciation and acknowledgement for a traditional family model (see also Marques-Pereira and Paye 2001).

But perhaps more important is the institutional setting of pillarisation, which gave 'free choice' its meaning. Because of the ideological and religious heterogeneity of society, it is believed that citizens should have free choice to decide, for instance, which schools their children attend. Belgian parents can choose between a Catholic or a secular school (and in the Netherlands between different religious schools). This principle of choice also applies to hospitals, sports clubs, homecare organisations, and the like. Freedom of choice would be an empty concept if the state did not guarantee choice. Pillarised societies are therefore characterised by 'subsidised freedom': the state must have respect for people's choices and enforce pluralism and diversity (Groof 1983). Free choice in the pillarised societies of Belgium and the Netherlands can be translated into the objective of 'state pluralism': the state enforces a pluralist society. This also means the state always has to be neutral in its outcomes.

Finally, the pillarised system not only shapes the origins of free choice, it also allows for a lively competition between providers of services. Both social democratic and Christian democratic organisations have been involved in the 'business of childcare'. If they provided good services, they could attach clients (or voters) to them. Both pillars have pushed the state to give more money to childcare. They have had much impact on governmental decisions (Hellemans and Schepers 1992). The institutional setting also demands that the state share money equally between the pillars, so that if Christian democratic organisations asked for money (often from their own minister), the Socialist organisation would also receive their share. With this system services were difficult to freeze, as it is difficult to say no to your own 'family member'.

In sum, Flemish childcare developed first of all because of the microeconomic necessity of working women. When many women worked in the 1960s and 1970s, they paid so many premiums to the state that investments in childcare were made. Besides, women increasingly wanted to work and stressed the need for childcare. Free choice became the crucial concept, largely embraced by Christian democratic forces: women should not only have the choice to stay at home, but also to work. Moreover, the typical structure of Belgian society, pillarisation, plays a double role in childcare policy: it gives meaning to the concept of free choice and creates what Pierson (1994) calls 'lock in effects'. The state can no longer withdraw its support. But while the right to receive care in Flanders is impressive and may in practice be universal, its motives are not: childcare is based on a labour market paradigm, it has to help women participate in the labour market.

The Netherlands: Taking a Jump

The Netherlands has always been a childcare laggard, together with the UK, Ireland, and southern European countries such as Spain. Until the late 1980s, as table 6.1 shows; only two percent of young Dutch children (aged 0-3) used state-financed childcare. For a long time, childcare was considered as an antiphon to a modern welfare state: in a decent welfare state, families should be able to afford to have their at children home. This changed only in the 1990s, when the increase in women's labour market participation became a policy target. Then the percentage of children who went to state-funded services more than doubled, and in the late 1990s nearly one-fifth of young children (aged 0-3) used state-subsidised childcare. In contrast to Denmark, few Dutch children go to childcare every day. The norm is that five days a week is not good for children's development; day care is commonly used two or three days a week (Portegijs et al. 2002). Although Dutch childcare is just a shadow of the Flemish and Danish arrangements, the rapid increase is extraordinary. While in the mid-1990s waiting lists were a huge problem, more recently childcare for children under age four is less problematic, and shortages are more of an issue for after-school care.

The organisation of state-subsidised care and the logic behind Dutch childcare is rather unique in Europe, as it developed in partnership with employers. The big increase in childcare in the Netherlands is due to two successive 'Stimulative Measures on Childcare' that the government launched in 1990 and were in place until 1996. These measures reveal the dominant ideology towards the state: the state contributes only when both employer and employee pay for childcare. Employers are supposed to buy *bedrijfsplaatsen* (company places) for their employees in childcare institutions. Over the years, employers' contributions became increasingly important. In 1990, the state paid 58 percent, parents 26 percent, and employers 14 percent. In 1996, this ratio changed to 36:21:40. In 1999 it was 29:19:49. As employers' contributions increased substantially, contributions made by the state decreased (Keuzenkamp and Oudhof 2000; Portegijs et al. 2002).

Dutch childcare policy is built on the trust of collective corporate arrangements. The drawback of this manner of organising childcare is that not all employers pay for childcare, they only do so when they fall under collective agreement (about 80 percent of employees in the Netherlands are), but these agreements also have to include childcare arrangements. Less than half of the collective agreements in the Netherlands (45 percent) include any childcare arrangement (Portegijs et al. 2002). Only employers that employ many women (for instance in the care and welfare sector) have good agreements. This in turn attracts mothers to work in these sectors, so gender segregation in the labour market can be reinforced by this specific childcare policy.

Another measure was taken in 1996, subsidising childcare specifically for single parents and allocating a sum of money for childcare for these parents. As explained in the chapter on social security, since 1996 lone mothers with children over age four are obliged to work. The social democratic Minister Melkert arranged that lone mothers should be able to receive affordable childcare, so there are various flows of state subsidies. To give an impression of the distribution of places available for children: in 1999 for children under age three there were 10,700 private places available, 35,600 company places, 14,600 subsidised places, and 1,700 places allocated to lone parents (Portegijs et al. 2002).

Although the Stimulative Measures in the Netherlands support child-care centres as well as family daycare that are connected to state-subsidised bureaus, these official childminders are not popular at all. Less than five percent of children aged 0-3 go to such families, in contrast to 21 percent who go to childcare centres (Knijn 2003; table 8.4). This is in stark contrast to Denmark and Belgium. Most popular in the Netherlands are unofficial, unregulated childminders, which will be discussed in chapters 7 and 8.

The Dutch system for financing and organising childcare resulted in care being relatively cheap for lone mothers while incredibly expensive for dual-earners (see table 6.3). Not deterred by the expense, higher-income families are more likely to use childcare than low-income families. The reason is simple: highly educated mothers are more likely to work (Portegijs et al. 2002). As in Flanders, the Matthew principle is in place, but not when it applies to lone mothers, who are a little more likely to use state-funded childcare – at least when they do work. This is not the case in Flanders, as we have seen.

In 2005, a new law on childcare was implemented – called the Basic Childcare Services Act. This title is very misleading as the organisation principles remain the same: employers, employees, and the state are jointly responsible for childcare. What does change is that parents are made into real consumers: via the tax system they receive their state component so they can go to the childcare market and compare prices and quality. Municipalities are no longer allowed to offer childcare: childcare centres are obliged to become commercialised. This law has been seen as the crowning stage of the implementation of the liberal notion of free choice. Again, employers are not *required* to pay for childcare, they are *asked.* If they do not pay, the state will make up some of the deficit for low-income families. The Christian democratic Minister De Geus has argued that the state filling in the gap for unwilling employers is a disincentive for employers to take childcare responsibility. Critics regard the law as a missed opportunity to establish childcare as a basic service that is open to all children and is based on the well-being of children (Schreuder 2001). From 2007 onwards, the scheme changed again. Because many employers failed to pay contributions it is now obligatory to contribute to childcare.

The Rise of Neo-liberalism in the Netherlands

Why did the Netherlands lag behind in the development of childcare? And why is the design of its childcare policy built upon trust between employers and employees? Until the late 1980s, most political and social parties – Christian democratic, liberal and social democratic – believed that women's place was in the home (Bussemaker 1993). In the 1950s and 1960s nearly all Dutch mothers were at home, while Danish and Flemish women entered the labour market. Dutch male breadwinners, as Plantenga (1993) puts it, were rich enough to afford a woman at home, in contrast to Belgian breadwinners. The pillarised organisation of society also contributed, as it helped to keep norms in place. Childcare at that time was regarded as something that would be immoral in a well-developed welfare state such as the Netherlands. For this reason, public childcare services were only sporadically established in cities where there was a 'demonstrated need' and for cases with an 'abnormal' family situation (Bussemaker 1993).

In the 1970s, childcare became a political issue: women from social democratic and communist backgrounds (and not the Christian democrats as in Belgium) became strong advocates for public childcare. But the women's movement itself lacked consensus on the question of whether childcare was important for women; moreover, the movement was not strong enough and had not built a viable, recognised constituency in the political arena. Dutch opponents of childcare always argued that bringing your child to childcare was only in the self-interest of mothers and would endanger the welfare of children (Bussemaker 1993, 1998; see also Singer 1989).

It was not until the late 1980s and early 1990s that childcare became a serious political issue. At that time, the welfare state was criticised in two ways. First, it was argued that the welfare state contributes to an immoral ethos: people would become dependent on the state and this causes selfishness (Adriaansens and Zijderveld 1981). To prevent this culture of dependency, the state should decentralise responsibilities and make the family responsible again for the well-being of society. In the Netherlands this became a Christian and social democratic critique of the perverse consequences of the state, but one framed in neo-liberal language. Dutch politicians became strong advocates of the market and the community. Secondly, as in the rest of Northwestern Europe, it was argued that the welfare state was too expensive. A report by the Scientific Council for Government Policy entitled 'A Working Perspective' (WRR 1990) summarised the problem and in so doing marked a turning point, particularly for women. The report said that in the Netherlands a large amount of human capital was wasted because women were largely inactive. And for a sustainable welfare state, particularly in light of the aging of society, the Dutch needed to invest in female labour market participation and therefore in childcare.

In the 1990s, all political and corporatist parties agreed that childcare was necessary to raise women's productivity. The Dutch government understood that the substantial number of inactive women contributed to the crisis of the welfare state. Using a macroeconomic rather than a microeconomic rationale, as in Belgium, the state introduced the first Stimulative Measure and reserved 300 million guilders for investment. It is telling that this money was derived from the extra tax revenue generated by dual-earner couples (chapter 5).

The organisational foundation of childcare was shaped in the 1990s, at a time when the state was experiencing large deficits. The language of the market, which was spoken by Christian democrats but obviously also by social democrats and liberals, became predominant in Dutch social policy. Why? In the Netherlands, democratisation and secularisation led to the erosion of the pillarised system. In the 1980s most of the pillarised movements merged and the end of pillarisation marked a new era. The vacuum was filled by a new ideology of the state and society relationship – that of neo-liberalism. The new language described society as a market of individuals, rather than as persons tied to pillars. As Duyvendak (1997) points out: faith in God became faith in the market. According to this ideology, the state should facilitate and not obstruct the natural processes of the market as it used to. According to Knijn (1998: 89), the language of the market has far-reaching consequences: it offers the image that 'transforming public goods into private goods sold for profit in a free market can reshape clients into consumers who have freedom to select the care they need'. Parents thus became consumers rather than clients.

At the same time, neo-corporatism, popularly called the *poldermodel*, gained importance. In seeking a solution for the economic crisis of the 1980s, the Dutch government fell back on an old habit: cooperation between the social partners. In a famous meeting in Wassenaar in 1982, already described in chapter 5, unions and employers' organisations reached a consensus about the rigid renovation of the welfare state, the freezing of wages, and the promotion of part-time jobs to redistribute employment and raise the historically low rates of female employment (Visser and Hemerijkck 1997; Trommel and van der Veen 1999). Many politicians are convinced that the economic boom in the 1990s – the Dutch miracle – is the result of a pact between trade unions, employers' organisations, and the state. Due to the successful cooperation between the partners and the (alleged) success of the Dutch solution, childcare – because it is a relatively new type of service – could be developed strictly according to the ideology of the *poldermodel*. Hence the organisation and payment structure of Dutch childcare and the existence of company places at childcare facilities; the latter will nevertheless disappear when the 2005 law is implemented.

Dutch-Flemish Differences

While both Flanders and the Netherlands have a strong Christian democratic basis and are part of the same 'family of nations', their history of
childcare is very different. The two pictures described above point to the
fact that a strong political consensus against working women existed in
the Netherlands. This could also hold true because in the Netherlands,
at least in the 1950s and 1960s, families were rich enough and the pillars
could conserve gender norms which positioned women outside the labour
market. In addition, the Dutch women's movement was too fragmented to
change this ideology. In Belgium there was more pressure, especially on
the Christian democratic party, to support women's employment outside
the home. Initially this was due to economic necessity and then, from the
1970s onwards, because the women's movement had a crucial position
within the political establishment. Consequently, childcare policy was
shaped much earlier and also according to the Christian democratic interpretation of free choice, which stresses childcare's institutionalisation.
In the Netherlands, childcare policy developed because of a macro-economic rationale: women need to work in order to maintain a sustainable
welfare state. Childcare was shaped much later in a period in which the
state had little money to spend. The notion of free choice is shaped by an
individual and market paradigm.

The final question is why the Flemish notion of free choice assumes
a strong state intervention while the Dutch notion does not. Why is Belgium not intoxicated with the language of the market to the extent that it
too is guided by a Liberal notion of free choice in its childcare policy? In
contrast to the Netherlands, pillarisation in Belgium is still the most important system of subsidising and delivering welfare. In the Netherlands,
democratisation and secularisation have been much stronger. Moreover,
the pillars became trapped by the state that subsidised them. By accepting
state subsidies, they were no longer powerful (van Doorn 1978). By contrast, in Belgium the political elite connected to each of the pillars – and
thus the heads of childcare services, trade unions, education, and the like
– have always been powerful. The pillars 'overruled' the state, not the
other way around as in the Netherlands (Hellemans and Schepers 1992).

The state guarantee of having a free choice is necessary to pacify differences and to create consensus and stability in the system (Lijphart 1968).
Much more than in the Netherlands of today, Belgium needs a system
to keep the nation together. The Belgian political scientist Huyse (1983)
pointed out that there are no less than three ideological folds: between

socialists and Catholics, between employers and employees, and between French- and Dutch-speaking Belgians. Much of public policy is focused on gluing these rifts and keeping the nation-state as it is. Childcare policy is part of that.

England: Lethargic but Finally on the Move

Of all four countries, the UK has the lowest level of state-subsidised childcare and is the least likely to reach the Lisbon criteria. The Conservative government that was in place from 1979 to 1997 never expanded childcare services. Childcare policy was at the margins of public policy. As table 6.1 shows, in the 1990s the level of state-subsidised childcare was just two percent for children under age three. Provided by the local authorities, these services are directed towards children who have strictly defined special needs. The local authorities' nurseries only provided spots for 24,000 children in 1994, a number which has been quite steady since the 1980s (Bull et al. 1994). This is only a fraction of the number of children cared for by the local authorities during the Second World War (Moss 1991).

Apart from caring for the 'most needy', the Conservatives left childcare to the responsibility of individuals and their employers. The market and employers were supposed to fulfil the demand for care: supply-side economics was the paradigm and employers were held responsible for the provision of childcare. The Conservative Member of Parliament Patten, for instance, argued that 'employers in this country must realise that the only way to defuse the demographic time bomb ticking away underneath them is by taking the initiative themselves to support family life and to support mothers who want to work' (Moss 1991: 137). This *laissez-faire* strategy turned out to be unsuccessful: day care was expensive, and the quality and availability variable depended on the region in which one lived. Despite the Conservative government's faith in the creativity of the market, the demands of parents have not been met. At the same time, employers did not develop childcare provisions either. Tax deductions, in place from 1984 until 1990, to stimulate employers to make childcare arrangements, had little success. Few employers did so (Brannen and Moss 1991). As a result, childcare shortages were constant (Day Care Trust 1997).

In line with a liberal view of the state, two tasks were nevertheless taken seriously: helping to connect supply and demand and to prevent excesses of the market. Since 1948, when nurseries were also regulated, childminders have been obliged to register at the local authority: it is otherwise illegal to care for a child in your home. Childminders have to reach minimum standards of safety and for facilities. A childminder is not allowed to care for more than three children under the age of five, including one of her own. These rules, surprisingly, are much stricter than in Flanders and Denmark. In the Netherlands childminders do not have to register at all. On the other hand, childminders in England do not get much support from the local authority in terms of education, training, supervision, or money (Moss et al. 1995).

Why the Conservatives Did Not Develop Childcare

During the Conservative area, childcare was not on the agenda because it was associated with spending and with debates on the ideology of motherhood. In the 1980s the Conservative party had a small membership rift between real classical liberals and moral authoritarians (Lewis 2003). The first were willing to leave it to women to decide whether to work and seek childcare. Here the liberal notions of freedom of choice and equal opportunities applied. The second strand is more suspicious of the desirability of mothers' employment. The authoritarians spread concerns about the morality of childcare. An example of the authoritarian mindset is presented in the study by Morgan (1996), published by the IEA, the conservative think tank, in which she mops the floor with the protagonist of childcare. Research shows, Morgan argues, that only the very best childcare can hope to equal the outcomes of children who are cared for at home, and most childcare is not of this high standard. But it is much too costly to have really good care institutions, and besides, a large number of women want to stay at home anyway, she argues. 'If the government has any duty to facilitate the successful rearing of the nation's children, it would do well to enhance the opportunities for parents to care for their own children. This is in line with most people's aspirations and with what we know is best for the welfare of most children' (Morgan 1996: 127).

This type of critique was more common under the Thatcher regime than under that of Major (1992-1997). In the early years, Thatcher herself opposed childcare strongly: it would lead to 'a whole generation of crèche children ... who never understood the security of home' (quoted in Ginsburg 1992: 173). But under Major's premiership there was a shift away from this antipathy towards working mothers (Lister 1996; Randall 2002). When Major was still the chancellor of the Exchequer he said:

> We have always made it clear that it is not for the Government to en-
> courage or discourage women with children to go out to work. But it is
> undeniable that an increasing number of mothers do want to return to
> work and many employers in private industry and in public services are
> keen to encourage them to do so. (quoted in Gardiner 1997: 212)

As time went by, and especially in the wake of the demographic time
bombs panic, government utterances were positively supportive of working mothers. A conservative MP even concluded that the importance of
childcare is not in dispute in the House (Randall 2002).

But the problem was that in conservative ideology childcare arrangements were essentially a private matter (Randall 1996). If parents wanted
to work they would have to find childcare on the market. Or as Conservative Edwina Currie put it in 1988,

> Our view is that it is for parents that go out to work to decide how best
> to care for their children. If they want to or need help in this, they
> should make the appropriate arrangements and meet the cost (quoted
> in Cohen and Fraser 1991: 9).

Moreover, for the Treasury-led perspective of Conservatives supplying
childcare would merely mean a 'dead-weight' cost: they would just pay
to people who already were in the economy (Gardiner 1997). They also
argued that the growth in women's employment had occurred without
government intervention supporting childcare; childcare had grown to
meet the demand anyway (House of Commons 1994/1995). Therefore, under Major the private and public sectors were *asked* in a friendly way to
develop services. The 1992 Manifesto summed up the government's childcare policy:

> We shall continue to encourage the development of childcare arrange-
> ments in the voluntary and independent sector and local authorities
> would be asked to ensure that the standards for which they are now re-
> sponsible under the Children Act would be applied sensibly. (Lister 1996)

The Conservative government also did not exactly give the women's movement a 'window of opportunity', to put it mildly. The women's movement
has been in the margins and feminists were isolated from the political
mainstream and political allies (O'Connor et al. 1999). Unlike Danish politics, British politics is known for its bureaucratic culture, and the British

system – no matter which party takes office – has been relatively centralised and difficult to penetrate for outsider groups, such as those associated with the women's movement. But perhaps more importantly, until the 1980s the British women's liberation movement hardly mobilised on the issue of childcare. Campaigns for issues that fit the liberal logic were much more successful, such as abortion rights and the campaign against rape (Randall 1996). From the 1980s onwards, women's organisations did make a claim on childcare, but at that time few listened on the other side. Indeed, at that time the Labour party seemed more receptive as it needed new constituencies, but women's organisations had little power.

Other advocates of childcare were not visible either. In England, local authorities were the only providers of state-subsidised childcare, but only for the most needy. These local authorities have always had different goals than those in Denmark; they are among the largest in Europe and very bureaucratic (Rhodes 1999). Under the Thatcher government a major operation took place which centralised the UK even more. After that, by introducing a purchaser-provider split, the provider function was removed from the hands of the local authorities. They became nothing more and nothing less than an organisational and controlling body, precisely in line with liberal notions of what a state should be (Lewis 1998). The local authorities could not serve as a protagonist of state-subsidised childcare either. As Pierson (1994) notes, the traditional activists against conservatism had all been dismantled.

New Labour

Since Labour took over the government, childcare investment did increase and a remarkable shift in policy took place. For the first time since the Second World War, the state has taken responsibility for the development of childcare. In 1998, the government presented the first National Childcare Strategy in their paper 'Meeting the Childcare Challenge'. The motivation behind the policy is very different from that of the previous period. In the introduction the government explained that 'the National Childcare Strategy is about supporting families. Families need childcare. Good quality childcare is good for children. And it helps parents to go out to work or to study' (CM3959, 1998). New labour's strategy includes four interventions: to subsidise start-up costs of nurseries in order to increase availability, to support children in deprived areas, to make childcare affordable trough tax deductions, and to invest in early education (Lister 2003; Lewis 2003).

The government promised to invest in nurseries and spent (in England) 470 million pounds over a five-year period. This money is earmarked to offer capital grants or support towards the start-up costs of out-of-school services. Showing its liberal genetics, the Labour government argues that this should not be seen as a system of continuous public support but as an investment. Consequently, this intervention has raised criticism. Aside from not covering running costs, the strategy offers no guarantee of the level of out-of-school services, argue critics such as Rake (2001). Then there is the investment in the well-being and education of children living in deprived areas. The Neighbourhood Nurseries Initiative will bring 45,000 affordable new childcare places to deprived areas, stipulates the National Childcare strategy.

In addition to making childcare available, the government aimed to make it affordable via substantial tax deductions. Both the Netherlands and Belgium have tax deductions for childcare, but none are as high as in the UK. The basic idea is that when parents have money to buy childcare, the market will also develop. The Labour party believes in investing in a demand-driven economy. The childcare tax deduction is part of the Working Families Tax Credit (WFTC). Only WFTC recipients can apply for the childcare credit. This credit helps working parents with the cost of registered and approved childcare, such as a registered childminder or a nursery. Care provided in one's own home is excluded, even when paid, along with any care provided by a friend or family member (Land 2001). Parents will be paid 70 percent of childcare costs, up to a ceiling. The condition is that lone parents and each partner in a couple work more than 16 hours a week. In practice the average childcare credit is 40.61 pounds a week and is used almost exclusively by lone mothers (nine out of 10 of claimants). This fits well with the government's aim to provide a childcare place for all children or lone parents and get 70 percent of them back to work by 2010 (Rake 2001).

Table 6.4	Children's day care facilities in thousands, 1997-2001, England			
	1997	*1999*	*2001*	*Difference 1997-2001*
Day nurseries (0-4)	194	248	285	+91
Play groups (0-4)	384	347	330	-54
Childminders (0-7)	365	337	304	-61

Source: DfES (2001)

Table 6.4 shows that a huge increase has taken place in children at nurseries. At the same time, the number of children in playgroups dropped. Since playgroups are less helpful for working mothers – children can only go for a limited number of hours – this indicates that working women have now managed to find a place for their children at a nursery. On the other hand, the number of children with childminders also decreased. The net investment is thus 'only' 30,000 places between 1997-2001. However, a further injection of funds was scheduled to take place and by 2005-2006 an additional 250,000 childcare places will be developed, promises the government (Lister 2003).

What may have had a bigger impact is the focus on early learning. Education is one of the main themes of the 'New Childcare Strategy' (Cm 3959). Early education is important for children, as it best prepares them to succeed in society. In addition, the UK needs a well-trained labour force. Labour therefore committed itself to pre-school nursery for all four year olds, extended to all three-year-olds in 2004. The claim was thus that every four-year-old would have the chance of a free education place. Huge investments were made. Of all three-year-olds in England, about 45 percent in 2000 and 90 percent in 2002 used some type of facility (school or nursery) (DfES 2002). From the point of view of working mothers, the education program is rather useless. The free place consists of a minimum of three 11-week terms of five weekly sessions lasting 2.5 hours. This does not allow parents to work (Rake 2001).

The fact that the first Childcare Strategy was one of New Labour's primary goals shows that in England a change of party indeed makes for a change in policy. Day nurseries were extended and financial investments were made, but to what extent political parties matter remains questionable. When Labour was in power before 1979, it did not develop childcare services although women worked anyway. As Lewis (1992a) argues, the Labour Party and trade unions have been dominated by a masculine ethos that has neglected the interests of working class women. When New Labour came into power in 1997 this was nevertheless profitable for women's organisations, which had built a good relationship with Labour when they were in the opposition.

Moreover, Labour's ideology towards childcare shows many remnants of the previous paradigm: ideologies are indeed path-dependent. The Conservative government under Major invested in early education (Randall 2002). Incentives for childcare mainly depart from demand-side economics, as parents have to stir the childcare economy. This was also a popular way of thinking under the Tories, in contrast to subsidising services as in Denmark. Labour's National Childcare Strategy is certainly not social democratic in the sense that it is based on universal claims. Despite Labour's belief that social policy should offer 'opportunities for all', the British system is more targeted than in the other countries, as evidenced by the specific support for lone parents. Childcare is still for the most needy, especially those in need of a working mother. However, the definition of need does include a much broader category of children and parents than under the Conservative governments.

Conclusion: The Origins and Outcomes of Childcare Policy

This chapter on childcare should answer three questions: which welfare state has indeed implemented the right to receive care, what are the origins of childcare policy, and what does the right to receive care mean for gendered citizenship: do women work *en masse* when childcare is available and affordable?

Denmark is indeed the European pioneer in childcare services: children – and not parents – really have the right to childcare services. Childcare is widely available and quite affordable. Surprisingly, Belgium, and particularly Flanders, comes second in the childcare league. Although childcare policy in Flanders developed in response to the needs of working women, it now has coverage rates nearly similar to countries like Sweden. The Netherlands and the UK, on the other hand, are historically characterised by low state investments in childcare. This changed in the Netherlands in the early 1990s, when working women were seen as necessary for a sustainable welfare state. Due to the design of the intervention – the state only pays if employers and employees also take financial responsibility – childcare remains expensive for dual-earner families. In England, childcare investments are even more recent and were launched by the Labour government in the late 1990s. Those who profit the most are lone mothers.

The second question is what are the origins of childcare intervention. Childcare services have always developed under the economic and social pressures of women going to work. In Ragin's terms (2000), women wanting to work is a *necessary* condition for the development of state-subsidised childcare, but it is not a *sufficient* condition: not all welfare states have been as responsive as the Danish or Belgian. England, for instance, was rather slow. It is striking that especially the traditional interpretation of social democratic or Christian democratic power regimes cannot fully explain the level of state intervention. In Denmark (and in the

Netherlands), childcare policy developed when consensus was reached on the necessity of investments, not because of the intervention of one party. The Christian democratic label is not very telling either: concepts of subsidiarity as well as free choice have various faces and were shaped by institutional settings and rival ideologies.

This chapter also highlighted other factors that shaped childcare interventions, such as the coherence and power of the women's movement, the political culture within a country, and the institutional setting.

The third question raised in this chapter was about the link between the right to receive care and gendered citizenship. At first glance, the link between mothers' employment patterns and childcare services is unmistakable. In low-service countries like the UK and the Netherlands, few mothers work and they hardly ever work full time. In high-service countries like Belgium and Denmark more mothers work and they are also more likely to work full time. State-subsidised childcare services seem a necessary or even a sufficient cause. On second thought, the cases of the UK and Belgium raise questions. Denmark and the Netherlands fit the model neatly.

In both the Netherlands and the UK employment rates of mothers increased during the 1990s, although in the UK less than in the Netherlands (tables 4.5, 4.6, 4.7). For the Netherlands, this is understandable as childcare became more available. How come British employment rates also increased while childcare investments were only made in the late 1990s? One hypothesis is that up to a certain level of female employment, state-subsidised childcare is not a necessary condition: informal sources can also resond to the childcare needs of working women. But if the aim is for employment to surpass a specific level, for example if all women want to participate in the labour market, it will be conditional upon having state-subsidised childcare. A second hypothesis is that a high level of state-subsidised childcare is necessary for full-time employment, but not for part-time work. Indeed, in the UK and the Netherlands – which have comparatively low levels of state investments in childcare – women often work part time. Full-time employment is more common in Denmark and Belgium, where state investments are higher. But there are more puzzles. Take the case of lone mothers. Why are lone mothers' employment rates similar in the UK and the Netherlands? (table 4.8) Looking at the availability and affordability of childcare, Dutch rates should be higher.

The Belgian case also raises doubts. Childcare in Belgium is relatively well developed – much more than one would expect from a regime typified as Christian democratic. Therefore, it is no surprise that Belgian mothers' employment rates are higher than the Dutch. But we can also look at it differently. If childcare facilities are so well developed – they reach Swedish levels – why don't more mothers work? Why do they not work more hours? Why are less-educated women more likely to stay at home, while childcare is affordable? This chapter shows that a steady increase of state-subsidised childcare took place in Flanders. While 17 percent of children used state-subsidised facilities in 1983, this rose to 41 percent in 2000. At the same time, mothers' employment did not boom; instead more women went to work part-time (chapter 4). The relationship between the existence of childcare services and type of employment is thus not that self-evident. Do countries have a cultural saturation point for mothers' employment?

Childcare services – the right to receive care – are of course part of the caring state as a whole. Perhaps Belgian mothers stay at home because of the substantial rights they have to give care? Belgium, after all, is a two-track welfare state: mothers have the right to choose between work and care. This however cannot fully explain the relative modesty of mothers' employment rates. The previous chapters also showed that the Danish welfare state has 'work disincentives' similar to the Belgian. Up to 1994 the unemployment benefit system could easily be used by Danish mothers to stay at home, as Belgian women did; both welfare states have incorporated a male breadwinner bonus in taxation, and both have substantial care leaves. Still, Belgian (as well as Flemish) women and mothers work less. Indeed, less-educated women in Belgium are most likely to stay at home. Some will argue that in Belgium highly educated women will use the childcare track and less-educated women will use the financial compensation available to them and stay at home. But even this is not true. The right to give care – implemented via tax policies, benefits, and the leave scheme – are not used exclusively by those who have the lowest employment rates, the less-educated mothers. The question thus remains: Why do Belgian women with good access to affordable childcare not work more?

The right to provide care and the right to receive care do not directly result in an ungendered citizenship practice in each country. The cultural approach would immediately stress the negligible role of welfare states. But in broad lines, the previous chapters have shown that the design of the welfare state does loosely relate to gendered citizenship – there are just a few anomalies. These puzzles do not falsify the welfare state's effects: they lead us to question how welfare states influence human actions. Doing so will help us to achieve a more profound understanding of the origins and outcomes of caring states. The next part of this book explores the cultural dimension of welfare states. In the next chapters the same domains of welfare regimes – social security, leave, and childcare services – will be analysed. In the next two chapters we will look more explicitly through the lens of 'ideals of care'. Perhaps this can contribute to solving some of the puzzles raised thus far.

7   After Full-Time Mother Care: Ideals of Care in Policy

Few welfare states univocally and exclusively support the ideal of full-time motherhood, today a fact that many welfare state theories have not taken into account. The previous chapters showed how the paradigm of full-time motherhood has changed in different countries at different paces and times. Two conditions for this paradigm shift stand out. Women themselves encouraged the dismantling of the full-time motherhood ideal. They did so by entering the labour force and pushing for change but they also used political force (often together with other political groups – sometimes liberals, sometimes trade unions). The second condition is economic necessity, although economic necessity takes different shapes: labour-market shortage, micro-economics (families need two incomes to reduce poverty), or macro-economics (women need to work to save the welfare state) are presented as reasons to support women's employment.

But this does not explain the extent to which states became engaged in policy, or which ideal of care came to be promoted as an alternative to the full-time mother-care model. This chapter analyses the ideals of care – again in the domains of childcare services and financial arrangements – that replaced the traditional ideals. And seeks to explain why a certain ideal of care becomes dominant in a country.

Denmark: The Ideal of Professional Care

In Denmark, the ideal of full-time motherhood – the male breadwinner model – ceased to be a dominant ideal long ago. From the 1960s onwards the Danish welfare state has had a relatively coherent care-and-work policy that was 'perfected' only in the mid-1990s with the 1994 Labour Market Reform and the formal right to childcare. The normative point of departure is that both women and men have the duty as well as the right to work while the state takes over caring responsibilities. For caring, another ideal has been put forward: the ideal of professional care.

Danish citizens do not feel they make use of state controlled care, they use what they see as professional care. It is a common expression in Denmark that 'every parent knows how to care for its own child, but you need a proper education to care for someone else's child' (int. 39, 50, 65). Day care in Denmark does not mean 'minding', it is supposed to improve the child's upbringing. As we saw in the previous chapters, the talents and aspirations of each individual child need to be developed while at the same time children are offered a possibility to feel attached to a larger community and become social and political citizens. This is even laid down in the 1998 Social Services Act. Childcare is more than the place where parents bring their children because they need care for them, it provides children with a type of care that parents can never provide.

The emphasis on professional care can be traced back to the childcare workers who played an important role in the history of state childcare. During the initial phase in the development of state childcare, the driving force came from individuals connected to pedagogical ideas like those of Fröbel and Montessori. Already in the late 1940s, the organisation of professionals working in childcare demanded a universal element in the law on childcare. Their objective was to accommodate children from different backgrounds, so facilities for children from well-off homes should also be funded. Their argument was that all children need social contacts, personal inspiration, and development. In the 1950s, professionalisation of childcare workers really took off. Common standards were defined and special training courses for childcare workers were established. In 1969 the education of professionals was extended to three years, strengthening the social-pedagogical aspects. The number of trained professionals, many of them women, rose significantly, as did the number of employees in childcare facilities (Borchorst 2002).

This went hand-in-hand with the growing importance of pedagogues in defining the childcare question. The first universal law for childcare, in 1964, shows that pedagogues' organisations were protagonists, flanked by the women's organisations who agreed on the issue of childcare (Bertone 2003). The alliance with the social pedagogues made it feasible to promote childcare that was not at the expense of children's interests.

> The women themselves said ... we want to join the labour market and become equal with our husbands, but it shall not be at the cost of the children or the elderly,

according to Bent Rold Andersen, the former Social Democratic minister (int. 40). Quality professional childcare would take the issue of women's work beyond the question of what the consequences are for children. It silenced the moral debate.

Until 1960, the more traditional Danish women's society (DK) promoted free choice for women. They believed that women themselves should decide if they wanted to work or not. In the 1970s, they moved towards defining children (rather than women) as the central objects of their claims for childcare. In this way, writes Bertone (2000) in her comparison of the Danish and Italian cases, the DK could avoid debates on whether married women should work or not. Also the Redstockings, an organisation that was part of the second wave of the Danish women's movement, first saw children's needs as secondary, but in the late 1970s they also recognised the importance of children's interests for quality childcare. The political scientist Dahlerup (1998,) once a Redstocking herself, writes that the demand for improved childcare centres for all children was crucial. The women's movement, traditional as well as second-wave, was strongly engaged in the discussion on pedagogical goals. It sided with the pedagogues in their claims for quality childcare. Also later, when childcare was under severe pressure in the 1980s, the pedagogues together with the women's groups were again among the most active forces against the cutbacks (Bertone 2000, 2003).

It is thus no coincidence Danish children are cared for by the best-trained workers compared to other countries: they are real professionals (OECD 2001). Childcare workers need three years of higher education and have a recognised title (social pedagogues). Unlike in many other countries, there is little wage differential between childcare workers and schoolteachers and ratios between child and staff are the lowest in Europe (3:1 for children up to age three) (OECD 2001). They are organised in a relatively strong trade union (BUPL), which is important as in Denmark the corporate channel is powerful (int. 39,43, 57, 65). In that sense, trade union strength, a feature of the social democratic regime, is important in understanding Danish childcare policy. Protecting the quality of care is considered one of the roles of social pedagogues. The higher their level of education, the higher the quality of care.

In the 1990s social pedagogues gained a new ally. The parents (and their organisation) have become powerful clients in the Danish system and now have a statutory voice in it. They often side with the BUPL in keeping the number of trained workers in childcare facilities as high as possible (int. 43, 57). When in the late 1990s the social democratic government decided to reduce the number of social pedagogues per child, there was an outcry in the media by professionals as well as parents. The system itself, as Pierson (1994, 2001) and Alber (1995) pointed out, created its own defenders. Childcare services resulted into a new constituency: powerful parents who, as individuals and collective actors, became important childcare advocates.

In short, the alliance between organised professionals and womens' groups, which in the 1980s and particularly the 1990s was strengthened by parents' organisations, is crucial to understand the content of childcare policy in Denmark. The ideal of professional care binds them together and solves the socially constructed dilemma in which children's interests are placed against women's interests. This opened up support from many political parties. The stress on the pedagogical function of childcare services also legitimised universal childcare services. The ideal of professional care can be seen as a precondition for claiming the right to receive care.

Surrogate Mothers as the Black Sheep of Childcare

The Danish welfare state also pays for family day care, (further discussed in chapter 8). Should this not be seen as stressing the ideal of the surrogate mother? Not at all. In Denmark, day care mothers – *dagpleje* as they are called – have always been opposed to professional care: they were never promoted as a substitute for mother care. In the period before the first law on childcare some political parties promoted the existence of state-employed day care mothers. Both social democrats and the bourgeois parties argued that family day care could be a more gradual break with the model of full-time caring (Bertone 2000). But when the 1964 law on childcare was written, day care mothers were considered to be a *nødlusning*, an 'emergency solution'. The future ideal was that all children would be cared for in day care centres by professionals. At that time, the Danish Women's Society (DK) was already very much against family day care as it would undermine the pedagogical ideal of childcare (Bertone 2000). Day care mothers were nevertheless a cheap solution, and in the rural areas of Denmark it was the only solution for childcare. And thus what was presented as an emergency solution became a structural local practice (int. 45, 65).

Two parties are traditionally in favour of family day care. One is Venstre, the right-wing farmers' party, although they did not actively promote the model. For them, this type of childcare was necessary in the countryside and day care mothers provided care in a homely atmosphere. Indeed, family day care is more a rural phenomenon than an urban phenomenon.

The second advocate were the municipalities, a crucial actor in the Danish political setting. Some rural municipalities pointed out that childcare centres could not survive in the countryside. Other municipalities had a financial and pragmatic argument: day care families are more flexible because they can be easily established and dismantled. Family day care is also cheaper for parents than a *vuggestue*, a childcare centre for the very young (int. 41, 43, 45, 48, 57, 65).

Initially, working conditions for the day care mothers were poor. But women organised in the trade union for public employees fought for workers' rights, and as a result the first collective agreement was made in 1971. The main issues were wages and the number of children, not training. Since then, day care mothers are no longer seen as an emergency solution, but as a 'supplement'. The government nevertheless explicitly stated it was better if children were cared for by professionals in day care centres. The trade union of social pedagogues (BUPL), women's organisations, and the social democrats strongly agreed: they were strongly opposed to family day care (int. 41, 48, 57).

In the 1980s it was a social democratic minister, Ritt Bjerregaard, who officially stated that day care centres and family day care have the same status. Family day care was no longer seen as supplementary. At the same time she stressed that family care can only be given to young children (aged 0-2). Older children should get professional care. She also demanded that municipalities stop building new day care centres, indicating that the reluctant acceptance of family care was not inspired by ideology or pedagogical motives but by an economic crisis. It showed a social democratic pragmatism that exchanged an ideal of (professional) care for a practical solution.

Due to the efforts of the family day care workers who used the corporate channel to gain proper wages and working conditions, today they are no longer the black sheep of childcare (int. 41, 48, 57). Nearly all have followed a basic course offered by their trade union, which consists of just 76 hours of training, and almost half followed a supplementary course in 1999. More recently, the Danish government set up a new 42-week training programme (int. 41, 48). In addition, the wages and working conditions of the 24,000 *dagpleje* are now relatively good, nearly as good as those working in childcare centres, and they are fully paid during sickness and maternity leave. Furthermore, about 1,000 supervisors employed at the municipalities give guidance and support to the childminders. Family day care workers are obliged to meet other day care mothers at least once a week, so that their children can meet other children. The idea behind this is that social contact is better for children' upbringing than when children are home alone with one mother (int. 41, 48). If parents who use day care mothers are critical, it is mostly of the lack of education of the childminder and the weaker pedagogical element involved in this type of day care (Bertelsen 1991). In that sense, this municipal family day care no longer fits the cultural ideal of the surrogate mother, it is closer to the ideal of professional care. To put it differently, after a long struggle, the ideal of professional care now also includes day care families. In Denmark, the dominant ideal in policy is that of professional care.

Intergenerational Care: Elderly as Individuals

In Denmark it has never been suggested that grandparents should take care of their grandchildren. Denmark has a strong policy of individualisation of the elderly (Koch Nielsen 1996). Since the 1974 Social Services Law, elderly people have had the right to receive care so that they can live autonomously from their families. The Danish elderly also receive by far the largest amount of care in Europe. While many welfare states had serious cutbacks in the mid-1990s, in Denmark 20 percent of the elderly (65+) still received homecare and six percent were living in residential settings (Anttonen and Sipilä 1996). The number of hours of home care that a needy person receives (five hours per week) is especially high compared to the rest of Europe (Rostgaard and Fridberg 1998; Rostgaard 2004).

In many other countries (including the Netherlands), family members can be asked to care for the elderly, but in Denmark home care is a right, even if a partner or daughter is available in the near surroundings. The 1974 law stipulates complete individualisation and it is even illegal for the municipality to demand a family member to help. A study from the mid-1990s shows that elderly people with children receive more formal support than those without. The explanation is that, rather than being involved in physical and practical care, children are good advocates for their parents (Juul Jensen and Krogh Hansen 2002). The elderly are thus not supposed to be dependent on their children but on the state. Conversely, children are not supposed to be dependent on their parents to provide care for their own children, thus their parents' grandchildren. The ideal of intergenerational care is absent.

This individualisation is not only a principle that applies to the elderly, it is central in Danish public policy. Unlike other countries, the Danish legal system even includes a 'Law on Individualisation' (Koch Nielsen 1996), which is the showpiece of the Radical Party. This law stipulates that all new legislation has to be assessed on whether it is based on the individual and not the family as legal entity. Exceptions are only allowed when good reasons are given. This is the case for social assistance, which is based on family-means testing. This notion of complete individualisation in Danish public policy has far-reaching consequences. It has for instance limited the conceptual space for another ideal, that of parental sharing.

Parental Sharing

Parents and children are not supposed to be dependent on each other, nor are partners. In other words, vertical and horizontal dependencies are not encouraged in Denmark. Individualisation is a key concept. This has had an impact on the discussion on the role of fathers. Danish policy distinguishes itself from the social democratic model, writes Sainsbury (1999a), as it lacks advanced policies for men's careers in the home and no statutory rights based on fatherhood. Although fathers' involvement have been on the agenda for a long time, it has not had much influence on the content of social policy.

In the 1980s, the Commission on Childcare had argued that fathers are important for the well-being of children and proposed the right to time off when a young baby is born – paternity leave. But the Commission stood rather isolated (int. 43, 58). Nowadays Danish fathers have this right but it came rather late, though not as late as in the UK. More recent debates on parental leave show that politicians are not very concerned about the lack of fathers' involvement in caring for their children. Their main concern is that children are away from home for too long when they are little, which is a critique of the ideal of professional care. Danish parental leave is aimed at ensuring that children spend time at home, with which parent does not matter. Gender equality or fair parental sharing is not the main issue (Borchorst 1999; Rostgaard 2002).

Rostgaard (2002, 2004) argues that in Denmark the father and mother are seen to have an equal position in the family, but the negotiation of time to care is considered a private matter. Freedom to choose is a central element. Parents are regarded as free-standing from each other and free in regard to gendered distribution of work in the family, thus being able to choose freely whether or not to take leave (Olsen in Rostgaard 2002). Therefore Danish politicians, unlike their Scandinavian neighbours, are against what they consider to be forcing fathers to take up care duties. Parental sharing is not an ideal that should be promoted by the state through incentives or punishments.

Danish labour market policy and labour market law have not promoted the notion of parental sharing either: individual part-time work has not been seen as a route toward redistribution of work and care; childcare taken up on a part-time basis has to be paid for full time; part-time work is not covered well in social security; and a part-time parental leave option has just recently been introduced , as discussed in chapters 6, 7, and 8. If people in Denmark decide to work part time, they say they work 'reduced hours', giving the impression that it is temporary and that they are still very committed to a career. Part-time work has connotations of having a marginal job or being marginalised.

Both the Danish government and the powerful trade unions (with 80 percent membership) have been very much against part-time jobs, which are not considered to be 'real' jobs. This trade union antagonism tends to have two causes, according to Blossfeld and Hakim (1997): one conscious and explicit, the other unstated and implicit. First, trade unions' patriarchal and sexist attitudes led unions to give unthinking priority to the interests of male members over the concern of any female members. Indeed, much more than in other Scandinavian countries, the Danish corporate channel is very male-dominated (Bergqvist 1999). Second, the trade unions' long campaign to establish and maintain the standard full-time permanent job as the norm meant that they were always explicitly opposed to other types of contracts, seeking to prevent their growth if not abolish them altogether. In Denmark, trade unions struggled for a general reduction of working hours. Individuals who gave in to part-time arrangements could get individual advantages but hurt the case for all. Part-time work, it was said, erodes solidarity between workers.

Finally, parental sharing has not been strong in the Danish care history because of the dominance of the ideal of professional pedagogical care. These ideals seem to conflict with each other. If professionals are so well equipped to care for children, and if it is so important for children to have the crèche experience, why would a parent, including a father, stay at home to share in the caring duties?

Flanders: The Ideal of Surrogate Mothers and Intergenerational Care

In Belgium the notion of full-time motherhood has never been the only ideal expressed in public policy. As described in chapter 5 and chapter 6, the notion of free choice has been crucial, most strongly promoted by

Christian democratic forces, although pressure from social democratic forces and economic necessity have also been decisive. Free choice in the Belgian pillarised context means that women have the right to stay at home and therefore tax allowances and leave schemes are in place to facilitate this. Also, unemployment benefits can be seen as an implicit financial compensation for caregiving. On the other hand, women should have the right to work; childcare services are thus affordable and available, and labour market schemes cater especially to (less-educated) women. In Belgium, women have the right to provide care as well as the right to receive care. While Hobson (1994) wondered if it was possible to validate both routes of working and caring, the Belgian welfare state seems to be a successful example. In other words, the undeniable stress on familialism does not necessarily mean that women should stay at home.

Chapter 5 on social security already showed that small steps have been set to limit the ideal of life-long full-time motherhood, and part-time employment and flexible leave are more intensively promoted. Is Belgium moving towards parental sharing? A close look at the development of childcare services also shows that the state has never been neutral. Do people really have a free choice? The type of childcare promoted strongly resembled the ideal of the surrogate mother.

Surrogate Mothers Triumphs Over Professional Care

Although it was never openly declared, Flemish governments, which always had a Christian-Democratic minister responsible for welfare, seem to prefer the ideal of the surrogate mother (int. 1, 6, 7). The official standpoint is that the state is neutral: the government does not prefer any type of childcare above another. 'The state has to follow parents' wishes', stresses the quasi-state organisation Kind and Gezin (1988). And since parents seem to prefer the system of formalised day care mothers, the state has to put people's preferences into practice.

Until the 1970s, the dominant type of state-subsidised day care in Flanders were day care centres. They were mostly an urban phenomenon, catering to working-class families in cities. Historically, they have been part of a medical-hygienic regime. The institutions were large, the staff was made up of nurses, and the places were labelled as beds (Hermans 1984). As a counterpart to them, organisations of day care mothers developed; they were seen as the answer to collective 'cold and formal' institutions as well as to the increased employment of rural women. The Catholic agrarian women's movement (KVLV-Katholieke Vrouwen van de Landelijke Beweging) was the first to call for childminding services: these were the founding mothers of state-subsidised family daycare. At that time, the Catholic women's movement was a very strong force and not only included the agrarian women (KVLV) but also the organisation of Catholic women workers (KAV). They had strong links with the political decision makers, and many women who attained a position in parliament or the government did so after a career in the Christian democratic women's movement (including Smet, whose important role was discussed previously in the chapter on social security).

The concept of day care mothers was not widely known – at that time grandparents cared for young children – the initiative was very new (int. 6, 16). When they launched their family daycare plan in the early 1970s, the agrarian women had to convince day care mothers to join in, they had to convince mothers to use the service and, last but not least, they had to persuade the government to fund the initiative. At that time, both mothers as well as potential childminders were suspicious though curious. The women organised in KVLV were motivated to set up a childminding service because they needed and wanted to be engaged in employment. Childcare at that time was often seen as a necessary evil. For this reason, the agrarian women argued in their pamphlet that 'bringing up children also at the "second" home is not necessarily worse, if the quality was guaranteed' (KVLV 1977: 5). Organised day care mothers, with the help of the state, could guarantee this level of quality: 'in the countryside many women and families are prepared, with some guidance and information, to give care successfully' (KVLV 1977: 6).

Another argument in support of the initiative was that organised day care mothers would activate family and neighbourhood life, which was allegedly eroding at that time too. This was especially powerful: rather than arguing that childcare would diminish family and community life – the Cinderella story – the women of KVLV stressed that this type of childcare would strengthen family and community life.

Financially speaking day care mothers were also surely an attractive bargain. The state only had to play a small role, just to ensure that people would support and help each other. Organising and subsidising day care mothers was very cheap compared to day care institutions. Since no buildings have to be rented – as children are cared for in a mother's home – and day care mothers do not receive wages for which tax and social security payments have to be paid, family day care is half the price of day care centres (int. 1, 6, 16).

The arguments the Catholic Agrarian Women (KVLV) used fitted smartly with Christian democratic interests – low costs and social cohesion – while at the same time concern was shown about the quality of care for children. The Catholic women thus sought an ideological alliance with their Christian democratic Party.

The initiative was 'crowned' in 1975: day care families would indeed be subsidised and a service could be set up. The mothers were paid fees and did not have to pay tax and social security premiums. They were not employees and were not professionals. They were not protected by social security. From then on, day care mothers were 'embraced' by the Christian democratic Party and the ministers in charge of childcare. The increase in childcare subsidies from the late 1980s onwards was to a large extent used for the development of the *Diensten voor Opvanggezinnen*, the 'Bureau for Day Care Families'. Today many more children are cared for by subsidised day care mothers than in day care institutions, and the number of children in family care continues to increase (this is discussed further in chapter 8).[6]

Services for childminding are now a much more universal practice, it is no longer a Christian democratic phenomenon only. It is true that as an urban phenomenon, crèches are very much associated with the social democratic movement. For a long time the social democrats were against family day care and strived for crèches as they treated all children equally and engendered solidarity between children. Consequently, most organisations for day care mothers – first in the countryside, later in cities – belong to the Catholic pillar. More recently, after the success of family day care services, the social democratic pillar also started to develop family day care networks, primarily in cities (int. 28).

The importance of formal and subsidised childminding in Flanders however is not only ideological: it was also an unintended consequence of tax policy. In 1987 a law was passed in order to allow parents to deduct BFR 345 per day (approximately 8.55 euros) from their taxable income when they use childcare, but only if their children are in registered and state-controlled facilities. This fiscal measure unintentionally 'whitened' the grey market of childcare; informally paid childminding has become a rare phenomenon in Flanders (Kind en Gezin 1997).

Subsidising day care mothers has been a way out of a deadlocked situation. As in many welfare states, in Belgium 'warm' care – represented by a dedicated mother who continuously cared for children – was contrasted with 'cold' institutional care, in which indifferent professionals cared for children for long hours. In the first case mothers have to sacrifice for their children, while in the second children suffer because of mothers' selfishness. Caring at home was weighted against day care institutions; the interests of children against the interests of mothers (Somers and Peeters 1991). In no way did the existing (urban) day care institutions resemble home-based care. Day care mothers provided an alternative to the cold professionals that was much more in keeping with the wishes and values of Flemish parents as well as Christian democratic ideology: children are cared for in homelike surroundings. This highlights the ideal of the surrogate mother: It is more appropriate for a mother to care for children, even though they are not her own children. This also helps explain the development of state-subsidised childcare under a Christian democratic regime. It is because of these surrogate mothers that state investments in childcare took place. The type of care promoted fit well with Christian democratic ideology, not only the ideology towards childcare but also the gender ideology that stressed (economic) dependency relations within the family.

It is important to stress that several ideals of care can operate at the same time, but also that one dominant ideal of care is often replaced by another. The Flemish quasi-state organisation Kind en Gezin has slowly tried to alter the model of the surrogate mother in the direction of professional care. Professional care has so far not been a strong ideal in Flanders, but Kind en Gezin (2003) increasingly stresses that childcare outside the home also contributes to the welfare of children. This is also underlined by the Flemish ministry (2000). One way of supporting professional childcare is to work on the improvement of the quality of care. The medical-hygienic regime has thus been transformed into a welfare regime with the concomitant education, training, and control. This however has not lived up to the OECD expectations (2001) yet, as the OECD finds Belgian childcare still too scholarly and worries about the low educational level of childcare workers. Moreover, about 75 percent of those employed in childcare services have not completed the lower level of professional training (Kind en Gezin 2003). In addition, staff-child ratios are the highest of all four countries (1:7 for children under age three.

The most recent move towards professional care is to grant surrogate mothers basic rights. Since April 2003, day care mothers receive social security rights such as pensions and unemployment benefits, although they are still not considered 'employees'. The Flemish federal state is putting 10 billion euros into this expansion of social security coverage. The reasons are pragmatic: first a court case deemed childminders to be employees increasing their rights, and secondly the number of women seeking jobs as family day care providers has decreased dramatically. Professionalisation may attract more people to work in childcare, perhaps even some men (Delva et al. 2003).

Intergenerational Care

Another dominant ideal in Flemish policy is that of intergenerational care. It is good when parents and children are dependent on each other and exchange care and trust. In Flanders, state-subsidised childcare is developed more than elderly care, which is in line with public support (Van Peer and Moors 1996). State services for elderly care are not widespread: 10 percent of the elderly received some kind of help in the mid-1990s, compared to 18 percent in the Netherlands, 26 percent in Denmark and 14 percent in the UK (Anttonen and Siplilä 1996; see also Jamieson 1991, OECD 1994b). Although home care has expanded more recently, statistics from the mid-1990s show that six percent of people aged 65 and over receive home help, which is less than in the Netherlands (eight percent) and much less than in Denmark (20 percent). In Belgium a limited number of people live in residential facilities (four percent).

In Flanders, home care is commodified – state-subsidised help is based on income. The law stipulates that 'priority is given to the most dependent and to those who are financially most needy' (*Belgisch staatsblad* 1988). In countries like Denmark and the Netherlands care services are more universal – selection takes place not on the basis of income but on the need for care (OECD 1994b). Care for the elderly is also based on the family. When children or other relatives can provide informal care, home care is denied (Baro et al. 1991). In addition, local authorities (OCMWs) that support the elderly have to collect all costs for financial and material services from spouses, parents, and children. This is no leftover from the past: the law was only enforced in 1983. Sociologists have warned that this liability for maintenance can disturb family relations (Lammertijn and Bavel 1996). Flemish local authorities know that and in practice they hardly enforce the law. Only when the elderly go to (expensive) nursing homes are the costs for these caring arrangements sometimes recovered (Meulders et al. 1990).

The ideal of intergenerational care is also visible in the Belgian tax system, being the only system that has specific deductions for dependants, such as children and elderly living in (although the elderly dependants should not be well-off). This is not an archaic remnant either. When the Christian democratic minister De Meester gave a lecture on family and fiscal policy, she dreamed about a gulf of 'moral sacrifice' in which grandparents cared for their children and children cared for their parents. She said: 'The state can perhaps push this trend a little?' (in Van Haegendoren and Moestermans 1994: 103).

Tax deductions for childcare also reflect the intergenerational ideal of care. When in 1987 the law was discussed which offered tax relief for state-recognised childcare, the influential Organisation for Big and Young Families (BGJG) and other family-minded forces argued that this would discriminate against all those families in which grandparents provide childcare. The amount they eventually gained however is less than in the case of childminders or crèches, but it does have an important symbolic meaning. Belgium is one of the few countries that provides direct financial support for the intergenerational care of children. Unmistakably, Belgian social policy emphasises the ideal of intergenerational care.

Parental Sharing

During the 1980s the Christian democratic movement became more favourable towards part-time work, especially because of the recession. Minister Smet even praised the Dutch 'one-and-a-half' model and wanted to mimic her Northern neighbours. She believed that this would give space to employers to hire more people and would be a more humane way of living (*De Standaard* 1995). As mentioned in chapter 5, Smet argued that part-time work should be considered as a decent job. At that time, part-time workers were awarded the same right to unemployment benefits as full-time workers.

Advocates of part-time work framed their arguments in gender-neutral terms: parents should have more time at home – time for children and time for the family, this was the issue, not gender equality (Marques Pereira and Paye 2001). Opponents of part-time work argue that it perpetuates the gender division of labour at home: it does not lead to fathers' involvement or parental sharing. Critics dismiss the one-and-a-half model saying that 'he will get the one job and she will get the half' (int. 29, 33, also Marques-Pereira and Paye 2001). If women work part-time, men have no need to help them out. To support the concept of sharing care duties, Smet launched a public campaign to encourage discussion of gender role stereotypes in relation to working and caring duties. Postcards were distributed of a woman repairing a car and a man ironing a shirt. It was striking that the campaign only dealt with domestic chores, not with men's role as fathers.

Belgian opponents of part-time work blame the Dutch model for seducing their policymakers (e.g., Marques-Pereira and Paye 2001). The next section shows that the Belgian welfare state is not heading for the Dutch model of parental sharing yet: Belgian part-time workers are still very likely to receive some extra pay (via social security or via the system of time credit), while Dutch men as fathers have received much more attention from the state.

The Netherlands: The Ideal of Parental Sharing

Until the mid-1980s, the dominant ideal in Dutch childcare policy was the ideal of full-time mothering (Bussemaker 1993). Few welfare states have been as consistent as the Dutch. This ideal had an impact on every area of social policy. In the late 1980s and particularly in the 1990s, this ideal changed: the women's movement stressed the importance of employment as the key to emancipation, and at the same time the Dutch Scientific Council published a report arguing that women's labour market participation was crucial to the survival of the expensive welfare state (WRR 1990). However, women did not receive the right to work, instead they were given the duty to work. An important icon of this paradigm shift is the new law on social assistance, described in chapter 5, which notably requires lone mothers to take up employment when their children reach the age of five.

Perks of the male breadwinner model are still lingering (Plantenga et al. 1999). In 1998, 25 billion Dutch guilders were still being spent on single breadwinner support (Bekkering and Jansweijer 1998). Yet, the care ideal that replaced the full-time motherhood model has been the ideal of parental sharing, which has been univocally preached by most political parties, trade unions, and the women's movement and consolidated in the 1990s. Ironically, this ideal is not suitable for lone mothers.

Parental Sharing

The Dutch ideal of parental sharing has been summarised and highlighted in one of the most crucial policy papers of the 1990s, 'Unpaid care equally shared' (Commissie Toekomstscenario 1995). The social democratic minister of employment (Melkert) formed a commission to develop scenarios on the future of paid work and unpaid care. The Commission found that the most desirable scenario was the 'combination scenario', meaning that that all people, men as well as women, should share available paid and unpaid work equally. In practice, they recommended a 32-hour workweek and investments in childcare, calling for professionals to take over some of the caring work, but certainly not all.

The combination model was the idea of women's organisations in alliance with academic women and had already been put forward by the Emancipation Council in the late 1980s. It tries to find a balance between the Dutch culture of 'self care' and improving women's position in the labour market, and clearly aims at gender equality outside and inside the home. Thus on the one hand, the Commission sided with the strong anti-Scandinavian sentiments that stressed that parents should do the bulk of the parenting themselves – 'if you choose to have children, you have to care for them yourself'. This shows, as Billig (1991) has pointed out, that ideals are constructed as the opposite of one another. But on the other hand, it was stressed that men should work less and women should work more: women now had too many small jobs and more investments in childcare were needed. The assumption was also that when men do more in the home, women would like to work more outside the home. The combination model pleads for a shift from the practice of the 'one-and-a-half' model to the 'twice-three-quarter' model (Plantenga et al. 1999).

The Purple government agreed with the Commission: the combination scenario, with its emphasis on parental sharing, should be the basic model for modernising the Dutch welfare state. In all policy papers and evaluation research since then the combination model has been the point of reference; it has become the policy target (e.g. Ministerie van Sociale Zaken 1996; Portegijs et al. 2002, 2004). One of the reasons, again, is that parental sharing is seen as not only fair, it is also considered to be as a pre-condition for women's increased labour market participation. Dutch policy is built on the assumption that if *he* does more in the home, *she* can work more outside the home.

Parental sharing means two things: part-time rather than full-time employment is the norm and while women should not reduce all their caring activities, men should be more involved in caring. Starting off with the latter, sharing care duties has received much attention in the Dutch public and governmental debate. The first emancipation policy paper stated that not only women should have choices, men too should be able to choose more freely (preferably choosing to provide more care). Rather unique in Europe, the central objective of emancipation policy was that men and women should not only be economically independent, but also 'care independent' (Ministerie van Sociale Zaken en Werkgelegenheid 1992). Both men and women should be able to care for themselves and their family members.

Encouraging men to take up care duties is primarily considered to be an issue of socialisation and consciousness raising. In 1993 a course on caring (*verzorging*) became part of the national curriculum throughout the country. All children up to the age of 15 were supposed to learn to care, although it was implicitly aimed at boys. The objective was to degender caring and emphasise the importance and difficulty of caring (Grünnel 1997). Men were also addressed more directly: the government intensively used the mass media to communicate the message that men should care. One advertisement on TV was set in the 1950s and featured the slogan 'who's that man who cuts the meat every Sunday'. The message was that absent fathers are not very modern. Such campaigns were also run in the early 1990s by one of the biggest trade unions: 'Hi, *I* am your dad think about a part-time job'. More recently, the Ministry of Social Affairs, with the support of the European Commission, started a multimedia project, which includes a website with information and discussion, a TV program on fatherhood, and all kinds of courses and public debates. Mass media and education have been important routes in the Netherlands to persuade men to give care.

Dutch care policy also supports the idea that men should have the *opportunity* to be fathers. Since many studies show that men want to work less and care more, allowing time for fathers to care is seen as the most important policy intervention (Ministerie van Sociale Zaken en Werkgelegenheid 1996). Hence the individual right to unpaid parental leave which came into force already in the early 1990s. In the Netherlands, however, no additional measures were made taken to make it financially attractive for fathers to take up care duties or to force them to engage in caregiving, as in the Nordic parental leave schemes. Instead, ideological persuasion and giving men the opportunity to become involved in care duties seems to be the policy strategy.

The importance of part-time work is the second important feature of Dutch government policy on parental sharing of childcare responsibilities. In the 1990s, part-time work was embraced by individuals, the state, and trade unions (Visser 2002). It was in the 1970s that many women who wanted to marry and become mothers asked their employers if they could work part time. Particularly in sectors experiencing labour market shortages, such as education and nursing, it became common for women to continue to work part-time after they married. In the late 1970s, more than one-third of all jobs in the service sector were part-time jobs. In the 1980s and 1990s this became even more institutionalised. Due to the lack of childcare facilities, part-time work was considered the most viable option because it was seen to be a compromise between working full-time and staying at home. Instead of 'all-or-nothing', part-time work developed as an alternative to not working at all (Plantenga 1996).

In the early 1990s, part-time work was thus approached positively while at that time the international community (EU and OECD) still saw part-time work negatively. In 'Shaping Structural Change: The Role of Women' the OECD (1991) presented part-time work as a reconfirmation rather than a negotiation of the implicit gender contract. Of course, in the 1970s and early 1980s Dutch trade unions and the women's movement were not positive towards this type of work either. As in most countries, they were worried about the marginalisation of part-time workers and their lack of social rights. The unions and women's organisations struggled with the dilemma of giving in to individual part-time work or supporting shorter workweeks for everyone, but after the Wassenaar Regulations (1982) part-time employment became a more feasible option. The Organisation of Employers asked their members to accept part-time work as it was an alternative for firing people in times of recession. They also found out that it was not too expensive to reorganise and reschedule labour in order to allow for part-time employment.

It was crucial that trade unions became pro-part-time. When in 1990 the FNV (trade union) pleaded for part-time employment, it was the first trade union in Europe do so (Visser 1999). The trade unions supported the demands of many female workers. Why women wanted to work part-time at that point is a matter for debate. Was it because they were afraid of losing their jobs during the recession? (Visser 2002) Was it because no childcare was available at that time? (Plantenga 1996) Or was it because they preferred to spend more time with their children? (Hakim 2000). In any event, the change in the trade union's position was a result of a strong women's lobby within the trade union as well as lobbying by external women's organisations. In addition, members of the trade unions increasingly worked part-time themselves, which also initiated a debate within the trade unions. The trade union policy of 'right to part-time work for men and women' and 'equal rights for part-time workers' is the trophy of years of women's union lobbying, argues Grünnel (2002).

Most rules discriminating against part-time workers have been dismantled since the 1990s (chapter 5). Part-time work has become a normal job with equal pay, labour market conditions, and social rights. Moreover, in the modernised Labour Time Act (*Arbeidstijdenwet*) of 1996 the definition of employee has been altered to 'employee with care responsibilities'. Employees must be able to combine work and care, and therefore find variable and personal solutions in matters of working time. The crown jewel so far has been the law, put forward in 1993 but not enacted until 2000, which gives individual workers (except in very small companies) the right to adjust working hours from full-time to part-time or vice versa, unless employers prove that compelling business reasons make this impossible (Grunnel 2002; Visser 2002). Finally, the 2001 Tax Reform gives people who combine work and care a symbolic sum of money (Dierx et al. 1999). Indeed, the Dutch welfare state is moving from a male breadwinner model to a combination model.

Professional Care and Surrogate Mothers

Pleas for the ideal of parental sharing have not only been promoted as the alternative for full-time motherhood, they are also the opposite of full-time professional care. The Scandinavian model was seen as a living nightmare for Dutch parents, professionals, and politicians. A strong consensus exists that that young children should be taken care of by their mothers: there is a strong culture of self care (Knijn 1994; Plantenga 1996). For a long time, in the Netherlands, as anywhere else, the opponents of childcare argued that such services were only in the self-interest of mothers and that working women endangered the well-being of their own children by sending them out of the home to be cared for. Childcare services were only acceptable for very needy women with low incomes who were unable to care for their children. The children's interests were played against mothers' interests in working. This was still visible in the 1980s. Eelco Brinkman, the Christian democratic welfare minister who rejected government-subsidised childcare, argued that

> many families no longer exist as such because both man and women
> have to work or want to work, and that value is considered more worthy
> than raising a child (quoted in Bussemaker 1993: 85).

The women's movement was not coherent and strong enough to break this dominant rationale of children's interests through which childcare was seen as a dangerous expression of mothers' self-interest (Bussemaker 1993). Although the second-wave women's movement – the feminist group Dolle Mina and the Man Woman Society (MVM) – carried out actions demanding more and free crèches, and childcare expanded, childcare did not become a universally available service (van Rijswijk Clerx 1981; Singer 1989). When the state finally intervened on a larger scale in the early 1990s, the influence of the women's movement was negligible, argues

Peters (1999). Some individual women nevertheless did have an impact, notably Minister D'Ancona (social democrats). The Christian democratic women's organisation also made a difference, as it argued against its party, which had always been opposed to universal childcare subsidies.

Social pedagogues and day care workers have not had a strong impact on governmental policy or childcare debates in the Netherlands either. The organisation of childcare centres (WKN) had little influence on childcare policy (Peters 1999). One of the reasons is that playground workers are overrepresented within this organisation. The playground movement became very strong in the 1970s. Set up by higher-class women and supported by the medical establishment, the playground movement stressed that full-time professional care was not in the interest of children. Their main aim was to help mothers with the pedagogical relationship with their children. As childrearing – at that time too – became more intense and expectations rose, mothers needed more support as carers and not as workers. According to Van Rijswijck Clerx (1981), the playgroup movement even hampered the development of childcare centres. Parts of the women's movement – MVM as well as Dolle Mina – also supported the playground movement as they thought it would at least lead to universal services. Rijswijk Clerx (1981) argues that the playground movement forgot the interests of working women; the playground movement was even at odds with women's interests. This movement helped strengthen the public perception that childcare centres were bad for children. Herewith the playground movement placed a break on the emancipation of women as workers.

Professional care is still not a strong ideal in the Netherlands. This was again revealed in the summer of 2002, when Riksen-Walraven, a professor of childcare, spread the news that bringing your child to a childcare facility can disturb the child's development. Although her intention in raising this warning was to encourage the government to improve the quality of care in day care centres, others used this as ammunition to argue for the closure of childcare centres altogether. A second indication that the ideal of professional care is weak is the staffing situation at state-subsidised centres. In terms of staffing the Netherlands takes an average position, with 4:1 child to staff ratios for the very young (0-1) and 6:1 for ages 1-4. Dutch day care workers are usually trained, but only for three years on a middle level. This is more than in Flanders – where training is on a low level – but less than in Denmark, where the level of training is high (OECD 2001). The ideal of professional care is thus neither widespread nor robust.

A second question is why surrogate mothers have never become an alternative to full-time mother care as was the case in Flanders. There is no obvious answer. More than in Belgium, childcare policy has been *laissez faire*, implementing a liberal notion of free choice. In 1984, when a tax deduction for childcare was introduced, the government argued that because of parents' own responsibility and free choice the cabinet preferred to give them a tax deduction instead of raising the budget for childcare. With this small policy intervention the Dutch government explicitly chose to indirectly stimulate informal childcare supply (Bussemaker 1993). Rather than putting forward the ideal of the surrogate mother, the government hoped that people would sort out their caring themselves, preferably informally.

At the same time, the women's movement and particularly the trade unions were fervently against childminding at home. They saw it as a disaster for women's labour market participation. Rather than trying to formalise such childcare, they simply ignored it. The Stimulative Measures, which are described in chapter 6, an important financial investment in childcare services, made it possible to set up bureaus for host families, as described in the previous chapter. But this, according to experts, may even have harmed the development of state-regulated childminders as the financial measure was mostly equipped for supporting the set up of day care centres (int. 70, 71).

Intergenerational Care

In Dutch social policy, partner dependencies (horizontal dependencies) have always been assumed and promoted, and also the modernisation of care – the ideal of parental sharing – is built upon solidarity within couples. Conversely, vertical solidarity, dependency of children on their parents and vice versa, has been rejected. While in Denmark both vertical and horizontal dependencies are diminished, in Belgium both types of family dependencies are reinforced. This final section on the Netherlands deals with the absence of the ideal of intergenerational care. Why is this the case?

The ideal of intergenerational care was eradicated from social policy as early as the 1960s. Unlike caring for children, caring for the elderly is considered a state responsibility. While the Danish state cares for the elderly as well as for children, the Belgian state cares for children and less for the elderly, while the Dutch state cares less for children than for the elderly. This has important consequences for childcare: in the Netherlands grandparents are not supposed to be involved in caring for their grandchildren. Dutch people – both the elderly and the younger generation – argue that the state rather than the family is responsible for elderly care. If the elderly are ill they want to be cared for by professionals, not by their children. For the elderly, the ideal of professional care is in place (Voorn and Meijer 1999; Dykstra 1998). The comparative statistics, presented in the section on Denmark, also show that the Netherlands is high in the league of care services, right after Denmark. This is especially due to a substantial number of elderly in residential care (Alber 1995; Anttonen and Sipilä 1996; Rostgaard and Fridberg 1998; Rostgaard 2004).

The rejection of intergenerational care – the right to individualisation of the elderly – can be traced back to the 1950s, the time of rebuilding a country that was hard hit by the Second World War. Many houses were destroyed during the war – although a shortage of housing was already foreseen in the 1940s – and at the same time a baby boom took place. There was a constant need for big houses, which were occupied at that time by elderly couples or individuals. Children often had to live with their parents. The idea was that if the elderly moved to and lived in residential care, this would solve the housing problem for families with children.

This was however not only a purely functional solution for the housing shortage; the state also wanted to pay back the elderly who had survived the war and had worked hard. It was felt that these elderly people should be relieved of all daily care burdens; this would particularly relieve women. The newly established residential homes were not aimed at frail, sick elderly people: both the housing and the services attached to them were universal. Class or income did not matter. The individualisation of the elderly was finished off by universal and individual pensions in 1965, when the financial responsibilities of children for frail parents were also cancelled. The elderly were now free from care burdens and dependencies (Bijsterveld 1996).

In the 1980s, the move from residential care to home care resulted in a re-evaluation of the principle of individualisation. First, formal elderly care was reduced. Residential care was broken down (literally), although home care did not fill the care gap. Unlike the Danish case, in the Netherlands state expenditure was not transformed from residential to home care: the budget of elderly care was significantly reduced in 1980 and 1983 (Goewie and Keune 1996) and did not expand between 1980 and 1990, unlike in many other European countries (Tester 1996). Home care became particularly scarce: in 1999, 23,000 people were on waiting lists. This caused a huge outcry. A court case in 2001 concluded that the Dutch elderly in need of care indeed do have a right to receive care, and in the late 1990s substantial investments in home care took place (Ministerie van Volksgezondheid, Welzijn en Sport 2002).

The increasing importance of home care revealed that the law on home care does not entail the same rights to individualisation as residential care. In fact, the provision of state subsidised care is only allowed when 'the necessary help is absent or insufficient in a dependable way by family, neighbours or volunteers' (art 10, paragraph sub d.e. Regeling Ziekenfondsraad). In the Netherlands a debate has started on what the financiers of home care can expect from children and other relatives. What type of caring obligations are 'normal'? Although this has been changing during the last decade, the elderly in the Netherlands still have more of a right to live independently from their family and children than in a country like Belgium. Intergenerational care is still not a dominant ideal in the Netherlands.

The United Kingdom: From Surrogate Mother to Professional Care

Up until Major's second term (the mid-1990s), the British government was still flirting with the notion of full-time mothering, despite a continuous discourse on the importance of working women. In the 1980s, the Conservative government even wanted to introduce a male breadwinner bonus in taxation. Had it not been so expensive, women would have been paid to stay at home. The ideal of full-time motherhood has thus long been under the surface of liberal policy. Under Major this slowly changed, as consensus arose that women should work outside the home. It still took until the New Labour government came into office in 1997 for a British government to wholeheartedly become committed to working women: the pendulum swung in the direction of facilitating women to work.

Due to both a liberal stance and the full-time motherhood ideal, the British state at that time did not actively support an alternative ideal of caring. Implicitly, the Tory government preferred the ideal of the surrogate mother over professional care and supported intergenerational care. Under New Labour childminding lost out to the ideal of professional care, although this ideal applies more to children older than three and is primarily aimed at education.

How Surrogate Mothers lost

In the UK, the ideal of professional care has received a boost under the New Labour program. Before that, state-subsidised professional care was out of sight, except for the most needy – children with specific problems, often from low-income families. As described in chapter 6, the Conservative governments – up until Major's second term – showed no consensus as to whether women should work or not. Regardless of the answer, caring for children was seen as a private matter.

At the same time, the women's movement was weak and was divided on the issue of whether professional childcare should be for a demand: they distrusted the state and questioned whether it could provide qualitatively good childcare. According to Randall (1996), the British women's movement was very cynical and suspicious of the service state; they could not imagine it could provide any good-quality services. This British distrust of the state is opposite to the Danish belief in the 'people's home'. Moreover, British feminists, as Randall shows, were until the 1980s very critical about having children at all, and were very fragmented when it concerned motherhood and employment. They wondered whether it was really women's choice to go out to work, or if it was just economic necessity; they were very critical of the capitalist and patriarchal workplace. Similar to the Dutch but unlike the Danish and Belgian women's movement, the British women's movement could not say in one voice: we want state-subsidised childcare!

At the same time, the Conservatives implicitly emphasised the ideal of the surrogate mother. If young children (aged 0-2) really had to be cared for by someone other than their mother, home-based care was the implicit ideal in social policy in the 1980s and early 1990s. The British childcare expert Moss writes:

> Childminding has received official support for several reasons, including its low cost and its flexibility but it has also been supported because it is regarded as the type of care closest to the ideal, that is, the child cared for by its mother. (Moss 1991: 134)

The Tory government in 1992 showed its empathy by a change of law which allowed childminding for children between ages five and seven. This was expected to lead to a boost in this practice. The ideal of surrogate mothers was also perceivable at an organisational level: many day care institutions at that time did not even admit children younger than age two. Reasons could be practical and commercial, caring for childred aged 0-2 is very intensive, but there could also be cultural reasons: professionals may not believe themselves that young children should be cared for outside a home (int. 37, 38).

In the early 1990s, most organisations in the field of childcare, the Equal Opportunity Commission, the Trade Unions Congress, major childcare organisations, and specialised scholars advocated a National Childcare Strategy (Daguerre and Bonoli 2003). When New Labour came into office they expanded the number of childcare places in nurseries to a large degree, and have planned further expansion (chapter 6). The New Childcare Strategy is based on the ideal of professional care rather than that of the surrogate mother. Indicative of a shift in policy was that childcare policy aimed at doubling the number of nursery places for three year olds, double the number of out-of-school places for school-age children, provide universal nursery education for all four-year olds, and improve childcare staff regulation and training (Baldock 2003). Under the Labour government the guidelines for childminding were also strengthened (Lewis 2003).

One reason why the ideal of surrogate mothers was no longer stressed under New Labour was its weakened support in public opinion or, more precisely, parents' wishes. Parents have been very dissatisfied with the childcare available and have especially lost trust in childminders (Thomson 1995, see chapter 8). As New Labour listened carefully to the middle classes it would be politically harmful to promote an ideal that was criticised so much by parents. Catering to the middle-class parents would be to support the ideal of professional care. Again we see a change of ideal.

As described in the previous chapter, the content of the ideal of professional care is early education, not so much the social-pedagogical care as has been advocated in Denmark. This stress on education for young children is not completely new. Even in the UK, ideological continuity is visible after a government change. If the Conservative government gave any attention to the provision of care for children, it was under this flag. The over-five initiative, for instance, a program running from 1993 to 1996, gave support for services providing care and recreation for school-age children. Moreover, in 1994 the Conservative government installed a voucher system to provide a pre-school place for all four-year olds. Each parent was given a voucher worth 1,100 pounds a year which could be used to buy a variety of approved services in the education or welfare system. Most parents however bought a place at school, which meant losing welfare services (Land and Lewis 1998).

New labour has invested in childcare for instrumental reasons, because it was seen to be strategic to combat poverty and social exclusion via social investment in children; it would also move the UK into the dual-earner model which was also one of New Labour's aims. Children are seen as either potential workers or childcare recipients who enable parents to earn a sufficient income. Or as Lewis (2003: 220) describes New Labour's policy:

thinking about childcare was thus framed primarily by an economic approach that saw childcare as a means of raising children's future prospects by improving early years provision and by allowing their parents (especially lone mothers) to earn.

Childcare is thus part of the new 'investment state'. These are also the grounds on which Esping-Andersen et al. (2002) plea for state investments in childcare services. Lister is very critical about this approach to childcare. She argues that it is the child as 'citizen-worker' of the future rather than the 'citizen-child' of the present who is invoked by the new discourse of social investment (2003: 437). In this line of thinking, childcare is not child-centred, she argues. It is not about the better lives that children will lead as children. This is very different from the Danish objective of professional care based on social and pedagogical goals. Lister (2003) also questions how stable this ideal of professional care can be. If children seem to matter instrumentally, not existentially, expenditure on them will only be justifiable where there is a demonstrable pay off.

Another question is how much the ideal of professional care is put into practice. Although child-staff-child ratios are average (4:1 public but 8:1 private for children aged 0-3), staff qualifications are comparatively low (OECD 2001). A survey found that 22 percent of day nursery heads and 33 percent of other day nursery workers had no qualifications (Lewis 2003). The OECD (2001) warns that childcare personnel in the UK is not well-trained, and working conditions and pay are low. Finally, the ideal of early education stresses that children younger than three should not have other childcare arrangements than a mother being at home. It may well be that, analogously to the Dutch playground movement, this ideal of care hampers the development of childcare for the very young (children under age three).

Parental Sharing

The importance of parental sharing as well as the focus on men are surely important breakthroughs of New Labour policy. Parental sharing is really a recent policy issue, even though commentators argue that the focus on men's involvement is still too weak (Rake 2001). For the first time in the UK, working times as well as men's involvement in caring have been discussed – first, by introducing limited leave schemes, as we have seen in chapter 5; secondly, by the possibility of reducing working hours; and thirdly, by installing a minimum wage, which should limit the necessity to work many hours per week (Daly and Rake 2003). Compared to the Dutch case, state support for parental sharing is limited, but the recent developments are crucial in the British context.

It is important to note that the Conservative government would never have put forward the notion of parental sharing. Even though one strand of conservatism does have a clear notion about who should do the caring – the mother at home – a stronger voice said these issues were private. This private view of the family can be illustrated well by a speech of the conservative Minister Virginia Bottomley. For her, the most important task for the state was

> to acknowledge the privacy of the family, stressing the responsibility of parents and the importance of keeping the state out of private family matters (in Jones and Millar 1996:4).

In addition, the Conservative government was more concerned about the economy than about the division of labour in the family. They rejected parental leave because it would impose 'added burdens on employers without regard to their impact on jobs', said Minister Forsyth (in O'Connor et al. 1999: 86). For conservatives the main argument is that state intervention would place a burden on employers, and their wishes are more important then those of parents.

Intergenerational Care

While parental sharing is a very recent policy objective, the implicit ideal of intergenerational care has a long history. Indeed, the UK has a long tradition of state support for the elderly. Residential care as well as home care have been important elements of local authority policy. In the UK there are no legal obligations between parents and children (Millar and Warman 1996). At the same time, since the 1970s policies towards elderly care went hand in hand with the notion of community care, which was supported by all parties in different times. This comes close to a (limited) ideal of intergenerational care. Moreover, British elderly care is based on the need principle. Those who suffer the most receive the most help.

The concept of community care, so crucial in British caregiving policy, has many meanings. According to Tinker et al. (1994) it not only involves public recognition of the importance of the family and caring within marriage – informal care – but also the recognition of the family's limitations. It invokes the idea of neighbours and friends helping but recognises a limit to the sort of care they will provide. Community care also means that people want to stay as long as possible 'in the community'. The notion became more crucial when the Conservative government came into office, and was made explicit in the 1990 National Health Service and Community Act. This act also organised the introduction of quasi-markets, where different care providers are supposed to compete for local authority money (Land and Lewis 1998).

In the UK, care policy for the elderly has been increasingly built upon selectivity. The money for the ever-aging population of elderly was limited, although unlike the Dutch case the budget still grew slowly (Baldock 2003). Comparative statistics show that in the mid-1990s the UK had nine percent of elderly (65+) people covered by home help and five percent in residential care (Anttonen and Sippilä 1996). This is more than in Belgium but less than in the Netherlands and Denmark. Cross-national research by Rostgaard and Fridberg (1998; also Rostgaard 2004) shows a darker picture: home help covers only five percent of the population, although it is given for a substantial number of hours (more than five hours per week). This indicates that the British home care scheme is highly selective: it caters to the worst-off citizens, the most needy. Only one-fifth of those with some degree of dependency were receiving home care in the mid-1990s. This means that a large number of frail elderly who are not frail or sick enough have to depend on informal sources. Those who receive informal care have been less able to receive home care since the mid-1990s (Baldock 2003).

Another indication of the ideal of intergenerational care is the support of informal carers. Uniquely in Europe, informal care in the UK has been financially supported by successive governments. Since 1976 the Invalid Care Allowance pays informal carers who put in long hours providing care a kind of wage-replacement benefit. Equally, the 1995 Carers (recognition and services) Act gave caregivers entitlements to have their needs assessed; i.e. they also have the right to get support from professionals. As Finch (1990) had foreseen in the late 1980s, care in the community has become 'care by the community'. Hence, although never stressed as such, the intergenerational ideal of care has become particularly strong in the UK as a consequence of the highly selective home care policy, the rhetoric on community care, and the stress on carers' rights.

This notion of intergenerational care does not fit with the recent childcare policy, which explicitly excludes informal, intergenerational care. Different from the Belgian situation, the UK's Childcare Credit excludes tax deductions when children are cared for by grandparents (Land 2001; Weelock and Jones 2002). In that sense, the British ideal of intergenerational care stands in a 'flamingo position': it stresses the importance of caring for the elderly but does not support childcare by grandparents.

Conclusion: Ideals of Care after the Full-time Motherhood Norm

This chapter demonstrates that the childcare paradigm has changed in all four countries. The ideal of full-time mother care has been eradicated in each country, though at different points in time. However, the policy responses to the moral predicament of care has varied from country to country. In other words, what is considered to be the most appropriate solution for providing childcare when parents are at work is country-specific. In Denmark, the full-time mother care model was in place only in the 1950s. The Danish alternative for the upbringing of children when mothers are at work is the ideal of professional care: social-pedagogical aims are placed central. Danish childcare is about socialising children as social beings as well as stressing their self-development. This ideal is not clearly related to specific political parties, such as the social democrats, but to the alliance of the women's movement with the organisation of childcare professionals, the social pedagogues (who were also women), and more recently with parents/clients.

In Belgium, free choice has been the articulate policy principle: women should have a free choice as to whether to work or not, and what type of childcare they need if they enter the labour market. But this free choice is not real. Flemish governments invested much more in the ideal of the surrogate mother, and childminders became linked to subsidised organisations. This ideal has been put forward by the women's group of the Catholic agrarian movement, which found a natural ally in the Christian democratic government – not only because it was a cheap solution, but also because this type of childcare is considered to be warm, motherly, and to strengthen social cohesion. In addition to the ideal of the surrogate mother, intergenerational care is an important policy objective. This is of course not a new alternative but is seen as a remnant of the past that should be allowed to live on.

In the Netherlands, the eradication of the ideal of full-time motherhood happened comparatively late. Women started to work in larger numbers only in the late 1980s. An alternative ideal of parental sharing was put forward and consolidated in the 1990s. This ideal is based on part-time employment and on seducing men to behave as caring fathers. The ideal of parental sharing is seen as an appropriate alternative for mother care: the child is still cared for at home, but now the father is involved too. The advocacy coalition for this ideal of care was the women's movement in the widest sense of the word – including scholars – together with the trade unions.

The British case, finally, is more mixed and at the same time shows clearer transformations. During the Conservative governments no clear ideals of care were put forward to offer parents an alternative care solution, although full-time motherhood as well as surrogate mothering and intergenerational care were implicit in many interventions. The Labour government has more clearly bid farewell to full-time mothering as well as to the surrogate mother, and shifted to the ideal of professional care, at least for children over age three. Different from the Danish case however is the fact that childcare is seen as education, which also limits the impact of the ideal for young children.

This chapter thus showed that in most countries women tried to organise themselves to find a way out of the deadlock situation in which the interests of children were played against the interests of women. Women, individually and in groups, have been vital in developing and striving for new policy ideals of care. The very moment women were able to ally with groups that were powerful in a specific country at that time – a governing political party, trade unions, professional groups, parents, or scholars (often women themselves) – new ideals arose and became paradigmatic. Specific ideals took shape mostly in relation to the existing care practice as well as the orientation of the women's movement, whose direction was different in each country. Whether women as actors had power is an important factor in understanding caring states, but what ideals of care they strived for is just as important. In other words, in understanding the development of new care ideals we have to reinterpret the recent history of welfare states and study various factors such as the orientation of the women's movement and the possibility to form (female) alliances with other dominant groups such as trade unions, professional organisations, the dominant political coalition and parents' opinions, or in other words, the advocacy coalition (Jenkins and Sabatier 1994) in the broadest sense.

While this chapter was devoted to ideals of care in policy, the next chapter focuses on ideals of care in practice. Are they the same in each country? Moreover, what are the consequences of embedding specific care ideals in welfare states? Do ideals of care indeed result in gender-specific employment and care patterns? How do ideals of care relate to citizenship?

8   How Welfare States Work: Ideals of Care in Practice

Care ideals are helpful in understanding the (changing) content and origins of caring states. The previous chapter showed that welfare states promote different ideals of care. But ideals of care also help to explain why mothers do or do not work. When mothers make decisions about work, they always refer to whether their children are cared for well. Appropriate care solutions that fit people's ideals are a necessary condition for taking up employment. This also entails that welfare states are more than a set of financial structures that limit and provide people's choices, as comparative welfare state theories often assume. Seemingly neutral procedures and structures embody particular values, norms, interests, identities, and beliefs. Social policy – through regulations, financial measures, and content of provisions – influences the normative structures that provide people with choices, but also limit those choices. In other words, a welfare state is a moral agent, as Wolfe (1989) has put it.

Welfare states give messages to their citizens about what the most appropriate way is to care for children when mothers are at work. In other words, the welfare state is not merely a merchant connecting supply and demand or a judge safeguarding justice and people's basic rights, but also a priest: it tries to tell people how to behave. The state is a messenger whose institutions help to shape appropriate behaviour. This means that social policy can also be read as a sermon, or a set of sometimes contradictory messages. The question is of course whether people still listen to this priest. Is the state still a source of moral authority? Or do people only follow their own life goals as Hakim (2000, 2003) argues?

This chapter shows that ideals in care policy indeed relate to care ideals in practice. Welfare states matter. Specific ideals of care also have an important impact on citizenship: different ideals of care relate to different gendered citizenship practices. For instance, the ideal of the surrogate mother produces different gendered patterns of paid employment, care, and income than the ideal of professional care. In fact, women's labour market participation can be hampered by some ideals of care, such as the surrogate mother ideal, and stimulated by others, like the ideal of professional care. In addition, specific ideals of care have a different impact on different categories of women (by age, class, or profession). The set of hypotheses presented in this section is illustrated with examples from the four countries.

Denmark: Professional Care

Denmark, as we saw in the previous chapter, was the first country that eradicated the model of full-time mother care from its social policy, and this is also true in practice. Today, the phenomenon of the housewife has practically disappeared: just 4 percent of women are engaged in full-time mothering (Eurostat 1997). More than in other Scandinavian countries, most parents (90 percent) also reject the husband as a sole provider (Ellingsaeter 1998). Most children, as described in the chapter on childcare, use state-subsidised facilities. Especially from age three and up, children go to childcare five days a week. Even when parents are at home – for instance due to unemployment – most parents want their children to go to day care, where highly professionalised workers care for them. They believe that children are better-off at day care than at home with their mother (Cristensen 2000).

Table 8.1   Care arrangements for children under three in percentage around 1990 and 2000, Denmark

Care arrangement for children under age three	1989/1990	1999/2000
No public scheme:	12	approximately 24
Private family day care	11	for informal
Grandparents and others		arrangements
Cared for at home by parents (not leave)	20	
Parents taking leave	9	approximately 25
Local government family day care	28	35
Local government childcare institution	20	21
Total	100	100

Source: Juul Jensen and Krogh Hansen (2003)

Many young children go to family day care nevertheless (table 8.1, see also chapter 6). But as was argued in the chapter 7, these women can no longer be labelled as surrogate mothers: they are closer to professional care.

In Denmark, as table 8.1 also shows, the ideal of the surrogate mother is not found in the market either (see also Mogensen 1995). The explanation must be the widely available and affordable state-subsidised facilities; other sources of paid childcare are rare. Also in line with messages found in social policy, few grandparents are involved in the day-to-day care of their grandchildren, especially compared to the other countries (Eurostat 1997). Danish research in the mid-1990s even showed that only one percent of young children were cared for by family and friends (Mogensen 1995). Grandparents do not provide childcare on a regular basis. They are more likely to provide help in emergency situations (Juul Jensen and Krogh Hansen 2003).

An interesting aspect of the Danish case is that the ideal of parental sharing is not really promoted in social policy, is not practiced, but is much more preferred. Danish couples work full-time (chapter 4) and parental leave is not taken by men (chapter 5). But if Danes are asked about their wishes, they either want to share the work and caregiving duties or they want the junior model: the man working full-time, the woman working part-time (Ellingsaeter 1998). In fact, in 1999 not more than three percent of parents preferred the dual-earner model, the most common Danish family model. This is not a recent phenomenon. Since the 1970s, few Danes have wanted the model of both partners working full time. Danish women and men do not want to work long hours, and never did. But the practice is the opposite (Christensen 2000: 149).

This indicates that Danish people do not follow what they put forward as 'preferences'. Denmark is a country that neatly fits Hakim's conditions (2000, see chapter 2) of a place where men and women for the first time in history have real choice over their lives, with equal opportunity policy and reproductive rights in place (see Siim 2000). But in this country people do not follow their work-life preferences or pursue their own life goals. On the contrary, they practice the ideal promoted in social policy, which they also support: the ideal of professional care.

Belgium: A Mammoth Alliance of Mothers

The Belgian case also shows clear linkages between policy and practice. Slowly, the ideal of full-time mothering is disappearing in policy and practice, more than in the UK and the Netherlands (table 8.2). Parental sharing, which is hardly alive as an ideal in social policy, has not yet gained much ground. Few Belgian fathers work part-time and if men take leave it is not for caring practices, although this is recently changing under the new Time Credit Scheme (chapter 5). The only ones who have listened to the call of part-time work are working mothers (chapter 4). Belgian mothers increasingly work part-time and, as we see in table 8.2, many more would like to do so.

Table 8.2		Actual and preferred employment patterns for two-parent families with children under six, 1998, three countries			
		Man full time/ woman full time (dual-earners)	Man fulltime/ woman part time (junior model)	Man full time/woman not employed (male breadwinner model)	Other (e.g., parental sharing, female breadwinner model)
BE	actual	46.0	19.4	27.3	7.3
	preferred	54.8	28.8	13.4	3.0
NL	actual	4.8	54.8	33.7	6.7
	preferred	5.6	69.9	10.7	13.8
UK	actual	24.9	31.9	32.8	10.4
	preferred	21.3	41.8	13.3	23.6

Source: OECD (2001)

When parents are at work, a mammoth alliance of mothers enables mothers to work. The first source of mothers are day care mothers: one-third of young children stay with them during the day. These day carers are unofficially called *onthaalmoeders* (the term *onthaal* has the connotation of a warm welcome). In contrast to Denmark, these women are surely 'surrogate mothers'. The second are the mothers of the working mothers: the grandmothers. They support their daughters' entering the labour market. This means that the ideal of the surrogate mother as well as the ideal of intergenerational care are present in both policy and practice. Flemish parents are generally very content with the practice of their care arrangements: they get the childcare they want (Vanpée et al. 2000).

Although literally every year fewer grandparents take care of their grandchildren, 84 percent of very young Flemish children are still cared for by grandparents (table 8.3). Or more precisely, they are cared for by grandmothers – often those from the mothers' side (Jacobs 1996; Vanpée et al. 2000). In other words, Flemish women have a social contract with their own mother, a contract fathers and grandfathers are not really part

Table 8.3	Care for children younger than 2.5, 1999, Flanders
Care arrangements	
Informal care	
Grandparents	84.3
Relatives, neighbours	13.9
Formal care	
Day care mother employed by a service	34.0
Private day care	9.8
Subsidised childcare centre	24.0
Private childcare centre	7.6
Other arrangements at home (au pair, nanny)	1.4

Note: Children begin school at age 2.5.
Source: Vanpée et al. 2000

of. About 60 percent of grandparents are regularly involved in caring for their grandchildren, providing care one day a week for at least five hours, many of them for two grandchildren. On average, the job these grandparents have is quite substantial. Their 'workweek' is nearly 26 hours (Hedebouw and Sannen 2002).

Although it is important that grandparents are a cheap solution for childcare, research on this practice also reveals that it is indeed fitting to speak about a culturally defined moral ideal of care. Grandparents not only feel a strong moral duty to support their children, they feel that they 'are the best carers when mothers work' (LISO 1991). They consider the responsibility given to them by their daughters as a recognition that they were good mothers. One working mother explained:

> My mother found it really terrible that I had registered my children at a kindergarten without asking her. I had thought that she would find it too heavy with my sister's baby and therefore I brought them to a crèche. But she was offended. (Van Haegendoren and Bawin-Legros 1996: 31)

Grandparents want to be valued above professionals, as they do not consider childcare facilities to be the best solution (LISO 1991, Van Haegendoren and Bawin-Legros 1996). Many parents, but also the grandmothers themselves, see care provided by grandmothers to be the best alterative to mother care. After all, who can care better than the mother's own mother?

The Netherlands: Surrogate Mothers

In the Netherlands, the ideal promoted in social policy is parental sharing. This resembles Pfau-Effinger's label for the Dutch model: the dual carer/dual breadwinner model (1998, 1999). But unlike other ideals, parental sharing is difficult to put into practice. Depending on calculations just 2.3 percent (Eurostat 2002) – six percent (Portegijs et al. 2004) to nine percent (Knijn and van Wel 2001a) – of parents with young parents actually 'share' (meaning both have a job of about 32 hours). Most of them are highly educated. On the other hand, Dutch couples are more likely to work part-time than in any other country (Eurostat 2002). And more than in other countries, men seem to be more involved in caregiving. Dutch fathers for instance are more likely to take parental leave than in other countries (chapter 5), and recent research shows that half of working mothers have a partner who stays at home to give care on one weekday (Portegijs et al. 2004). Thus, although fathers are more likely to care, parental sharing is too optimistic a label for the Dutch practice.

In practice, the ideal of parental sharing turns out as the junior model (he works full-time, she works part-time) : the woman, ironically, is doing the 'sharing' on her own. The problem may be that the ideal of parental sharing is the most preferred model for women, while most men prefer both working full-time. When women then become mothers they nevertheless abandon their preferred ideal of sharing: they want to practice the junior model (Portegijs et al. 2002). Is it because they have experienced men's absence of caring and stopped the fight for equal sharing, or because they really prefer to spend more time on caring? In any case, women are very adaptive to the policy that promotes the ideal of parental sharing. This may relate to the fact that they also have put forward this model, as the previous chapter shows. Men on the other hand seem less adaptive to this particular social policy, although some of them take up the moral messages and act upon this ideal. In short, the Dutch case shows that the caveat of the ideal of parental sharing is that 'it takes two to share'.

If children are not cared for by their parents, parents piece together a jigsaw of childcare. Least popular are host families, which are regulated childminders (4.4 percent; see table 8.4). More popular are childcare centres (21 percent). Highly educated parents prefer childcare centres as they value children having social contacts, but at the same time parents who use day care centres are the least content of all parents with their care solution (Portegijs et al. 2002, 2004). Most popular childcare are childminders (52 percent). This has really been a booming business. In 1987

Table 8.4	Use of types of childcare of all children in care, in percentage of the age category, 1999, the Netherlands				
	Childcare centre	Host family	Childminder elsewhere	Childminder at home	One or more
Age child 0-3	21	4.4	31	21	70
Child 0-12 single parent	7.6	1.9	26	17	58
Double parent 0-12	7.3	2.8	21.7	17	

Source: Knijn (2003), based on Portegijs et al. (2002)

only nine percent of young children of working parents were cared for by a private childminder (Knijn 2003, Portegijs et al. 2002).

In contrast to most other countries, these childminders are neither registered nor controlled, they are indeed market players. Many (although not most) of the children are cared for in their own home between their own toys; the childminders are nannies, while Danish and Flemish childminders nearly always take their children to their own home, where they play with other children. In the Netherlands, parents prefer their child to be brought up according to their own wishes in the kids' 'natural environment'. This is indeed the ideal of the surrogate mother. The parents who choose such childcare prefer a woman who is a mother herself and who has the qualities that are traditionally ascribed to a mother: loving, familiar, and fully available. They want the child to feel as if the parents were still at home, so the childminder is a good imitator of the care of the real mother.

Parents also try to find a person that they believe can pass on the values they find important. This is in contrast to a professional in a day care centre, the parents say, as she listens to various parents (and also follows her professional standards), while a childminder will only listen to them. Parents therefore believe that they can have a strong say in the upbringing of their child (Nievers 2002).

Clearly the most practiced childcare solution, the surrogate mother, is not explicitly promoted in Dutch social policy. More in line with the moral messages spread via social policy is the fact that grandparents are not substantially involved in caring. They of course do care for their grandchildren, but not for extensive hours, as in Flanders, so that their daughters can work (Eurostat 1997; Remery et al. 2000). Intergenerational care is hardly a practiced ideal in the Netherlands. Remery et al. (2000) show that the primacy of the family is not a shared belief: only 12 percent of the respondents said that they prefer care provided by the family. Moreover, very few highly educated families have a caring contract with their parents, while they are generally the parents most in need of care for their children. Remery et al. (2000) speculate that parents of highly educated people may be too old and frail because in the Netherlands highly educated women have children when they are age 30 and over. These grandparents also live further away. More recently, however, grandparents seem to be more involved in child-care, but only for a day or so per week (Portegijs et al. 2004).

The UK: Intergenerational Care and Moving Away From the Surrogate Mother

As in the Netherlands and Belgium, the full-time motherhood ideal in the UK is still practiced by nearly one-third of the couples with young children (table 8.2). The question here is: what ideal is practiced by the majority of women, the ones who have entered the labour force? Which ideal has replaced the ideal of full-time care is not clear though. Caring practice shows that intergenerational care is the most dominant practice, and more recently a shift has taken place from the ideal of the surrogate mother to professional care. This is perfectly in line with the transformation in caring policy described in chapter 7.

Strikingly, parental sharing is hardly part of the practice and mindset of parents. British men do not have a good record on this issue: British fathers are the least likely to be involved in caring for young children (Eurostat 1997). They are likely to work many hours a week, much more than their continental peers (chapter 4). In addition, those men who do work part-time do not do so because of childcare. Only 17 percent of all men working part-time do so because they spend time taking care of their children (Matheson and Summersfield 2001).

Since British parents could not depend on professional state-subsidised childcare, most of them bought care on the market, hiring childminders: surrogate mothers. Many of them are registered at the local authority, as parents only tend to trust these (Ford 1996). More recently, however, parents have moved away from childminding as a solution for day care. Table 8.5 shows that in the late 1990s nurseries were a much more common care practice than childminders. Although research is difficult to compare, in the mid-1990s the use of childminders were the most common care practice. At that time, childminders were responsible for a quarter of all children while nurseries cared for about 14 percent of the very young children (Thomson 1995, personal correspondence 1998). More recent statistics show that childminders only care for about 11 to 13 percent of young children (see table 8.5). Other research shows the same picture: children being cared for by childminders decreased from 365,200 in 1997 to 304,600 in 2001 (DfES 2001; chapter 6).

Table 8.5	Types of providers used for children aged 0-4 in England, 1999	
Type of care	0-2 (%)	3-4 (%)
Childminder	11	13
Daily nanny	2	2
Live-in-nanny	1	1
Babysitter	13	15
Creche/nursery	26	38
Playgroup	20	44
Nursery/reception class	10	30
Family centre	1	*
Out-of-school club	4	6
Ex-partner	5	5
Grandparent	64	57
Older sibling	2	3
Other relative or friends	37	36
Other	1	1
Base (unweighted)	1575	1071

Source: La Valle et al. (2000)

This decrease in the use of 'surrogate mothers' is probably related to the widespread dissatisfaction with childminders. All British parents have been very unsatisfied with their care arrangements, but this applies most to those using childminders. In the mid-1990s only four out of ten parents using childminders thought their childcare arrangements were 'very convenient' or 'very satisfactory' (Thomson 1995). Childminders have a very high turnover: parents change childminders more often than nurseries. Most parents said that they would prefer nannies, who would come to the childrens' homes, instead of childminders, and even more said they would prefer nurseries (Brannen and Moss 1991; Thomson 1995; Gardiner 1997).

What also contributed to the decrease in the use of childminders is that parents in the UK – unlike other countries in this book – are continuously exposed to media coverage of unreliable and untrustworthy childminders. Accidents have occurred in the UK as well as in the US which caused the death of small children. Research on lone parents and childcare (Ford

1996) showed that half of the respondents specifically referred to distrust of potential resources of care as one reason why they would have difficulty using childcare. They no longer see childminders as 'surrogate mothers' that are trustworthy, familiar or resemble themselves, but as unreliable strangers. One mother said:

> It always worries me because you see these programmes on the telly about these childminders that battered kids and that put me off it. Like these childminders that have sexually abused children they've been minding, that have been registered. No, I couldn't have a registered childminder. No. (Ford 1996: 128).

Parents seem to be in constant doubt about the quality of care; will the childminder really care well for their beloved child?

This move away from surrogate mothers is also visible at the policy level. In this case, the British government seems to have listened to the parents and taken their worries seriously. Consequently, childcare policy is moving towards the direction of professional care, at least for older children (age three and up).

Most British children are cared for by grandparents. Table 8.5 shows that grandparents are the most common source of caregiving for young children. As in Belgium, a mother often signs a social contract with her own mother, and this type of care is relatively cheap. Research by Weelock and Jones (2002) also shows that parents as well as grandparents see intergenerational care as 'the next best thing' if mothers go out to work. Outsiders or strangers who work in formal childcare centres do not give love to the children, the parents argue, and there is nobody they trust more than their own parents.

In general, British parents, in contrast to the other countries, still express their unhappiness with the childcare arrangements they have. Three-quarters of working parents said their current childcare arrangements were not ideal and the figure for poorer households and lone parents was even higher (La Valle et al. 2000). In an ideal world of affordable and accessible childcare, nearly one in five parents said they would prefer an informal carer, which is often a grandparent. The problem is, as Land (2001) and Weelock and Jones (2002) argue, that the ideal of intergenerational care is not sufficiently supported by social policy. The Childcare Strategy even excludes informal care. These researchers therefore plea for recognition rather than a downgrading, demotivating, and discouragement strategy of intergenerational care.

Policy, Practice, Preference

This section showed that ideals promoted in welfare states are indeed linked to actual practices, although the correlation is stronger in Denmark, Belgium, and the UK than in the Netherlands. People are thus indeed guided by the normative messages of welfare states. Their action is inspired by notions of 'what is the proper thing to do' and the state is still one of the moral authorities to offer such scripts. This section also indicates, in contrast to Hakim's theory (2000, 2003), that people cannot or do not want to follow their own preferences. In the Netherlands, Belgium, and the UK, where the male breadwinner/full-time caregiver model is still practiced on a substantial scale (about one-third of families with young children), this is not the preferred practice: more mothers want to work. In a country like Denmark, parents prefer to share the provision of care and have more time to engage in caregiving duties. But the practice is the opposite: in none of the other three countries do mothers and fathers work as many hours. Danish people work much more than they want to.

Individual preferences clearly cannot explain cross-national differences in work and care, but they are nevertheless important in another way. The British case shows that parental preferences can be important in explaining changes in social policy, albeit in a modest way. The recent Labour government moved away from the ideal of the surrogate mother, as parents no longer trusted this type of care. At the same time, the British case shows that preferences are not always implemented. Many British parents prefer that grandparents take care of their children, while state support for such type of care is lacking. Ideals of care are only enforced when they are advocated by a larger coalition of women's organisations and powerful actors (chapter 7).

Finally, of all policy ideals, parental sharing has been the most difficult to put into practice. Women are much more adaptive towards this ideal and want to work part time. This is not a strange conclusion, if one keeps in mind that women were also the ones who actively promoted this ideal (chapter 7). Men are less flexible though. As a result, the ideal of parental sharing in practice often transforms to the 'junior model'.

So far, we have discussed whether care ideals in policy affect care ideals in practice. Now we come to the last question, which is central to this book. What are the impact of ideals of care on women's citizenship? The next section outlines a 'light' theory on the consequences of ideals of care, illustrating these impacts with examples from the four welfare states.

Ideals of Care and Citizenship

How do ideals of care influence women's citizenship? This section discusses two hypotheses. The departing point of the first hypothesis is that social change is linked with the change of norms (March and Olsen 1989). This means that women's route to employment is paved with a different set of care ideals. In other words, when women want to enter the labour market, a new ideal of care has to replace the old full-time mother care model. Of course, women have always worked, even when the dominant norm prescribed that they stay at home. Up to a rather low level of female employment, welfare societies can even stick to the ideal of full-time mother care. Women are also able to sort out their own work-and-care problems individually, and some women work even though they are unhappy with their childcare arrangements.

The crucial point though is that employment rates only pass a critical level if women believe their children are cared for well. The majority of women are likely to work only when a solution is found for childcare that fits their notions of satisfactory care. This means that a new, robust, ideal of care must have the potential to fit parents' wishes. In Ragin's (2000) terms, the replacement of the ideal of full-time mother care with a new ideal in both policy and practice is a necessary (but not sufficient) condition for a substantial number of working women. Up to a specific level of employment, women can do without official alternatives, but beyond a critical level state intervention is necessary and can then even act as a catalyst (Leira et al. 2005).

This is illustrated by the British case. While the Conservative government, especially under Major, wanted women to work in the 1990s, no new ideal was univocally and institutionally supported. In other words: not only did a practical void exist, since affordable childcare was hardly available, but there was also a moral void. Families had no alternative ideal of caregiving. The state did not promote any ideas on how to care for children in a decade where women wanted and were supposed to work. If the Conservatives promoted an ideal – and they did so in a very manner – it was the surrogate mother. This however turned out to be a misfit: British parents increasingly distrusted this type of care. Although women have tried to find their own solutions, an entirely personal pick-and-mix strategy does not seem to lead to substantial participation rates for all British women.

This is different in the three other countries, where new ideals have been put forward. In the Netherlands, women's participation rates increased substantially when the government proposed a new ideal of care in the mid-1990s – rather late, in fact. The ideal of parental sharing had the relatively strong support of people as it fits with notions of self-care, the nuclear family, and gender equality. In Denmark the ideal of full-time mother care was quickly replaced from the 1970s onwards by the ideal of professional care, while in Belgium the government actively supported ideals such as intergenerational care and the surrogate mother, which also fit or had the potential to change preferences and practices.

In other words, women's employment increases when an alternative ideal of childcare is embedded in policy that fits or has the potential to fit with parents' ideals. The development of alternative care ideals is a condition for employment changes. A parallel can be drawn with Kuhn's (2003, or. 1962) description of paradigm shifts: a new paradigm can help to dismantle the old. This logic also predicts that, for instance, as soon as an alternative ideal of care is publicly supported in the UK, i.e. through laws or financial structures that fit people's notions about good enough childcare, mothers' employment rates will increase more rapidly. People simply cannot change behaviour radically without some change of ideal. Thus, without a moral and practical solution for how children are cared for, mothers will hesitate to enter the labour market.

So far the relation between the bare existence of ideals of care and employment rates. A second question is how can the changes and differences in gendered employment, care, and income patterns in the four countries be explained? The second set of hypotheses is that the different alternative ideals of care – parental sharing, surrogate mothers, intergenerational care, and professional care – go hand in hand with specific citizenship practices, just as was the case of full-time mothering. Ideals of care relate to specific gendered patterns of paid employment, care, and income.

Table 8.6 presents the hypothetical relationship between ideals of care and ideals of citizenship, showing how ideals of care can reinforce as well as improve the hierarchy within gender relations. To make it even more complicated: some ideals are profitable for 'certain dimensions of citizenship' for 'some categories of women', as noted by Hakim (2000), while other dimensions or categories of women loose. The indicators for citizenship used here are the same as in the earlier chapters: (a) labour market participation, (b) participation in caregiving, (c) income and economic dependency relations, and the overall questions: (d) to what extent do ideals of citizenship change the hierarchical relations between men and women, and (e) how do ideals of citizenship gender or degender caregiving. The table also shows that welfare states are more than Janus-faced, they have many ambivalent features. In the following pages I will discuss the impacts that each of the ideals of care have on citizenship.

Table 8.6 Ideals of care and citizenship

	Full-time motherhood	Parental sharing	Intergenerational care	Professional care	Surrogate mother
Who cares	Mother (f)	Parents (m/f)	Grandmothers (f)	Professionals (m/f)	Quasi mother (f)
Where	Home	Home	Home and quasi-home	Outside the home	Home/quasi-home
Consequences for women's employment	Low	High in numbers, low in volume, high in part time	Low for grandmothers (45 plus), high for daughters	High full time	Moderate
Consequences for women's income	Low	Medium, interdependency	Low for older generations, high for younger generations	High	High for working mothers, low for surrogate mothers
Consequences for participation in caregiving	High for women, low for men	Medium for men and women	High for older generation, low for younger generation	Low for parents	High for surrogate mothers, low for working mothers, low for fathers
Potentially degendering caring	No	Yes	No (yes)	Yes	No

Full-time Mother Care

As has been well-documented, the consequences of the ideal of full-time motherhood is that it reinforces women's second-class citizenship. The ideal is built upon the notion that a mother needs to care full time for her children. No time is left for working outside the home and paid employment is considered harmful for those in need of care. This leaves women financially dependent on men. Men on the other hand have little potential to be involved in caregiving. While women are locked in the private sphere, men are locked out. Thus this ideal reinforces caring as a feminine phenomenon and is extensively based on partner dependencies. Household dependencies are common. Since this has been well documented and the ideal is slowly fading away, the consequences of the other ideals are more interesting to investigate. By and large the other four ideals of caring have developed as alternatives to the ideal of full-time motherhood.

The ideal of the surrogate mother as well as that of intergenerational care, which will be discussed first, come closest to the ideal of full-time motherhood: they do not contest caring as a gendered phenomenon, yet both models give opportunities to certain categories of women.

Surrogate Mothers

The ideal of the surrogate mother, in practice often a childminder, allows other women – often highly educated – to take up paid employment and become financially independent. The ideal is thus based on hierarchal class dependencies between women. Gregson and Lowe (1994) describe the phenomenon of the surrogate mother as 'servicing the middle classes', and O'Connor et al. (1999: 35) speak about better-off women 'off-loading' care work onto other women of less-advantaged social status (for example immigrants and poor women).

In all countries this book focuses on, highly educated women are indeed more likely to use formal childcare, thus also childminding. In the UK childminders are less educated and wages are extremely low, between 1 and 3.5 pounds per hour per child in the late 1990s (Day Care Trust 1998). Dutch and Flemish research nevertheless shows that within these regimes class differences are less pronounced. In Flanders, the surrogate mothers are not women with little or no education; many have an average level of education. Some are even trained as caregivers, often in the health care sector (Werkgroep Vlaamse Diensten voor Opvanggezinnen 1992). Interestingly, these surrogate mothers are particularly sought after by lower middle-class parents. Highly educated as well as much less educated women prefer childcare centres (family day care) (Vanpée et al. 2000). In that sense, lower middle-class women are 'servicing' other women of the same social strata. Moreover, the money that *onthaalmoeders* receive is not negligible, as for a long time they did not have to pay tax and premiums. When they care for four children, income is quite substantial and excedes the rate of pay earned by professional childcare workers. Most of them enjoy the freedom of being self-employed and see themselves as entrepreneurs (Werkgroep Vlaamse Diensten voor Opvanggezinnen 1992).

A study by Nievers (2002) also shows that Dutch surrogate mothers are less dependent on the family they work for than the family is on them. Due to scarcity of childminders and the intense relationship between the caregiver and the parents' child, parents are very dependent on the childminder. In fact, the Dutch (unregulated) childminders are not really 'mothers' but 'grandmothers'. These older women are literally 'grey ladies', especially because they are not poor – their husbands often earn a decent living. In fact, the childminder's family can even be more well-off than the family she works for. As in Flanders, a class divide in caring should not be exaggerated. Because of the inverse dependency relation, Niever's study is aptly entitled 'We Have to Cherish Her'.

However, what is at stake in both countries is women's citizenship. Although this has recently changed in Flanders, surrogate mothers were completely dependent on their partner for security. Day care mothers did not pay any social security premiums. Since they were not considered to be professionals but to be mothers who have expanded their caregiving activities, they had no social rights. The ideal of the surrogate mother assumes that these 'mothers' are dependent on their husbands.

The practice of the ideal of the surrogate mother has thus important consequences for the citizenship potential of certain categories of women. In addition, as with the ideal of full-time mothering, the consequences of its moral undertones are strong. The ideal of the surrogate mother perpetuates the notion that caregiving is a feminine phenomenon and is best performed in the home, preferably by someone who resembles the mother. Professionalisation of care is no issue here. The underlying assumption is that care is still best performed by the mother: other types of care are always surrogate. This legitimises a low citizenship status for carers and legitimises the moral notion that for children, the mother should be at home if possible. Surrogate mothers are nearly as good as real mothers, but the idea of childminders being second-best constantly puts a moral pressure, the pressure of guilt, on working mothers. In other words, the ideal of the surrogate mother reinforces the norm that the appropriate behaviour for mothers is still to be at home.

This helps to explain one of the main puzzles raised in this book. Why don't Belgian mothers participate more in the labour market, given that their welfare state so closely resembles the Danish state? The level of childcare is also equal to the Swedish, yet Belgian mothers have lower rates of employment. The 'light theory' of ideals of care thus argues that this relates to the type of childcare being offered – the fact that Flemish policy has promoted the ideal of the surrogate mother for a long time. This ideal projects the moral message that mothers still care best for their children. This has contributed to an incremental increase of mothers' employment. As soon as institutional barriers for part-time work were lifted in Belgium, mothers reduced their working hours. Full-time work is less of an option for working women if in the end mothers are perceived to be the take the best care of their children. This is emphasised by the ideal of intergenerational care, which is also strong in Belgium.

Intergenerational Care

Like the ideal of the surrogate mother, the ideal of intergenerational care also does not degender caring. This ideal maintains that care is best performed in the home, by someone who resembles the mother most, and that is her mother. Daughters or daughters-in-law on the other hand, are thought to be the best caregivers when parents grow old. This ideal perpetuates notions of care and gendered citizenship: children and the elderly are best cared for at home by a woman, preferably by a family member whose care stems from feelings of benevolent love. An important difference from the ideal of the surrogate mother is that this ideal does not directly reinforce class differentials but generational differences between women (although it does so indirectly). The generation of 'daughters' is much more able to participate in the labour market and be economically independent than the generation of 'mothers' and 'grandmothers', but less likely to be able to participate in caregiving. This may also lead to strong dependencies within the extended family.

These generational differences are somewhat visible in the employment statistics of older women in the four countries. In 2000, just 15 percent of Belgian women aged 55-65 were employed, in the Netherlands 26 percent, in Denmark 46 percent and in the UK 41 percent (Eurostat 2001b). Of course, older women's employment rates relate to many factors, such as their past careers or pension policy. British rates, in contrast to the other countries, do not fit the intergenerational practice. Older British women are involved in childcare but they nevertheless work. At the same time there is some evidence that grandmothers in the UK are more eager to stop working or work less because they want to care for their grandchildren, not only because they want to support their daughters in their labour market earnings but also because they very much enjoy providing care. They see it as a reward in and of itself or feel that it is a second chance at parenting that will keep them 'young at heart and fit in mind and body'; it is a form of a 'social career' (Weelock and Jones 2002).

The ideal of intergenerational care does have some indirect class effects. In most countries, the provision of regular informal care by relatives, particularly grandparents, increases with decreasing social class (La Valle et al. 2000; Vanpée et al. 2000; Remery et al. 2000). Flemish research, for instance, shows that particularly less-educated parents and parents with less money are happy with care provided by grandmothers. Highly educated parents instead are more hesitant: they fear the problem of spoiling , a problem that grandparents readily admit that they contribute to. Grandmothers living in rural areas are more involved in caregiving than those living in the big cities (Hedebouw and Sannen 2002). The regional factor is again important in understanding differences between women (Vanpée et al. 2000), and categories of class still matter.

Lone working mothers are also strongly dependent on informal sources of childcare, particularly on grandparents in many of the countries, but especially in the UK and the Netherlands (e.g., Ford 1996; Storms 1995; Knijn and van Wel 1999). This is certainly another consequence of economic concerns as it is the cheapest solution available, but as Ford (1996) argues, it is also their wish, not in the least because the grandmother can substitute the role of the absent father. One lone mother quoted by Ford says of her mother: 'I do involve her a lot, because his dad's not involved' (1996: 122). The other side of the coin, according to the same study, is that informal arrangements require a great deal of attention and create the feeling that another person is doing you a favour, while at the same time lone parents need the stability and continuous care of a trustworthy person such as a family member.

Intergenerational care has consequences for women's work because on the one hand it allows daughters to work but at the same time does not degender caregiving. As grandfathers and fathers are hardly involved, it reinforces the motherhood norm. In that sense it does not fit well with a high level of full-time female employment. But there are other reasons why intergenerational care does not facilitate full-time work for women. As Brannen and Moss (1991) explain, women who depend on informal care become considerably indebted to relatives who look after their children. Full-time workers do not have time to 'pay back' informal caregivers.

Professional Care

The next two ideals, professional care and parental sharing, could be considered to be from a different planet than the ideals discussed above. They contest the notion that caring is best performed by 'mothers'. These two ideals do challenge the notion that childcare by 'other people' is a necessary evil. Professional care or parental sharing are positive alternatives to full-time mother care and are considered to improve the upbringing of children.

The ideal of professional care means that all women, both as mothers and as professionals, can achieve the possibility of working and being relatively economically independent. Professional care corresponds with universalism. In theory, the notion of professional care has the potential to degender caring, as professionals can also be men. In practice they hardly ever are. Few men are involved as professional childcarers, even in Denmark (OECD 2001).

Professional care means that care is valued, as it is paid for, but it may also result in citizens having less time to care for their loved ones. Professional care as an ideal implies that care performed by a professional – a pedagogue, a nurse, a home carer, or a teacher – is just as good or even better than care for the elderly or children provided at home by a mother or daughter. This significantly changes the traditional logic of what is appropriate, legitimising women's entry into the labour market, as it may even be viewed as better for the children when professionals rather than family members are primarily responsible. In fact, it is the only ideal in which women receive moral support to work full-time. The ideal of professional care significantly reduces the guilt felt by employed parents.

Finally, professional care reduces intergenerational family dependencies as well as partner dependencies. Women can work full time and can earn a professional-level salary. This gives a large group of women the possibility to develop themselves professionally and receive concomitant wages and recognition as workers. It also enhances the financial position of these female workers, although care work always pays less than other types of jobs.

Denmark is the icon of the ideal of professional care: this ideal is strongly embedded in both policy and practice. The ideal of professional care in Denmark and the relative lack of it in Belgium, the Netherlands, and the UK may explain why this is the only country in which mothers not only have high employment rates but also have moved, and are still moving, towards full-time work. Even though many parents say they want to spend more time with their children, there is in fact little need for it, as childcare is as professional as they want it. The underlying idea is that during the day a child is better-off at a care centre than at home, because this helps the child to become a real social being, a social citizen. This light theory of professional care implies that as soon as other welfare states promote a professionalisation strategy for young children, mothers' employment will increase, but only if the content of the care fits the wishes of parents.

Two places are therefore particularly interesting at the moment and should be monitored. In Flanders, the quasi-state organisation Kind en Gezin and the Flemish government are investing in professionalisation, as described in this and previous chapters. If this strategy proves successful, in a decade or so there is a big chance that mothers will work more and move again towards full-time work. In the UK, the ideal of professional care is now being stressed for children over age three. The key theme is education, which is rather different from the Danish social pedagogical goals. Such an ideal of care may legitimate mothers of children over three to enter the labour market. At the same time, it may imply a barrier for mothers with younger children, as it may stress that professional childcare is only good for older children. These two cases offer good test cases of this light theory. Future research may show whether they support this theory.

Parental Sharing

The ideal of parental sharing also strongly contests the ideal of full-time motherhood. It assumes that children are better cared for when both parents are involved. Sharing the parenting duties means that fathers are involved in caring and are also valued for their (specific) input in raising the child. Since fathers then have to reduce their labour market participation, they become more economically dependent on their partner. At the same time, women are more likely to participate in the labour market and become less economically dependent on their male partner. All in all, parental sharing is based on partner dependencies, but in contrast to the male breadwinner model it departs from interdependency between partners simultaneously on all levels: work, care, and income.

The Netherlands is certainly the test case for such a hypothesis. What are the practical consequences of such an ideal? It is indeed no coincidence that so few Dutch mothers work full time. Parental sharing stresses that children need to be cared for in a home environment and spend more time with their parents. The problem is that fathers are less adaptive to the model. The ideal of parental sharing often turns out to be the junior model in reality, although Dutch parental leave for public employees has been very successful in attracting fathers because this leave is well paid. The caveat of the ideal is that women's citizenship is entirely dependent on the hope that men will do more in the home. But if he doesn't want to participate in caregiving, or the household income does not allow him to, what happens to a woman's aspirations? Perhaps the woman will not be able to work as much as she would like to.

The ideal of parental sharing can also result in two distinctions between women. The first is between highly and less-educated women. Highly educated women are more likely to partner with a man who works part time, or are more able to persuade their partners to work full time. Highly educated parents practice the ideal of parental sharing more often; nearly 17 percent of highly educated couples with children share childcare duties, while as many as half of them prefer this model (Knijn and van Wel 2001a; Portegijs et al. 2002).

Second, lone mothers have less to gain with the ideal of parental sharing than married women. Lone mothers have no one with whom to share caring duties. In the Netherlands, the combination scenario lies at the heart of emancipation policy. It assumes a certain level of childcare services (though not too high), a 32-hour job, the financial sharing of childcare costs, and economic interdependency between partners. While these assumptions may be inadequate for married mothers, they certainly are for lone mothers. Lone mothers in fact may be supported more by another ideal of care, that of professional care. It is no coincidence that employment rates as well as poverty rates for example for Danish lone mothers, where professional childcare is more widely available, are better than the Dutch (chapter 4).

Care Ideals and Citizenship

This light theory of ideals of care and its consequences for gendered citizenship can be summarised as follows: parental sharing and professional care share the ideal that women should enter the labour market. Paid employment is regarded as positive and care has the potential to be degendered, i.e., men are also considered to be good caregivers as either sons, fathers, or professionals. This opens up a space to challenge the logic of appropriateness and legitimises different types of behaviour. While parental sharing assumes partner interdependencies and strongly correlates to part-time work, the notion of professional care goes along with full-time employment. In other words, parental sharing cannot be combined, practically or morally, with full-time labour for both men and women while professional care cannot be combined with much time to care.

In the other two models, surrogate mothers and intergenerational care, mothers remain at the heart of care. This does change the logic of appropriateness somewhat, but not the gendered notion of caring. In the end, it may even reinforce rather than contest the ideal of full-time motherhood since it implicitly reproduces gendered notions of care. This has huge consequences for gendered citizenship. The women who work as caregivers are often fully dependent on their husbands. In the case of grandmothers they are dependent on their husbands for income, while for surrogate mothers they are dependent for social security. While the ideal of the surrogate mother may produce class differences between women, especially in liberal regimes, generational differences are produced by the ideal of intergenerational care.

Conclusion: The Moral Impact of Welfare States

This chapter shows that welfare states are more than a set of financial structures that limit and provide people's choices, as comparative welfare state theories assume. Seemingly neutral procedures and structures embody particular values, norms, interests, identities, and beliefs. Social policy – through regulations, financial measures, and the content of provisions – influences the normative structures that provide people with choices and also limit those choices.

Considering ideals of care contributes towards an understanding of the changes in as well as the cultural consequences of welfare states. When women have babies they do not reach for a calculator to decide whether they will work or not: they ask themselves, what would be the most appropriate way to care for my child when I am away? If this type of care is in place, women are more likely to work. Ideals of care provide the answer to the moral predicament of work and care. Women do not or cannot follow their individual care preferences. Women, more than men, are adaptive to the different ideals promoted in welfare states. In other words, there is a close link between the ideals of care promoted in social policy, as described in the previous chapter, and real practice.

Finally, specific ideals of care produce differences in women's citizenship across countries. The dominance of the ideal of professional care in Denmark, for instance, has been a crucial vehicle for mothers' full-time employment. It has been a very effective ideal for reducing guilt: why would women stay at home when their children are better-off together with other children, guided by professionals? The dominance of the ideal of intergenerational care and in particular the surrogate mother in Flemish social policy helps to explain why mothers there do not continue to work full time. The type of care promoted by the state has helped women enter the labour market but at the same time sends the message that the most appropriate care for children is that provided by a child's own mother. No wonder that Belgian mothers' employment levels do not match those of Danish mothers and that part-time work has become more popular, even though childcare is fully available and affordable. Welfare states are thus still a source of moral authority.

9 Conclusion: Care and the Cultural Dimension of Welfare States

For women, welfare states matter. But they matter in a different way than is often assumed. Welfare state scholars often presume that diversity in women's employment across Europe is based on financial (dis)incentive structures embedded in welfare states. In other words: if childcare is available and affordable, most mothers will work. If tax and benefit schemes have no financial employment obstructions, women will work. Welfare states are captured as structures of financial incentives and disincentives (e.g., Esping-Andersen 1990, 1999; 2002; Lewis 1992a, 1997b; Sainsbury 1996, 1999; O'Connor et al. 1999; Daly and Rake 2003). Policymakers at European as well as national levels also argue along those lines. It is no coincidence that 'financial incentives' have been the keywords in European welfare state restructuring. The crucial task has been minimising (financial) traps so that people are encouraged to work.

This book shows that such an approach cannot sufficiently explain the gendered division of labour and care and the most recent changes in the four countries of this study: Denmark, Belgium, the Netherlands, and the UK. Instead, welfare state analysis would improve by making use of the concepts of culture and care. Both concepts come together to form the explanatory notion of 'ideals of care'.

Puzzles

This book shows that there is no simple correlation between the design of welfare states and women's employment. Take the British case. British mothers have the lowest employment rates of all four countries. In 2003, only 52 percent of mothers (of children aged 0-3) worked compared to the Netherlands (70 percent), Belgium (63 percent) and Denmark (72 percent) (Eurostat 2005; chapter 4). At the same time, given the financial structures of the welfare state more British mothers are expected to work. The British tax regime has a long history of being favourable towards working women. In addition, benefits are comparatively low: both the insurance scheme and social assistance produce the highest poverty rates of all countries (chapter 5). British mothers are thus financially encouraged to work. Still, mothers have not taken up paid employment to the same extent as in the other countries. Indeed, the availability and cost of childcare are also important factors in terms of whether mothers will work, and childcare in the UK is particularly expensive (chapter 6). Even taking this into account, British mothers would be financially better-off working, yet they do not enter the labour market en *masse*.

A similar story holds when comparing Dutch and British lone mothers. Many of them receive social assistance. After a cost-and-benefit analysis they would still be financially better-off working, but employment rates in both countries are similarly low. In 1999, only 38 percent of lone mothers (with children 0-6) worked in the Netherlands and 34 percent in the UK (OECD 2001; chapter 4). So why don't they work more?

Take also the comparison between the other two countries of this study, the Danish and Belgian welfare states. Danish mothers' employment rates have always been higher than the Belgian – not only today but also in the early 1990s, when 61 percent of Belgian mothers and 70 percent of Danish mothers with a child under age three worked (chapter 4). In both countries mothers have always been more likely to work full time. More recently, however, Belgian mothers increasingly work part time, while Danish mothers increasingly work full time. Welfare state analysts point out that the Belgian welfare state is of the conservative or Christian-democratic brand: it discourages mothers from working (Esping-Andersen 1990, 1999; Gornick et al. 1997; Sainsbury 1999a; Cantillon et al. 1999). If we look more closely, the way welfare states care is more similar than expected.

Let us consider whether caring is financially compensated. Not only in Belgium but surprisingly in Denmark too, a system of fiscal care theoretically supports caregivers to stay at home. They both include a 'single breadwinner bonus' (chapter 5). The benefit system also shows similarities – at least until the mid-1990s. At that time in Denmark the onus was on the duty (and right) to work. Before that, Danish mothers could use unemployment benefits to stay at home if they wanted to do so. Access to unemployment insurance was good and control negligible, but mothers did not use benefits to stay at home (at least not on a large scale). In Belgium, where women also had high access to unemployment benefit, this was used as a 'wage for bringing up children'. When in 1991 this possibility was reduced and financial compensation was cut, women did not go out to work, they withdrew from the labour market (De Lathouwer et al. 2003). Moreover, both Danish and Belgian parents have the possibility of paid parental leave, although it is true that until recently Belgian leave could be longer, while in Denmark more rights were attached to leave and it was better paid (chapter 5). Still, these rights to care cannot explain the substantial differences between both countries.

Childcare services may then be more important for explaining women's employment levels, but in both countries childcare is well available and affordable. In Denmark, as the regime typologies predict, 56 percent of children under age three used state-subsidised childcare in 1999. This is 41 percent of young children. Flemish childcare services – unlike what is expected in such a regime – reached Scandinavian levels and are similar to Swedish rates. Both countries are in the top rank of the 'childcare league' (Bradshaw and Finch 2002; chapter 6).

Comparative welfare regime theories can thus not fully explain why employment rates for Belgian mothers are lower than the Danish. It cannot explain recent changes either: why do Belgian mothers increasingly work part-time (chapter 4)? Given such a high level of childcare, it is surprising that there are not more Belgian mothers working, and working more hours. Comparative welfare regime theories also cannot explain why Dutch mothers work more than Belgian mothers nowadays, while historically Dutch women hardly worked (Pott-Buter 1996; Plantenga 1996).

The Welfare State as a Cultural Catalyst

Welfare state analysis has difficulties explaining these cross-national differences. This is not just empirical 'noise', as the countries studied are representative of the dominant explanatory welfare regime models (Esping-Andersen 1990, 1999, 2002; Lewis 1992a). One of the reasons why such welfare analysis falls short is because it is based on inadequate assumptions about the way mothers decide how much to work or to provide care. The comparative welfare regime approach is often implicitly and sometimes unintentionally based on an image of *homo economicus*, for want of something better. Micro-level studies (Hochschild 1989, 2003; Duncan and Edwards 1999; Duncan et al. 2004; Finch and Mason 1993; Knijn and van Wel 1999) show that mothers' actions are not primarily based on economic cost-and-benefit analyses. They do not base their decision-making exclusively on the financial costs of childcare nor on the financial (dis)incentives embedded in tax and benefit policy. In other words, a mother is not primarily the *homo economicus* welfare state scholars tend to presume. 'To work or to care' is above all a moral predicament.

As care responsibilities are gendered, women in particular are concerned about what happens to care when they take up paid employment. Hence for women's decisions about work, care is crucial. This means that women are more likely to engage in paid employment when they find a solution for care, but this solution should fit their notions of what good care is (see also Lewis 2003). European mothers only take up a job when they are satisfied with the solution for childcare. Good quality childcare – which suits their view of what constitutes satisfactory care – is a necessary condition for going to work.

A more suitable approach towards understanding women's decisions is therefore to study what March and Olsen (1989) call 'the logic of appropriateness'. Women's (and men's) human actions are based on what they think is most appropriate in a given context. This is also a very different point of departure of human behaviour than the 'preference person'. According to Hakim (2000, 2003a), women's preferences can only explain diversity and change in Europe. Danish women work more because they want to work, British women work less because they want to care. Hakim argues that individuals pursue their own life goals and that this leads to diversity within Europe. Indeed, micro-level studies show that women make active decisions about work and care and that these decisions are rational. They are also relational however and people take into account moral considerations. The *homo complex* or *homo morales* which is adaptive to notions of appropriateness comes closer to the care reality than the image of human behaviour that only refers to preferences or financial motives.

Welfare state studies would thus gain if their focus did not lie exclusively on the structure of financial (dis)incentives, but on how welfare states influence the logic of appropriateness. Financial schemes are then studied as an indication of what is appropriate, while intentions behind policies, symbols, laws, and implementation practices are also taken into account. A welfare state is a moral agent, as Wolfe (1989) rightly suggests. Even the most liberal welfare state – in this book the UK – is not neutral. Welfare states send culturally defined moral messages. A state is not only a lawyer drawing up contracts between citizens and between citizens and the state, or a merchant connecting supply and demand, but also a priest trying to give people an interpretation of the world and of the most appropriate behaviour in a specific context. Of course, not everybody listens to the state, as not everybody listens to a priest. In democratic systems, citizens themselves also influence which images states can promote. Its symbols and scripts are nevertheless important in people's daily lives. In Western European societies the state is still a crucial moral institution (see also Rothstein 1998).

This means that we have to bring sociology, and more specifically cultural theories, back into the study of welfare states. However, the problem is that cultural theories – those put forward by Hakim (1998, 2000, 2003) as well as by Pfau-Effinger (1998, 1999) – tend to downplay the role of the welfare state in their theoretical frameworks, and locate culture primarily as a power that radiates from below. But the welfare state is not something that is the opposite of or separate from culture. Culture is located *within* rather than outside the welfare state (see also van Oorschot 2003; Clarke 2004).

Ideals of Care

This book presents a cultural analysis of welfare states. In the case of caring and paid employment, welfare states send culturally-defined moral images of satisfactory care in the form of ideals of care. An ideal of care implies a definition of what is good care and who gives it. These ideals of care are embedded in welfare states and their regulations, laws, and implementation processes. Each welfare state promotes specific ideals of care, which change over time.

Reading the childcare policies and care practices in the four countries, five ideals can be traced. As in a cultural analysis (Pfau-Effinger 1998), these ideals compete with each other, but in one country only one or two are dominant. The first ideal is that of *full-time motherhood*, which was in place after the Second World War in most West European welfare states. This ideal is no longer hegemonic (Lewis 1997a). When women entered the labour market, new ideals arose or old ones were revived.

The second ideal is that of the *surrogate mother*. According to this model, good care is still best provided by *a* mother, even if it is not *the* mother of the children. Care is provided by a childminder, babysitter, or family member and because it is offered in the caregiver's home, it most closely resembles home-based care. Surrogate mothers are considered to have the same kind of qualities that mothers have – motherly warmth, attention, and patience – but they remain substitutes.

The third ideal is *parental sharing*. This model is based on the assumption that men are able to care for children just as well as women. Advocates for this model sometimes go so far as to argue that an increase in fathers' care would be better for children. Another line of reasoning is that it would be more just for women, who now also work outside the home, if men took up some of their responsibilities. This increases gender equality. Parental sharing is rooted in two ideas: that both the care provided at home and paid employment should be shared, and thus both partners work on a part-time basis. The ideal of parental sharing is subversive because it degenders caregiving.

The ideal of *intergenerational care* is based on the notion that the first generation (grandmothers) cares for the third generation (children). In return, the second generation (the daughters who are now mothers) will care for the grandparents when they age. This is not just a calculated system of family exchange. It also guarantees good childcare in the eyes of the parents, because who could care better than the mother's mother? She is not only experienced and can be trusted more than anyone else, she will also love the children the most. The ideal of intergenerational care is not gendered in theory, but still is in practice. Grandmothers, daughters, daughters-in-law, and granddaughters are the ones most likely to provide care.

The ideal of *professional care* strongly contests the ideal of full-time motherhood because it maintains that professionals provide a different type of care than that provided by mothers, but offer something extra that should still be a part of every child's upbringing. Professional care is sometimes considered to be even better than parental care, as it offers professional guidance to children and socialises them. In the model of professional care, the education of professionals guarantees quality. Professional care often takes place in childcare centres or is part of the educational system, and its purpose is defined in various ways: to improve children's welfare, enhance their development, socialise them, or prepare them for school or for the labour market. Crucial to the ideal of professional care is the fact that caregivers are educated and are accountable in a professional way.

Care ideals are a detailed instrument to capture an often too broadly and vaguely defined notion of culture and gender culture. Culture is most poorly described with a few nouns like traditions, values, beliefs, norms, and practices. At best, culture is defined as shared values legitimating different patterns of social practices (Freeman and Rustin 1999; Inglis 2004). Gender culture is not a very useful concept either, at least when it only refers to the dilemma of whether women want to work or want to care, as it usually does. Surveys often ask people to respond to statements like 'being a housewife is just as fulfilling as working for pay' or 'a working mother can have an equally intimate relation with her children as a mother who does not work' (Halman 1999/2000; Kalmijn 2003). This is also how Pfau-Effinger (1998) tries to capture gender culture. The answers to such surveys however, do not correspond with employment practices (Hakim 2003b).

This book argues that what provides the most insight into women's and men's changing employment and care patterns is not an analysis of whether or not women want to work, but of what is considered to be the most appropriate form of childcare when mothers are at work. Studying ideals of care can provide more detailed information than more general notions of 'gender culture'. One can throw further using a small stone.

Care Ideals and Citizenship

How do ideals of care affect gendered citizenship? The 'light theory' of care ideals helps to explain the cross-national differences and changes in women's and men's gendered division of work, care, and income in three ways. First, this study shows that without state support of an alternative ideal for full-time motherhood, women's employment would be hampered. Up until a certain level of employment, women – sometimes together with men – will be able to make their own arrangements. To put it differently, state investments in childcare are important but they are not a necessary condition towards increasing mothers' employment. If employment rates 'need' to go beyond a specific level, such as the Lisbon target of 60 percent of women in employment by 2010, state intervention becomes decisive in meeting that goal. Such logic is not only visible in the four countries of this study but also in Spain, Norway, and Italy, as Leira et al. (2005) show.

This study shows that welfare state support is not only a necessary condition in practical terms but is also needed to fill a moral void. Only when a new care ideal has been put in place will full-time motherhood become outdated and mothers will enter the labour market. After the full-time motherhood norm, an alternative ideal of care supported by welfare policies is an important pre-condition for mothers' employment on a large scale. A parallel can be drawn with Kuhn's (2003, or 1962) description of paradigm shifts: a new paradigm helps dismantle the previous.

The British case illustrates what happens when a welfare state does not promote an alternative care ideal, and there is no new 'logic of appropriateness'. While British women – more than in Belgium and the Netherlands – have always been financially encouraged to work (see the work incentives in taxation), they have not entered the labour market *en masse*. The problem is that for a long time, during the 18 years of Conservative dominance, no appropriate alternative for care was presented. Support for care policy was off the agenda. If the Conservatives had any ideal of care it was that of surrogate motherhood in the form of childminders, but they promoted childminders as a solution for care while parents increasingly distrusted them. The promoted ideal of care has to fit the image that citizens, or more precisely that parents have of 'appropriate care'. Otherwise the ideal will be very short-lived, like that of the British childminders (chapters 7, 8). It is thus an important insight into the cultural approach towards welfare states that the norms of parents matter a great deal, as policy has to fit parent's preferences (Pfau-Effinger 1998, 1999; Hakim 2000, 2003).

The story of the UK is much different than those of the other three countries. In Denmark the ideal of professional care reflected a kind of care that parents felt was appropriate and was promoted by social policies for several decades, while in Flanders the ideal of the surrogate mother and intergenerational care have been the most dominant alternatives since the 1980s, although the first is also undergoing change. In the Netherlands, since the 1990s parental sharing has been the governmental ideal, supported by many parents. Unlike the British case, in the past decades an appropriate ideal of care was established in the Netherlands, one that fit with parents' wishes.

Secondly, some ideals of care perpetuate gendered notions of care while other ideals are more subversive. In other words, the ideal of the surrogate mother and intergenerational care perpetuate the gendering of care. The more gendered the caring, the more difficult it is for mothers to justify taking on paid employment. Surrogate mothers, often but not always childminders, are considered to have the same kind of qualities mothers have – motherly warmth, attention, patience – but they remain substitutes. This means that it remains preferable for children to receive motherly warmth and attention provided by their real mother. The same story applies to intergenerational care. This is not just a neutral, calculated system of family exchange, it is also based on the normative assumption that childcare is best performed by the mother's mother.

Care in both ideals is still assigned to mothers. If such images of appropriate care were supported in public policy, not all mothers would want to work, and certainly not for long hours. These gendered notions of care hamper mothers' (full-time) employment. As soon as it is possible

– financially or career-wise – mothers would want to spend more time with their children. Hence the lower employment rates of Belgian mothers compared to the Danish (and recently to the Dutch), as well as the tendency to move towards part-time jobs. The kind of care promoted in the Belgian welfare state – intergenerational as well as surrogate motherhood – attracts women to work less rather than more.

Parental sharing and professional care, on the other hand, can theoretically degender caregiving. Parental sharing assumes fathers will be more involved in caring duties and mothers less so. It assumes a decrease of fathers' working hours and an increase of mothers' employment. Women and men become interdependent. The Dutch welfare state promotes such an ideal. The 'combination scenario' is based on the idea that when men work less, women work more. Indeed, the ideal of parental sharing has paved the way for mothers' spectacular entrance into the Dutch labour market. Since the ideal of parental sharing disconnects women from being the only person responsible for caring, mothers have also started to work.

At the same time, this study shows that the ideal of parental sharing has difficulty coming into practice fully (in any country). The actual consequence of parental sharing is that it reinforces the notion that full-time work is not appropriate, and women are especially sensitive to this moral message. Women, not men, are more likely to work on a part-time basis. In other words – ironically – women are more adaptive to the ideal of parental sharing than men. The caveat of the ideal of parental sharing is thus that it takes two to share. On the other hand, Dutch men are slightly more likely to shoulder care responsibilities than elsewhere. The promotion of parental sharing thus has had some impact on men's behaviour – albeit more watered-down – than is promoted in the Netherlands.

Professional care, supported and practiced in Denmark, is the best 'guilt-reduction strategy' for working mothers and stimulates them to work full-time. Only the ideal of professional care goes hand in hand with high full-time employment rates for mothers. This ideal assumes that children are best-off when they are cared for by professionals who are highly educated and that such care contributes to the upbringing of children. Danish childcare workers are the most highly educated among such workers in all four countries. These professionals are seen as able to do things that parents cannot: they can raise children to be social citizens. This also means that it is not appropriate to take care of children at home. In Denmark, the ideal of professional care has released parents from heavy care responsibilities. It has made full-time employment for both fathers and mothers fully legitimate. Danish parents do not have to work to make ends meet. They work the number of hours they do because childcare is not only available and affordable, it is also professional. It offers the child more than when mothers stay at home to provide care.

Finally, specific ideals affect different categories of women. Women are to often seen as one category. The ideal of intergenerational care limits the possibility of women of the older generation to be involved in paid employment or even gives them a double burden. Especially in Belgium and the UK, older women are heavily involved in caring for their grandchildren, which limits their employment careers. The ideal of the surrogate mother also supports (higher) middle-class womens' working but reduces the citizenship of childminders, who often lack social security rights and earn little. It assumes that these women are dependent on their husbands. In some countries, notably the UK, the ideal of surrogate motherhood reveals class differences. Interestingly, this is not the case in Flanders or the Netherlands, where surrogate mothers are more often middle-class (chapter 8). Moreover, the ideal of parental sharing is not very useful to lone mothers as they have no one with whom to share care duties. They may need a different ideal of care, for instance that of professional care. Hence the low employment rates of Dutch and British women. The ideal of professional care brings employment opportunities to all women. It does not exclude certain categories of women. Therefore the Danish employment rates for women have been the highest in Europe.

Analysis from the perspective of care ideals not only helps to understand changes in womens' employment during the last two to three decades but also helps us to understand the many anomalies and puzzles of the welfare states presented in this book. Welfare states do matter for the gendered division of labour, care, and income, but we can only understand how they matter when we add a cultural dimension to the analysis. As the comparative welfare regime approach rightly shows, the welfare state is an important catalyst for women's participation in work – although less for men's participation in care. It is especially a cultural catalyst. The role of the state is pivotal for women's participation in the labour market, much more so than cultural theories would have us think.

Such a cultural welfare state approach also questions the effectiveness of employment policy that is dominant in Europe. In Lisbon, the European leaders came together to set targets for women's and men's employment rates. If Europe wants to hold the broad ambition of solidarity with the needy, now and in the future, it needs more growth and more people at work, argued the high-level group formed to review the Lisbon strategy

(European Communities 2004: 12). This book shows that it is no easy task to raise (all) women's employment rates across Europe. Simply changing the financial incentive structures of social policy is certainly not sufficient. Employment practices only change when ideals of care change. In other words, new employment patterns only arise when an 'appropriate' solution is found for care in each country.

The caveat is that this should fit the country-specific ideals of care that parents have. This may be a difficult conclusion, as at the same time this book shows that the ideal of professional care is more likely to result in the highest full-time employment rates for mothers compared to other ideals. It is most inclusive for all women and is the best strategy for reducing the guilt that mothers feel when leaving their children to go to work, yet this ideal may not be suitable for all European welfare states.

Origins of Welfare States

In this book welfare states are studied through a 'care lens'. This has shed new light on how welfare states work and how they affect people's lives. Another advantage of looking at caring states is that it helps to rethink the development and origins of welfare states. Are the stories of welfare states, often built upon an analysis of social security and workmen's protection, similar to the stories of caring states? It is now common to argue that welfare state austerity cannot be explained by the same theories as its erasure. Power resource theory is helpful in understanding the origins of social policy (Esping-Andersen 1990; O'Connor et al. 1999), whereas neo-institutionalism or 'the new politics' is helpful for understanding its recent history (Pierson 1994, 2001; Alber 1995).

This book shows that class-based power resources, especially the approach of the three welfare regimes, are useful as a heuristic frame but cannot fully explain the origins of and changes within care policy. We have come across many empirical anomalies and puzzles within the regimes. As is well documented, in the liberal model of the UK caregivers are protected from market forces: caregivers such as lone mothers are offered specific benefits (chapter 5; see also Lewis 1992a; O'Connor et al. 1999). Less documented is that in the Danish case, a representative of the social democratic model, a single breadwinner bonus in taxation is still in place, although individualisation of taxation took place much earlier than in other countries. This is however not a trophy of the social democrats but of the liberals (chapter 5). More important however are the significant differences within the Christian democratic world. Flemish childcare levels are much higher than the Dutch; they almost reach Scandinavian levels. Why does a so-called Christian democratic welfare state invests nearly as much in childcare as social democratic regimes?

In addition, it is unclear whether specific ideologies have a direct effect on the 'women-friendliness' of welfare states. Liberalism or Christian democracy do not necessarily oppose women's right to work – on the contrary – while social democratic dominance does not necessarily promote women's citizenship. This is not only because the right to give care is often under pressure, but also because in each country social democrats have struggled with the question of what is more important, class or gender. In the Netherlands this is aptly labelled as the 'Mrs. Philips' dilemma – should this woman be viewed as the wife of a rich man or as an individual without beneficial ties (chapter 5)? In reality, in many countries gender tends to lose.

To understand differences in the origins and development of caring states, institutional factors are important. More useful for understanding Flemish childcare policy than the often-stressed concept of subsidiarity is the concept of free choice. In the Belgian context it means that the state should support both working women and those who want to stay at home. Such interpretation of free choice opposes its liberal interpretation, which stresses that choice does not need state intervention. The stress on state support for enabling choice is shaped by the Belgian institutional framework of pillarisation. The point of departure is that people should be able to choose their own schools, hospitals, and insurance according to their own background. This manner of societal organisation is vital for Belgium as a nation-state; it is necessary to keep rival ideologies, beliefs, and languages together (chapter 6).

Ideals of Care and Policy Origins

Care ideals are not only helpful for studying policy outcomes but also policy origins. Following the full-time motherhood norm, new ideals of care have been proposed. These new ideals are often a way out of the deadlocked situation in which mothers' interests are placed against children's. Institutional care was regarded as 'cold' while mother's care was considered to be 'warm'. Especially working women benefited from ending such moral debates. It is therefore no coincidence that alternative ideals of care were often proposed by women, although always in alliance with more powerful actors in the specific welfare regimes, such as the political party in government, professional organisations, women in trade unions, and newly-established client organisations such as those for parents. This was often an alliance between women within and outside women's groups.

It is therefore impossible to study the origins of care policy without including women's power resources and women's actions (Skocpol 1992; O'Connor et al. 1999; Naumann 2005). It was not only important whether women had power and their actions fit the institutional setting of a country (Skocpol 1992), but also what women (as collective agents) wanted (O'Connor et al. 1999; Naumann 2005). What has been the direction of the care dreams of the women's movement (in a broad sense): which ideal of care was considered appropriate when mothers went to work?

In the Netherlands, the ideal of parental sharing and the stress on part-time work can be traced back to the women's movement, which promoted the sharing of paid and unpaid work in alliance with women working in the pro-part-time trade union. In Denmark, professional care has been promoted by the women's movement along with the pedagogues. In Flanders, the ideal of the surrogate mother – in this case organised childminders – has been put forward by the Catholic Agrarian Women's Movement, which was supported by the Christian democratic party. In the UK, on the other hand, the women's movement distrusted the state as a service provider and was very hesitant to get involved in childcare policies (chapter 6).

This cultural welfare state approach borrows much from gender-based power resources: care policy is understood as the result of a political battle between normative ideals. Ideals of care that are promoted always counter other ideals (Billig 1991; Pfau-Effinger 1998). Welfare states are not composed of sedimented values. Social policy is not a mere reflection of culturally embedded ideals. Ideals have to be promoted by a powerful alliance to become embedded in social policy.

Finally, looking at which care ideal has been dominant also helps to understand the composition of welfare states, and especially to what degree investments took place in childcare services. Flemish childcare services are much more developed than in the Netherlands because the state largely invested in surrogate mothers. It invested in state-subsidised family day care – that is, mothers who receive pay but have no workers' rights. This is not only a cheap solution but also fits well with the Christian democratic ideology that stresses solidarity within the community, motherhood, and dependence within the family. State investments could then take place and lead to a top ranking in terms of European provision of childcare. In the Netherlands, investments in state-subsidised professional care were lower because of the emphasis on parental sharing. Children, according to this view, are best-off when fathers as well as mothers are involved in childcare. This is seen as a 'warm' solution.

In Denmark, by contrast, professional care is not considered to be 'cold'. In the 'people's home', the Scandinavian label of the state, it is 'warm'. Such an ideal of care is a pre-condition for the universalisation of childcare. When professional childcare is not seen as a 'pleasure' for working women but as important for the well-being of children, it is more logical that all children should have the right to professional childcare. Thus ideals of care also help to explain the content of the childcare policy in place, for instance how much state support takes place and whether childcare services are universal or targeted (chapter 7).

Looking Through the Lens of Caring

The study of welfare states – of origins and outcomes – benefits from taking into account caring, not only as a cultural and moral practice as described above but also as a normative point of departure and as a set of policies. Such an approach can also help to explain cross-national differences in gendered employment and income patterns (Anttonen and Sipilä 1996; Daly and Lewis 1998; Jenson and Sineau 2001; Daly 2002; Daly and Rake 2003; Anttonen et al. 2003; Bettio and Plantenga 2004).

The problem with many social policy studies are the concepts used to capture the outcomes of welfare states, such as de-commodification (Esping-Andersen 1990) or de-familialisation (Esping-Andersen 1999, 2002; Lister 1994; McLauglin and Glendinning 1996). These concepts position citizenship as being independent from either the market or the family. Considering care, both in terms of receiving and giving, not only questions notions of independence but also cuts through all boundaries: it has no assigned location. Care can be provided by states, markets, families, and by childminders (paid by the state or the parents), grandparents, fathers, mothers, or professionals. Most important for the citizenship of caregivers – who are primarily women – is under which conditions and terms care is given (chapter 2).

Looking at welfare states through the lens of care also forces us to rethink the normative concept of citizenship that is central to the study of welfare states. This book stresses that in a European conception of citizenship, care should be recognised in addition to work. This is important because care is part of living the life of a human being, it can contribute to human flourishing: people should also have the possibility to provide care. In addition, when care is valued well it may also lead to a degendering of care. This will increase gender equality as both women and men are freer to choose to work and/or to care. Finally, caregiving will be increasingly important in the light of aging societies and the socio-economic future of the welfare state.

In much welfare state analysis, and especially in social democratic and feminist traditions, care is often described as the work of Cinderella. Care is considered to be a burden that keeps women from working. The best solution is when the state takes over this 'unpaid work' and pays professionals for it. At the other end, the Christian democratic and communitarian traditions see caregivers as Snow Whites: caring is a joy, a moral attitude that spreads social cohesion. It is women's gift to society. People should take an example of this moral attitude. Citizens should not care less, but care more. Both care stories are fairytales. In the real world caring can go either way. Caring can be hard work, but also a pleasure. It can destroy family ties but also strengthen them. All depends on the conditions under which care is given and how much (moral) force is used.

When T.H. Marshall described the concept of citizenship he did not include care, but his definition of 'citizenship as participation in the community' easily allows for the inclusion of caregiving. Including care in the concept of citizenship means that people, both men and women, have a freer choice as to whether or not they want to care or not. Citizenship would then mean the right to care and the right not to care, but without locking a person into one activity. In other words, the right to give care as well as to receive care are important for modern welfare states. These rights indicate how welfare states care and under which terms care is provided (see also Knijn and Kremer 1997).

These rights are not utopian. Care is increasingly becoming part of citizenship in European welfare states (Daly 2002; Jenson and Sineau 2001; Anttonen et al. 2003). This book shows that the four welfare states have also given special attention to the right to receive care. In recent decades, childcare services expanded in all countries – although the headlines vary and so do the level of affordability and availability of care. Denmark is still the pioneer: all children older than age one now have the right to professional childcare services (chapter 6).

At the same time, the right to give care is under pressure. Parental leave can indeed be considered to be a genuine new care right that is gaining ground in all countries (chapter 5). But so far, it does not seem to compensate changes in social security. In many countries – the UK, the

Netherlands, and Belgium – implicit as well as explicit care rights existed which have now have been (partly) dismantled. The right to care lost out to the obligation to work (Lister 2003; Orloff 2006; chapter 5). In other words, participation in work – both as a right and a duty – has become the dominant translation of citizenship.

In *Why We Need a New Welfare State* Esping-Andersen et al. (2002) promote a new welfare architecture that actively supports mothers' employment, specifically by subsidising childcare. Working women are seen as the weapon against child poverty and the saviours of the economy and the welfare state. At the same time, women have to deliver more babies, as European birth rates are too low. Although this modern 'Beveridge plan' offers an important break from the traditional male breadwinner welfare state model, it raises some questions.

First of all, what are men supposed to do when women enter the labour market *en masse* and rescue the welfare state: sit back and wait? When women become more active outside the home, perhaps men can be asked to become – a little – more active inside the home. In Lisbon, EU targets were set to increase female workforce participation. No targets have been set for male care participation. But if women are expected to work *more*, should the Lisbon agreement not demand that men work *less*?

Time to care should not be a right for only one category of citizens. This right used to be confined to women only, but today both men and women want and need time to care. Wouldn't it be a missed opportunity if a European conception of citizenship only included the right to work and not the right to care? A modernised interpretation of citizenship needs to recognise caregiving in society.

Appendix I   Governments In Belgium, Denmark, The Netherlands and the UK 1980-2000

Table Ia	Governments in Belgium, 1980-2000		
	Prime minister	*Party composition*	*Character*
1979-1980	Martens I (CVP, Christian democrats)	Christian democrats (CVP/PSC) Social democrats (PS/SP) and FDP	Centre left
1980-1980	Martens II (CVP)	Christian democrats and Social democrats	Centre left
1980-1980	Martens III (CVP)	Christian democrats, Social democrats and Liberals	Mixed
1980-1981	Martens IV (CVP)	Christian democrats and Social democrats	Centre left
1981-1981	Eyskens (CVP)	Christian democrats and Social democrats	Centre left
1981-1985	Martens V (CVP)	Christian democrats and Liberals	Centre right
1985-1987	Martens VI (CVP)	Christian democrats and Liberals	Centre right
1987-1988	Martens VII (CVP)	Christian democrats and Liberals	Centre right
1988-1991	Martens VIII (CVP)	Christian democrats, Social democrats and People's party	Mixed
1991-1992	Martens IX (CVP)	Christian democrats, Social democrats	Centre left
1992-1995	Deheane I (CVP)	Christian democrats and Social democrats	Centre left
1995-1999	Deheane II (CVP)	Christian democrats and Social democrats	Centre left
1999-2003	Verhofstadt (Liberals)	Liberals, Social democrats, Green party	Mixed (rainbow coalition)

Source: Kuipers (2004), www.premier.fgov.be

Table Ib	Governments in Denmark, 1980-2000		
	Prime minister	*Party composition*	*Character*
1982-1984	Schlüter (Conservatives)	Conservatives, Liberals, Centre democrats, Christian people's party (minority)	Centre right
1984-1987	Schlüter (Conservatives)	Conservatives, Liberals, Centre democrats and Christian people's party (minority)	Centre right
1987-1988	Schlüter (Conservatives)	Conservatives, Liberals, Centre democrats and Christian people's party (minority)	Centre right
1988-1990	Schlüter (Conservatives)	Conservatives, Liberals and Social liberals (minority)	Centre right
1990-1993	Schlüter (Conservatives)	Conservatives and Liberals (minority)	Right
1993-1994	Nyrup Rasmussen (Social democrat)	Social democrats, Social liberals and Centre democrats, Christian people's party (majority)	Left
1994-1998	Nyrup Rasmussen (Social democrat)	Social democrats, Social liberals and Centre democrats (stepped out in 1996) (minority)	Left
1998-2001	Nyrup Rasmussen (Social democrat)	Social democrats and Social liberals (minority)	Centre Left
2001-	Fogh Rasmussen (Right-wing Liberals)	Liberals, Christian people's Party (minority)	Right

Note: In Denmark minority governments are possible and very common.
Source: Green-Pedersen (2000)

Table Ic   Governments in the Netherlands, 1980-2000

	Prime minister	Party composition	Character
1982-1986	Lubbers I (Christian democrats)	Christian democrats, Liberals	Right
1986-1989	Lubbers II (Christian democrats)	Christian democrats and Liberals	Right
1989-1994	Lubbers III	Christian democrats and Social democrats	Centre left
1994-1998	Kok I	Social democrats, Liberals and Social liberals	Mixed (Purple Coalition I)
1998-2001	Kok II	Social democrats, Liberals and Social liberals	Mixed (Purple Coalition II)

Table Id   Governments in the UK, 1980-2000

	Prime minister	Party composition	Character
1979-1983	Thatcher	Conservative	Right
1983-1987	Thatcher	Conservative	Right
1987-1990	Thatcher	Conservative	Right
1990-1992	Major	Conservative	Right
1992-1997	Major	Conservative	Right
1997-2001	Blair	Labour	Left

Source: O'Driscoll (2002)

Appendix II   List of Interviewees

Belgium

Interviews took place in spring and summer 1997

1. Bea Cantillon, director, Centre for Social Policy, University of Antwerp, UFSIA.
2. Agnes Bode, Family Services, Familiehulp, Catholic Organisation for Homehelp, Brussels.
3. Jef Breda, University of Antwerp/UFSIA, Antwerp.
4. Bea van Buggenhout, Catholic University Leuven, Leuven.
5. Bea Buysse, Research Office Child and Family (Studiedienst Kind and Gezin), Brussels.
6. Yvan Daelman together with Jannie Hespels, Thuishulp, Social Democratic Organisation for Home Help, Brussels.
7. Lieve De Lathouwer, Centre for Social Policy, University of Antwerp, UFSIA.
8. Christian Deneve, director, Research Office Ministry of Labour, Brussels.
9. Walter van Dongen, Centre for Population and Family Studies, CBGS, Brussels.
10. Gilbert Dooghe, Centre for Population and Family Studies, CBGS, Brussels.
11. Wilfried Dumon, Catholic University Leuven, Leuven.
12. Mark Elchardus, Free University Brussels, VUB, Brussels.
13. Theresa Jacobs, University of Antwerp, UIA, Antwerp.
14. Ria Janvier, University of Antwerp, UIA, Antwerp.
15. Mieke van Haegendoren together with Greet Verreydt, Limburg University Centre, Diepenbeek, Hasselt.
16. Mia Houthuys, director, Catholic Women of the Agrarian Movement, (KVLV), Leuven.
17. Dirk van Kappelen, director, Regional Employment Office, Antwerp.

18. Walter Kaesen, Ministry of the Flemish Community, Department of Welfare, Brussels.
19. Marleen Lambrechts, Ministry of the Flemish Community, departement of Family and Welfare.
20. Frans Lammertijn, Catholic University of Leuven, Leuven.
21. Magda Linthout, together with Patricia van Dessel, Catholic Women Workers Movement (KAV), Brussels.
22. Ive Marx, Centre for Social Policy, University of Antwerp/UFSIA.
23. Fons de Neve, director Research Centre of the League of Young and Large Families (BGJG), Brussels.
24. Hedwige Peemans-Poullet, Committee Liasons des Femmes, Universite des Femmes, Brussels.
25. Patricia Sabbe, Organisation of Flemish Cities and Municipalities, Brussels.
26. Mieke Slingerland, Family Help and Help to Elderly of the Agrarian Movement, Leuven.
27. Berenice Storms, University of Antwerp/UFSIA.
28. Linda van Torre, Socialist Day Care Services, Brussels.
29. Linda Turelinkx, Christian Democratic Trade Union (ACV), Brussels.
30. Lieven Vandenberghe, director, Child and Family (Kind en Gezin), Brussels.
31. Lieve Vanderleyden, Centre for Population and Family Studies, C.B.G.S, Brussels.
32. Joris Vanseveren, advisor on career breaks, Ministry of Labour, Department of Unemployment, Brussels.
33. Myriam Van Varenberg, chairperson, Council of Equal Opportunities, Brussels.

UK

Interviews took place in spring and summer 1998

34. Ruth Lister, University of Loughborough, Loughborough.
35. Jane Millar, University of Bath, Bath.
36. Clare Ungerson, University of Southampton, Southhampton.
37. Peter Moss, Thomas Coram Institute, London.
38. Beryl Braggs, Council of Wiltshire, childcare services.

Denmark

Interviews took place in autumn and winter 2000

39. Peter Abrahamson, University of Copenhagen, Copenhagen.
40. Bent Rold Andersen, former minister of social affairs, Social Democrat, social researcher.
41. Christina Barfoed-Høj, Trade Union of Public Employees, FOA, Copenhagen.
42. Thomas Boje, University of Roskilde, Roskilde.
43. Anette Borchorst, University of Århus, Århus.
44. Hanne Marlene Dahl, Trade Union for Public Employees (FOA) Copenhagen.
45. Jan Dehn, Organisation of Municipalities, KL, Copenhagen.
46. Liesbeth Denkov, Ministry of Social Affairs, Copenhagen.
47. Bent Greve, University of Roskilde, Copenhagen.
48. Karen Halling-Illum, Trade Union of Public Employees, FOA, Copenhagen.
49. Torben Hede, Ministry of Social Affairs, Copenhagen.
50. Finn Kenneth Hansen together with Henning Hansen, Centre for Alternative Social Analysis, CASA, Copenhagen.
51. Hans Hansen, Danish National Institute for Social Research, Copenhagen.
52. Kurt Hjørtso Kristensen, organisation of municipalities, KL, Copenhagen.
53. Helle Holt, Danish National Institute for Social Research, Copenhagen.
54. Peter Foxman, Ministry of Taxation, Copenhagen.
55. Per Kongshøj Madsen, University of Copenhagen, Copenhagen.
56. George Leeson, research director, Danage, Ældresagen, Copenhagen.
57. Stig Lund, Trade Union for Childcare Workers, BUPL, Copenhagen.
58. Mogens Nygaard Christoffersen, Danish National Institute for Social Research, SFI, Copenhagen.
59. Sanne Ipsen, Centre for Alternative Social Analysis, CASA, Copenhagen.
60. Aase Olesen, former member of the Social Commission, former member of parliament, Radikale Venstre, Copenhagen.
61. Yvonne Olesen together with Lilly Søndergaard, Labour Market Office (arbejdsmarkedstyrelsen), Copenhagen.
62. Liesbeth Pedersen, Danish National Institute for Social Research, SFI, Copenhagen.

63. Klaus Petersen, University of Copenhagen, Copenhagen.
64. Merete Platz, Danish National institute for Social Research, Copenhagen.
65. Neils Plough, Danish National Institute for Social Research, SFI, Copenhagen.
66. Anne Birte Ravn, University of Aalborg, Aalborg.
67. Birte Siim, University of Aalborg, Aalborg.
68. Michael Teit Nielsen, Organisation for Elderly, Copenhagen.
69. Claus Ryde, Ministry of Labour, Copenhagen.

The Netherlands

Interviews took place over the period 1996-2004

70. Marianne Duvalier, director, Women's Alliance, Utrecht.
71. Josette Hoex, Netherlands Institute of Care and Welfare, NIZW, Utrecht.
72. Janneke Plantenga, University of Utrecht, Utrecht.
73. Hetty Pott-Buter, University of Amsterdam, Amsterdam.

Notes

1   Other ways to analyse care in welfare states can be found in Anttonen and Sippilä (1996), Anttonen et al. (2003), Daly (2002), or Bettio and Plantenga (2004).

2   In addition to or instead of the class-based interpretation, it has been stressed that other power resources have been important in shaping or obstructing collective welfare arrangements, such as Christian democracy (Van Kersbergen 1995), the petty bourgeoisie (De Swaan 1990), and the old establishment (Hoogenboom 2004).

3   Becker more recently argued that many economists, including himself, have relied excessively on altruism to tie the interests of family members together. He proposes including guilt, affection, obligation, anger, and fear of physical abuse as factors that need to be taken into account (Nussbaum 2000).

4   Hochschild (1995, 2003) uses different ideals than the ones I propose. She distinguishes between traditional, postmodern, cold modern, and warm modern ideals of care. These models are not only normative a priori, they also cannot explain the differences between the four countries. Hence I developed new ideals of care.

5   This chapter is based on a secondary analysis of six surveys covering the 1980-2000 period: the OECD Labour Force Study, the European Labour Force Study, the (European Community Household Panel 1994 (ECHP), the Employment Options for the Future Survey (EOFS), and the Luxembourg Income Study (LIS). It is necessary to use that many sources because there is no comparative labour force survey that can answer all of the questions raised in this chapter. One of the main problems in data selection for this study is the fact that the European Labour Force Survey tends to lack recent information on employment patterns of Danish parents. The main problem of the OECD Labour Force Study is that, in contrast to the EU surveys, its focus on motherhood and fatherhood is only recent. Historical developments can hardly be chased. As the tables will show, OECD labour force statistics and European Labour Force surveys show different employment and part-time rates, but the patterns are by and large the same.

6   In the French-speaking region organised day care also exists and has grown substantially between 1988 and 1993, yet day care institutions are much more common than in Flanders. Jenson and Sineau (2001) calculated that for children under age three, more than 9,000 children use family day care and more than 10,000 children are in day care centres. In the Flemish region more than 11,000 children are in day care centres and 19,000 in family day care.

References

Abott, P. and C. Wallace (1992) *The Family and the New Right*. London: Pluto Press.

Abrahamson, P. and C. Wehner (2003) *Welfare Policies in the Context of Family Change: The Case of Denmark*. Available at http://www.york.ac.uk/inst/spru/research/summs/welempfc.htm.

Adriaansens, H. and A. Zijderveld (1981) *Vrijwillig initiatief en de verzorgingsstaat: Cultuur-sociologische analyse van de beleidsproblemen*. Deventer: Van Loghum Slaterus.

Alber, J. (1995) 'A framework for the comparative study of social services'. *Journal of European Social Policy* vol. 5, no. 2: 131-149.

AMS/Arbejdsmarkedstyreldsen (2001) *Statistics on Leave 1995-2000*. Unpublished.

Andersen, D. and A. Apeldorn, H. Weise (1996) *Orlov- evaluering af orlovsordningerne*. Copenhagen: SFI.

Andersen, B.R. (1987) 'The Quest for Ties Between Rights and Duties – A key question for the future of the public sector'. In A. Evers et al. (eds.) *The Changing Face of Welfare*. Aldershot: Gower.

Andersen, D (1998) *Frit valg af dagpasningsordning. Evaluering af forsøgsordningen*. Copenhagen: SFI.

Andries, M. and L. De lathouwer (1996) *De politieke houdbaarheid van een selectief sociaal beleid: lessen uit de jaren tachtig*. CSB-berichten. Universiteit Antwerpen/Ufsia: Centrum voor Sociaal Beleid.

Andries, M. (1997) *De Belgische sociale zekerheid in de typologie van de welvaartsstaten*. CSB-berichten. Universiteit Antwerpen/Ufsia: Centrum voor Sociaal Beleid.

Anttonen, A. and J. Sipilä (1996) 'European Social Care Services: is it possible to identify models?' *Journal of European Social Policy*, vol. 6, no. 2: 87-100.

Anttonen A. and J.Baldock J. and J.Sipilä (eds.) (2003) *The Young, the Old and the State: Social Care Systems in Five Industrial Nations*. Cheltenham: Edward Elgar.

Archer, M. (1996) *Culture and Agency: The Place of Culture in Social Theory*. Cambridge: Cambridge University Press.

Arts, W. and J. Gelissen (2002) 'Three Worlds of Welfare Capitalism or More? A State-of-the-Art Report' *Journal of European Social Policy*, vol. 12, no. 2: 137-158.

Atkinson, T. and John Micklewright (1989) 'Turning the Screw: Benefits for the Unemployed 1979-88'. In A. Dilnot and I. Walker (eds.) *The Economics of Social Security*. Oxford: Oxford University Press.

Baldock, J. (2003) 'Social Care in the United Kingdom: A Pattern of Discretionary Social Administration'. In A. Anttonen and J. Baldock and J. Sipilä (eds.) (2003) *The Young, the Old and the State. Social Care Systems in Five Industrial Nations*. Cheltenham: Edward Elgar.

Bannink, D. (1999) 'Het Nederlandse stelsel van sociale zekerheid. Van achterblijver naar koploper naar vroege hervormer.' In Trommel, W. and R. Van der Veen. (eds.) *De herverdeelde samenleving. Ontwikkeling en herziening van de Nederlandse verzorgingsstaat*. Amsterdam: Amsterdam University Press.

Barbalet, J.M. (1988) *Citizenship. Rights, Struggle and Class Inequality*. Milton Keynes: Open University Press.

Baro, F. et al. (1991) 'Home Care Services in Flanders, Belgium'. In A. Jamieson (ed.) *Home Care for Older People in Europe: A Comparison of Policies and Practices*. Oxford: Oxford University Press.

Beck, U. (1992) *Risk Society: Towards a New Modernity*. London: Sage.

Beck, U. and E. Beck Gernsheim (2002) *Individualization: Institutionalized Individualism and Its Social and Political Consequences*. London: Sage.

Becker, G. (1981) *A Treatise on the Family*. Cambridge: Harvard University Press.

Beckers, M. and M. Verspagen (1991) 'Een weg vol hindernissen. De werkloze moeder en het recht op WW' *Nemesis*, no. 5: 32-37.

Bekkering, J.M. and R.M.A. Jansweijer (1998) *De verdeling van arbeid en zorg: prikkels en belemmeringen*. WRR Werkdocument. Den Haag: WRR.

Bennet, F. (2002) 'Gender Implications of Current Social Security Reforms'. *Fiscal Studies* vol. 23, no. 4: 559-584.

Bertelsen, O. (1991) *Municipal Domestic Day-Care and Parents*. Copenhagen: SFI.

Bertone, C. (2000) *Whose Needs? Women's Organisations' Claims on Child Care in Italy and Denmark*. Ph.D. dissertation, University of Aalborg.

Bertone, C. (2003) 'Claims for Child Care as Struggles over Needs: Comparing Italian and Danish Women's Organizations'. *Social Politics*, vol. 10, no. 2: 229-255.

Bergqvist C. (ed.) (1999) *Equal Democracies: Gender and Politics in the Nordic Countries*. Oslo: Scandinavian University Press.

Bettio, F. and J. Plantenga (2004) 'Comparing Care Regimes in Europe'. *Feminist Economics*, vol. 10, no. 1: 85-113.

Billig, M. (1991) *Ideology and Opinions*. London: Sage.

Bianchi, S., M. Lynne, M. Casper, and P.K. Peltola (1996) 'A Cross-National Look at Married Women's Economic Dependency'. *Luxemburg Income Study, Working Paper Series*. Working Paper No. 143. Luxemburg: Ceps/Instead.

Bielinski, H. and A. Wagner (2004) 'Employment Options of Men and Women in Europe'. In *Changing Life Patterns in Western Industrial Societies*. J. Zollinger Giele and E. Holst (eds.) Amsterdam: Elsevier.

Blossfeld, H. and C. Hakim (eds.) (1997) *Between Equalization and Marginalization: Women Working Part-Time in Europe and the United States of America*. Oxford: Oxford University Press.

Bock, G. and P. Thane (1991) *Maternity and Gender Policies: Women and the Rise of the European Welfare States 1880-1950s*. London and New York: Routledge.

Bonke, J. (1999) *Income Distribution and Economic Well-being within European families*. Working paper. Copenhagen: SFI.

Bonoli, G. (1997) 'Classifying Welfare States: a Two-dimension Approach' *Journal of Social Policy* vol. 26, no. 3: 351-72.

Bonoli, G. (2000) 'Public Attitudes to Social Protection and Political Economy Traditions in Western Europe' *European Societies*, vol. 2 no. 94: 431-452.

Borchorst, A., (1985) 'Velfaerdsstat og bornepasning: ligestilling, pasning eller paedagogik?' *Kritiske Historikere* no. 1: 32-56.

Borchorst, A. and B. Siim (1987) 'Women and the Advanced Welfare State – A New Kind of Patriarchal Power?' In A. Showstack Sassoon (ed.) *Women and the State*. London: Hutchinson.

Borchorst, A. (1999) 'Den kønnede virkelighed – den kønsløse debat'. In J. Goul Andersen et al. (eds.). *Den demokratiske udfordring*. Hans Reitzels Forlag.

Borchorst, A. (2002) 'Danish Child Care Policy: Continuity Rather than Radical Change'. In R. Mahon and S. Michel (eds.) *Child Care Policy at the Crossroads: Gender and Welfare State Restructuring*. New York: Routledge.

Bradshaw, J. and N. Finch (2002) *A Comparison of Child Benefit Packages in 22 Countries*. Research Report No. 174. Department for Work and Pensions. Leeds: Corporate Document Services.

Brandt, B. and E. Kvande (2001) 'Flexible Work and Flexible Fathers' *Work, Employment and Society* vol 15, no. 2: 251-267.

Brannen, J. and Moss P. (1991) *The Managing Mother: Dual Earner Households after Maternity Leave*. London: Unwin Hyman.

Bruning, G. and J. Plantenga (1999) 'Parental Leave and Equal Opportunities: Experiences in Eight European Countries' *Journal of European Social Policy* vol. 9, no. 3: 195-209.

Bull, J. et al. (1994) *Implementing the Children Act for Children Under 8*. Thomas Coram Research Unit. London: HMSO.

BUPL (1999) *Velfærdanalyse fra BUPL.* Copenhagen: BUPL.

Bussemaker, J. (1993) *Betwiste zelfstandigheid. Individualisering, sekse en verzorgingsstaat.* Amsterdam: SUA.

Bussemaker, J. (1998) 'Rationales of Care in Contemporary Welfare States: The Case of Childcare in the Netherlands'. *Social Politics,* 5: 70-96.

Bussemaker, J. and K. van Kersbergen (1994) 'Gender and Welfare States: Some Theoretical Reflections'. In D. Sainsbury (ed.) (1994) *Gendering Welfare States.* London: Sage.

Bussemaker, J. and K.van Kersbergen (1999) 'Contemporary Social-Capitalist Welfare States and Gender Inequality' in D. Sainsbury (ed.) (1999) *Gender and Welfare State Regimes.* Oxford: Oxford University Press.

Bijsterveld, K. (1996) *Geen kwestie van leeftijd. Verzorgingsstaat, wetenschap en discussies rond ouderen in Nederland, 1945-1982.* Amsterdam: Van Gennep.

Callender, C. et al. (1997) *Maternity Rights and Benefits in Britain 1995.* Research Report no. 67. London: HMSO.

Cantillon, B. (1994) 'Reflecties bij de discussie individualisering-gezinsmodulering' in M. van Haegendoren and H. Moestermans (eds.) *Naar individuele rechten in de sociale zekerheid? De pensioenen en de werkloosheid in de kijker.* Leuven/Amersfoort: Acco.

Cantillon, B. and A.Thirion (1998) *Wegen naar een activerende verzorgingsstaat. Tussentijdse balans van het PWA-experiment.* CSB-Berichten. Universiteit Antwerpen/Ufsia: Centrum voor Sociaal Beleid.

Cantillon, B. (ed.) (1999). *De welvaartsstaat in de kering.* Kapellen: Pelckmans.

Cantillon, B. and G. Verbist (2003) *Sociaal-economische levensomstandigheden van eenoudergezinnen in België.* CSB-berichten. Universiteit van Antwerpen/ Ufsia: Centrum voor Sociaal Beleid.

Cass, B. (1994) 'Citizenship, Work, and Welfare: the Dilemma for Australian Women'. *Social Politics,* vol. 1: 106-124.

Centraal Bureau voor de Statistiek / CBS (1993) *Sociaal-economische-maandstatistiek.* No 2. Rijswijk: CBS.

Chamberlayne, P et. al. (1999) *Welfare and Culture in Europe. Towards a New Paradigm in Social Policy.* London: Jessica Kingsley.

Christensen, E. (2000) *Det 3-årige barn.* Copenhagen: SFI.

Clarke, J. (2004) *Changing Welfare, Changing States.* London: Sage.

Cm. 3805 (1998) *New Ambitions for Our Country: A New Contract for Welfare.* Secretary of State for Social Security and the Minister for Welfare Reform. London: Department of Social Security.

Cm. 3959 (1998) *Meeting the Childcare Challenge.* Department for Employment and Education, Ministry for Women. London: DfEE.

Cm. 620. (1998) *New Ambitions for Britain*. Financial Statement and Budget Report. 17 March 1998. London: House of Commons.

Cmnd. 8093 (1980) *The Taxation of Husband and Wife*, presented by the Chancellor of the Exchequer by Command of her Majesty. London: HMSO.

Cmnd. 9756 (1986) *The Reform of Personal Taxation*, presented by the Chancellor of the Exchequer. London: HMSO.

Cohen, B. and Fraser, N. (1991) *Childcare in a Modern Welfare System. Towards a New National Policy*. London: Institute for Public Policy Research.

Commissie Toekomstscenario's Herverdeling Onbetaalde Arbeid (1995) *Onbetaalde zorg gelijk verdeeld*. Den Haag: Vuga.

Compston, H. and P. Konshøj Madsen (2001) 'Conceptual Innovation and Public Policy: Unemployment and Paid Leave Schemes in Denmark' *Journal of European Social Policy*, vol. 11, no. 2: 117-132.

CPAG/Child Poverty Action Group (1996) *Jobseeker's Allowance Handbook*. London: CPAG.

Daguerre, A. and G. Bonoli (2004) *Child Care Policies in Diverse European Welfare States*. Paper presented at the Conference of Europeanists, March, Chicago.

Dahlerup, D. (1998) *Rødstrømperne. Den danske Rødstrømpebevægelses udvikling, nytænkning og gennemslag 1970-1985*. Copenhagen: Gyldendal.

Dahrendorf, R. (1988) *The Modern Social Conflict: An Essay on the Politics of Liberty*. London: Weidenfeld and Nicholson.

Daly, M. (1996) *Social Security, Gender and Equality in the European Union*. European Commission, Directorate General V/ Equal Opportunities for Women and Men.

Daly, M. and J. Lewis (1998) 'Conceptualising Social Care in the Context of Welfare State Restructuring' in J. Lewis (ed.) *Gender, Social Care and Welfare State Restructuring in Europe*. Avebury: Ashgate.

Daly, M. (1999) 'The Functioning Family: Catholicism and Social Policy in Germany and Ireland' *Comparative Social Research*, vol. 18: 105-133.

Daly, M (2000a) *The Gender Division of Welfare: The Impact of the British and German Welfare States*. Cambridge: Cambridge University Press.

Daly, M. (2000b) 'A Fine Balance: Women's Labor Market Participation in International Comparison'. In F. W. Scharpf and V.A.Schmidt (eds.) *Welfare and Work in the Open Economy: Diverse Responses to Common Challenges*. Oxford: Oxford University Press.

Daly, M. (2002) 'Care as a Good for Social Policy'. *Journal of Social Policy*, vol. 31, no. 2: 251-270.

Daly, M. and C. Rake (2003) *Gender and the Welfare State*. London: Polity Press.

Daycare Trust (1997) *The Child Care Gap*, briefing paper 1. Childcare Now. London: Daycare Trust.

Daycare Trust (1998) *Sharing the Costs of Childcare, briefing paper 2.* Childcare Now. London: Daycare Trust.

Debacker, M. and L. De Lathouwer and K. Bogaerts (2004) *Time Credit and Leave Schemes in the Belgian Welfare States.* Paper presented at TLM.net conference, 'Quality in Labour Market Transitions: A European Challenge,' 26 November.

DE/DHSS (1981) *Payments of Benefits to Unemployed People: Rayner Scrutiny.* Department of Employment/ Department of Health and Social Security. London: HMSO.

De Lathouwer, L. (1996) *Twintig jaar beleidsontwikkeling in de Belgische werkloosheidsverzekering.* CSB-berichten. Universiteit Antwerpen/Ufsia: Centrum voor Sociaal Beleid.

De Lathouwer, L., K. Bogaerts, and K. Van den Bosch (2003) *Schorsing artikel 80 gewikt en gewogen. Een evaluatie vanuit herintrede, behoefte en verzekeringsperspectief.* CSB-Berichten. Universiteit Antwerpen/Ufsia: Centrum voor Sociaal Beleid.

De Lathouwer, L. (2003) *Reforming the Passive Welfare State: Belgium's New Income Arrangements to Make Work Pay in International Perspective.* Paper for the conference 'Social Security and Participation in Social and Economic Life' Fiss, Sigtuna, Sweden, 14-16 June 2003.

Dean, H. and Shah, A. (2002) 'Insecure Families and Low-Paying Labour Markets: Comments on the British Experience'. *Journal of Social Policy*, vol. 31, no. 1: 61-80.

Delva, A. and B. van Bergen and M. van de Wiele (2003) *Kinderopvang. Onthaalmoeders en hun statuut. Karel de Grote Hogeschool.* Unpublished.

Denis, B. (1995) *Het effect van arbeidsherverdeling op de positie van vrouwen op de arbeidsmarkt. Een analyse aan de hand van loopbaanonderbreking.* Onderzoek uitgevoerd in opdracht van Vlaams Ministerie van Leefmilieu en Tewerkstelling. Brussel: Riar/IISA.

Deven, F. (1998) 'Belgium as a Cross-roads for Child Care in Europe'. In J. Schippers et al. (eds.) *Child Care and Female Labor Supply in the Netherlands. Facts, Analyses, Policies.* Utrecht: AWSB.

Deven, F. and T. Nuelant (1999) 'Parental Leave and Career Breaks in Belgium'. In P. Moss and F. Deven (eds.). *Parental Leave: Progress or Pitfall? Research and Policy Issues in Europe.* Brussels/The Hague: CBGS/NIDI.

DFE (1993) *Oversigt over rådighedsvurderingernes udfald.* Copenhagen. Unpublished.

DfES (2001) *Statistics of Education: Children's Day Care Facilities March 2001.* No. 8/01. London: DfES.

DfES (2002) Statistics of Education: Provision for children under Five Years of Age in England. January. No 08/02. London: DfEs.

Dienst Opvanggezinnen van de Landelijke Beweging v.z.w. (1992) *Enquête bij opvanggezinnen.* 28 March Unpublished.

Dierx, J.R. and Y.K Grift and.J. J. Schippers (1999) *Emancipatie-Effect Rapportage. Verkenning belastingstelsel van de 21ᵉ eeuw.* Utrecht: Universiteit Utrecht/ Economisch Instituut/CIAV.

Dilnot, A. (1989) 'Not Her Own Income: The Reform of the Taxation of Marriage'. In M. Brenton and C. Ungerson (eds.) *Social Policy Review.* London: Longman.

Dilnot, A. (1992) 'Social Security and Labour Market Policy'. In E. McLaughlin (ed.) *Understanding Unemployment: New Perspectives on Active Labour Market Policies.* London/New York: Routledge.

Dilnot, A. and Kell, K. (1989) 'Male Unemployment and Women's Work'. In A. Dilnot and I. Walker (eds.) *The Economics of Social Security.* Oxford: Oxford University Press.

Dingeldey, I. (2001) 'European Tax Systems and Their Impact on Family Employment Patterns'. *Journal of Social Policy,* vol. 30, no. 4: 653-672.

Dogan, M and D. Pelassy (1990) *How to Compare Nations: Strategies in Comparative Politics.* Second edition. Chatham: Chatham House Publishers.

Douglas, M. (1986) *How Institutions Think.* Syracuse: Syracuse University Press.

Douglas. M. and S. Ney (1998) *Missing Persons: A Critique of Personhood in the Social Sciences.* Berkeley/Los Angeles/London: University of California Press.

DS/Danmark Statistik (1999a) *Statistisk Tiårsoversigt.* Copenhagen: DS.

DS/Danmark Statistik (1999b) *Statistik Årbog.* Copenhagen: DS.

DS/Danmark Statistik (2002) *Børns Levevilkår.* Copenhagen: DS.

DSS (1996) *Statistics on Social Security.* London: DSS.

DSS (1997) *Statistics on Social Security.* London: DSS.

Duncan, S. and R. Edwards (1999) *Lone Mothers, Paid Work and Gendered Moral Rationalities.* Basingstoke: McMillan.

Duncan, S. and B. Pfau-Effinger (2000) *Gender, Economy and Culture in the European Union.* London and New York: Routledge.

Duncan, S. and R. Edwards and T. Reynolds and P. Alldred (2004) 'Mothers and Child Care: Policies, Values and Theories'. *Children and Society,* 18: 254-265.

Duyvendak, J.W. (1997) *Waar blijft de politiek? Essays over paarse politiek, maatschappelijk middenveld en sociale cohesie.* Amsterdam: Boom.

Dykstra, P. (1997) *Employment and Caring.* Working Paper 1997/7. The Hague: NIDI.

ECNC/European Commission Network on Childcare (1990) *Childcare in the European Communities 1985-1990*. Brussels: European Commission.

ECNC/European Commission Network on Childcare (1996) *A Review of Services for Young Children in the European Union 1990-1995*. Brussel: European Commission.

Elingsaeter, A.L. (1998) 'Dual Breadwinner Societies: Provider Models in the Scandinavian Welfare States'. *Acta Sociologica*, vol. 41: 59-73.

Esping-Andersen, G. (1990) *The Three Worlds of Welfare Capitalism*. Cambridge/Oxford: Polity Press.

Esping-Andersen, G. (1999). *The Social Foundations of Postindustrial Economies*. Oxford: Oxford University Press.

Esping-Andersen, G. and D. Gallie and A. Hemerijck and J. Myles (2002) *Why We Need a New Welfare State*. Oxford: Oxford University Press.

Etherington, D. (1998) 'From Welfare to Work in Denmark: An Alternative to Free Market Policies?' *Policy and Politics*, vol. 26, no. 2: 147-161.

Etzioni, A. (1993) *The Spirit of Community: Rights, Responsibilities and the Communitarian Agenda*. London: Fontana Press.

Eurobarometer (2004) *Europeans' Attitudes to Parental Leave*. Eurostat: Brussels. Relations and Social Affairs. Unit V/A.1. Brussels.

European Commission (EC) (2000) *Employment in Europe*. Directorate General for Employment, Industrial Relations and Social Affairs. Unit V/A.1. Brussels.

European Commission (EC) (2003) *Employment in Europe*. Directorate General for Employment, Industrial Relations and Social Affairs. Unit V/A.1. Brussels.

European Commission (EC) (2004) *How Europeans Spend Their Time: Everyday Life of Women and Men*. Data 1998-2000. Brussels.

European Communities (2004) *Facing the Challenge: The Lisbon Strategy for Growth and Employment*. Report from the High Level Group chaired by Wim Kok. Novemner. Luxembourg: European Community.

Eurostat (1997) 'Family Responsibilities – How are they Shared in European Households?' *Statistics in Focus: Population and Social Conditions*, no. 5.

Eurostat (2001a). 'Earnings of Men and Women in the EU: The Gap Narrowing but Only Slowly'. *Statistics in Focus: Population and Social Conditions*, theme 3/5.

Eurostat (2001b) 'Employment Rates in Europe – 2000'. *Statistics in Focus: Population and Social conditions*, theme 3/8.

Eurostat (2002). 'Women and Men Reconciling Work and Family Life'. *Statistics in Focus: Population and Social Conditions*, theme 3/9.

Eurostat (2005) 'Gender Gaps in the Reconciliation between Work and Family Life'. *Statistics in Focus: Population and Social Conditions*, theme 4.

Evans, M. (2003) 'New Deal for Lone Parents: Six Years of Operation and Evaluation'. In J. Millar and M. Evans (eds.) *Lone Parents and Employment: International Comparisons of What Works*. Department for Work and Pensions. Bath: Centre for Analysis of Social Policy.

Evers, A. et al. (1987) *The Changing Face of Welfare*. Aldershot: Gower.

Fagan, C. (1996) 'Gendered Time Schedules: Paid Work in Great Britain' *Social Politics*: 72-106.

Fagan, C. (2001) *Gender, Employment and Working Time Preferences*. Dublin: European Foundation for the Improvement of Living and Working Conditions.

Ferrera, M. (1996) 'The Southern Model of Welfare in Social Europe'. *Journal of European Social Policy* vol. 6, no. 1: 17-39.

Finansministeriet (1995) *Budget. Redegørelse*. Copenhagen: Ministry of Finance.

Finch, J. and D. Groves (ed.) (1983) *A Labour of Love: Women, Work and Caring*. London: Routledge/Kegan Paul.

Finch, J. (1989) *Family Obligations and Social Change*. Cambridge: Polity Press.

Finch, J. (1990) 'The Politics of Community Care in Britain'. In C. Ungerson (ed.) *Gender and Caring: Work and Welfare in Britain and Scandinavia*. Hemel Hempstead: Harvester Wheatsheaf.

Finch, J. and J. Mason (1990) 'Gender, Employment and Responsibilities to Kin'. *Work, Employment and Society*, vol. 4, no. 3: 349-367.

Finch, J. and J. Mason (1993) *Negotiating Family Responsibilities*. London/New York: Routledge.

Folbre, N. (1994) *Who Pays for the Kids? Gender and the Structures of Constraint*. London: Routledge.

Ford, R. (1996) *Childcare in the Balance: How Lone Parents Make Decisions about Work*. London: Policy Studies Institute.

Fraser, N (1989) *Unruly Practices: Power, Discourse and Gender in Contemporary Social Theory*. Minnesota: University of Minnesota Press.

Fraser, N. (1990) 'Struggle Over Needs: Outline of a Socialist-Feminist Critical Theory of Late-Capitalist Political Culture'. In L. Gordon (ed.) *Women, the State and Welfare*. Madison: The University of Wisconsin Press.

Fraser, N. Gordon, L. (1994) 'Dependency' Demystified: Inscriptions of Power in a Keyword of the Welfare State'. *Social Politics*, vol. 1, no.1: 4-31.

Fraser, N. (1997) 'After the Family Wage: A Postindustrial Thought Experiment'. In B. Hobson and A.M. Berggren (eds.) *Crossing Borders: Gender and Citizenship in Transition*. Stockholm: Swedish Council for Planning and Coordination.

Freeman, R. and M.Rustin (1999) 'Introduction: Welfare, Culture and Europe'. In P. Chamberlayne et al. (eds.). *Welfare and Culture in Europe: Towards a New Paradigm in Social Policy*. London: Jessica Kingsley.

Gallie, D. and S. Alm (2000) 'Unemployment, Gender and Attitudes to Work'. In D. Gallie and S. Paugam (eds.) (2000) *Welfare Regimes and the Experience of Unemployment in Europe*. Oxford: Oxford University Press.

Gallie, D. and Paugam, S. (eds.) (2000) *Welfare Regimes and the Experience of Unemployment in Europe*. Oxford: Oxford University Press.

Gardiner, J. (1997) *Gender, Care and Economics*. London: Macmillan.

Gelissen, J.P.T.M. (2002) *Worlds of Welfare: International Comparative Social Studies*. Leiden: Brill.

Gershuny, J. and O. Sullivan (2003) 'Time Use, Gender, and Public Policy Regimes'. *Social Politics*, vol. 10, no. 2: 205-227.

Giddens, A (1991) *Modernity and Self-Identity: Self and Society in Late Modern Age*. Cambridge: Polity Press.

Gillibrand, E. and J. Mosley (1998) *When I Go To Work I Feel Guilty: A Working Mother's Guide to Sanity and Survival*. New York: Thorns.

Ginsburg, N. (1992) *Divisions of Welfare: A Critical Introduction to Comparative Social Policy*. London: Sage.

Goewie, R and C. Keune (1996) *Naar een algemeen aanvaarde standaard. Opvattingen en normen over de inzet van gezinsverzorging*. Utrecht: Verwey-Jonker Instituut.

Gornick, J.C, Meyers, M.K., Ross, K.E. (1997) 'Supporting the Employment of Mothers: Policy Variation across fourteen Welfare States'. *Journal of European Social Policy*, vol. 7, no. 1: 45-70.

Graaf, de P.M. and W.C. Ultee (2002) 'United in Employment, United in Unemployment? Employment and Unemployment of Couples in the European Union in 1994'. In D. Gallie and S. Paugam (eds.) *Welfare Regimes and the Experience of Unemployment in Europe*. Oxford: Oxford University Press.

Graham, H. (1983) 'Caring: A Labour of Love'. In J. Finch and D. Groves (eds.) *A Labour of Love: Women, Work and Caring*. London: Routledge and Kegan Paul.

Gregson, N. and M. Lowe (1994) *Servicing the Middle Classes: Class, Gender and Waged Domestic Labour in Contemporary Britain*. London and New York: Routledge.

Green-Pedersen, C. and M. Haverland (2002) 'The New Politics and Scholarship of the Welfare State'. *Journal of European Social Policy*, vol. 12, no. 1: 43-51.

Green-Pedersen, C. (2002) *The Politics of Justification: Party Competition and Welfare State Retrenchment in Denmark and the Netherlands from 1982-1998*. Amsterdam: Amsterdam University Press.

Grift, Y. K. (1998) *Female Labour Supply: The Influence of Taxes and Social Premiums*. Ph.D. thesis. Amsterdam.

Groof, de. J. (1983) *Pluralisme: kind van de democratie?* Leuven: Davidsfonds.

Grootscholte, M. J. A. Bouwmeester en P. de Klaver (2000) *Evaluatie Wet op ouderschapsverlof. Onderzoek onder rechthebbenden en werkgevers.* Eindrapport. Den Haag: Ministerie van Sociale Zaken en Werkgelegenheid.

Grünnel, M. (1997) *Mannen die zorgen, zijn de kerels van morgen. Hoe jongens, dertigers en vijftig-plussers zich laten aanspreken op onbetaald werk.* Utrecht: Jan van Arkel.

Grünnel, M. (2001) *Mannen zorgen. Verandering en continuïteit in zorgpatronen.* Amsterdam: Aksant.

Gustafsson, S.S. and M. Bruyn-Hundt (1991) 'Incentives for Women to Work: A Comparison between The Netherlands, Sweden and West-Germany'. *Journal of Economic Studies*, vol. 18, nos/6: 30-65.

Guy Peters, B. (1998) *Comparative Politics: Theory and Methods.* London: Macmillan Press.

Hakim, C. (1999) 'Models of the Family, Women's Role and Social Policy: A New Perspective from Preference Theory'. *European Societies*, vol. 1, no. 1: 33-58.

Hakim, C. (2000) *Work-Lifestyle Choices in the 21st Century: Preference Theory.* Oxford: Oxford University Press.

Hakim, C. (2003a) *Models of the Family in Modern Societies. Ideals and Realities.* Aldershot: Ashgate.

Hakim, C. (2003b) 'Public morality versus personal choice: the failure of social attitude surveys' *British Journal of Sociology*, vol. 54 no. 3, pp. 339-345.

Hall, P.A and R.C.R. Taylor (1996) 'Political Science and the Three New Institutionalisms'. *Political Studies*, XLIV: 936-957.

Halman, L (1999/2000) *The European Values Study: A Third Wave.* Source book of the 1999/2000 European Values Study. WORC. Tilburg University.

Hansard (1989) *House of Commons: Second Reading of the Social Security Act*, 10 January, col 714.

Hays, S. (1996) *The Cultural Contradictions of Motherhood.* New Haven and London: Yale University Press.

Hedebouw, G. and L. Sannen (2002) *Grootouders of andere familieleden en kinderopvang.* Leuven: HIVA.

Hellemans, Staf. and R. Schepers (1992) 'De ontwikkeling van corporatieve verzorgingsstaten in België en Nederland.' *Sociologische Gids*, 5-6: 346-364.

Hemerijck, A. and J. Visser (2003) *Policy Learning in European Welfare States.* Unpublished paper.

Henkes, K and Siegers. J and K. van den Bosch (1992) 'Married Women on the Labour Market: A Comparative Study of Belgium and the Netherlands'. *Bevolking en Gezin*, no 1: 77-99.

Hermans, A. (1984) 'Wie zal er ons kindeke douwen? Uit de voorgeschiedenis van de kinderdagverblijven'. *Het Kind*, 1: 13-24.

Hernes, H. (1984) 'Women and the Welfare State: The Transition from Private to Public Dependence'. In H. Holter (ed.) *Patriarchy in a Welfare Society*. Oslo: Universitetsforlaget.

Hernes, H. (1987) 'Women and the Welfare State: The Transition From Private to Public Dependence'. In A. Showstack Sassoon (ed.) *Women and the State: The Shifting Boundaries of Public and Private*. London/New York: Routledge.

Hobson, B. (1990) 'No Exit, No Voice: Women's Economic Dependency and the Welfare State'. *Acta Sociologica*, vol. 33, no. 3: 235-250.

Hobson, B. (1994) 'Solo mothers, social policy regimes and the logics of gender'. In D. Sainsbury (ed.) *Gendering Welfare States*. London: Sage.

Hobson, B. and J. Lewis, B. Siim (2002) *Contested Concepts in Gender and Social Politics*. Cheltenham: Edward Elgar.

Hobson, B. and R. Lister (2002) 'Citizenship'. In B. Hobson and J. Lewis, B. Siim (2002) *Contested Concepts in Gender and Social Politics*. Cheltenham: Edward Elgar.

Hochschild, A. (1989) *The Second Shift: Working Parents and the Revolution at Home*. London: Piatkus.

Hochschild, A. (1995) 'The Culture of Politics: Traditional, Postmodern, Cold-modern and Warm-modern Ideals of Care'. *Social Politics*, fall: 331-346.

Hochschild, A. (2003) *The Commercial Spirit of Intimate Life and Other Essays*. San Francisco and Los Angeles: University of California Press.

Hoeflaken, van W. (2000) 'Korting voor huisvrouwen'. NRC *Handelsblad*, 16 september.

Hooge, J. and H. de Witte (1996) *De teruggetrokkenen: verdwenen van de arbeidsmarkt? Opvolging en diepere analyse van het type 'teruggetrokken' onder de werkzoekenden*. Leuven: Hoger Instituut voor de Arbeid.

Hoogenboom, M. (2004) *Standenstrijd en zekerheid. Een geschiedenis van oude orde en sociale zorg in Nederland (ca. 1880-1940)*. Boom: Amsterdam.

House of Commons (1994-1995) *Mothers in Employment. Employment Committee. Volume 1: Report and Proceedings of the Committee*. First Report. London: HMSO.

Huyse, L. (1983) 'Breuklijnen in de Belgische samenleving'. In L. Huyse and J. Berting (eds.) Als in een spiegel? Een sociologische kaart van België en Nederland. *Tijdschrift voor Sociologie*, nrs 1/2: 9-25.

Inglis, F. (2004) *Culture*. Cambridge: Polity Press.

Jacobs, T. (1996) 'Grootouderschap: demografische en sociologische aspecten'. In A. Marcoen (ed.) *Grootouders tussen mogen en moeten*. Leuven/Apeldoorn: Garant.

James, S. (1992) 'The Good-enough Citizen: Citizenship and Independence'. In G. Bock, G. and S. James (eds.) *Beyond Equality and Difference: Citizenship, Feminist Politics and Female Subjectivity*. London and New York: Routledge.

Janoski, T. (1998) *Citizenship and Civil Society: A Framework of Rights and Obligations in Liberal, Traditional, and Social Democratic Regimes*. Cambridge: Cambridge University Press.

Jenkins-Smith, H.C. and P.A. Sabatier (1994) 'Evaluating the Advocacy Coalition Framework'. *Journal of Public Policy*, vol. 14, no. 2: 175-203.

Jenson, J. (1997) 'Who Cares? Gender and Welfare Regimes'. *Social Politics*, no. 4: 182-187.

Jenson, J. and M. Sineau (2001) 'Comparing Childcare Programs: Commonalities Amid Variety'. In J. Jenson and M. Sineau (eds.) *Who Cares? Women's Work, Childcare, and Welfare State Redesign*. Toronto: University of Toronto Press.

Jones, H. and J. Millar (1996) *The Politics of the Family*. Aldershot: Avebury.

Jonge, de, P and Kam, de C.A. (2000) 'Wieg, wig en werk'. *Economische Statistische Berichten*. 20/10: 840-842.

Joshi, H. (1992) 'The Cost of Caring'. In C. Glendinning and J.Millar (eds.) *Women and Poverty in Britain: The 1990s*. Hemel Hempstead: Harvester Wheatsheaf.

Juul, S. (1998) *Faelleskab og solidaritet in Danmark*. Copenhagen: SFI.

Juul Jensen, J. and H. Krogh Hansen (2002) *Denmark: Surveying Demand, Supply and Use of Care. Care Work in Europe*. Aarhus.

Kager, P. (1999) 'Belastingplan 21ᵉ eeuw' *Nemesis*, no 2: 36-41.

Kalmijn, M. (2003) 'Country Differences in Sex-role Attitudes: Cultural and Economic Explanations'. In W. Arts and J. Hagenaars and L. Halman (eds.) *The Cultural Diversity of European Unity: Findings, Explanations and Reflections from the European Values Study*. Leiden: Brill.

Kessler-Harris, A. (2003) 'In Pursuit of Economic Citizenship'. *Social Politics*, vol. 10, no. 2: 157-175.

Keuzenkamp, S. and K. Oudhof (2000) *Emancipatiemonitor 2000*. Den Haag/Voorburg: SCP/CBS.

Keuzenkamp, S. (2001) 'Kinderopvang in cijfers'. *Tijdschrift voor de Social Sector*, vol. 55, no.7/8: 22-27.

Kilkey, M. and Bradshaw, J. (2001) 'Making Work Pay Policies for Lone Parents'. In J.Millar and K. Rowlingson (eds.) *Lone Parents, Employment and Social Policy: Cross-national Comparisons*. Bristol: Policy Press.

Kind en Gezin (1988) *Kinderopvang: een groeiende keuze van ouders. Studie van en voorstellen voor kinderopvang in Vlaanderen*. Brussel: Kind en Gezin.

Kind en Gezin (1997) *Blauwdruk beleidsplan kinderopvang.* Brussel: Kind en Gezin.

Kind en Gezin (1997) *Jaarverslag 1996. 10 jaar Kind en Gezin.* Brussel: Kind en Gezin.

Kind en Gezin *(2001) Jaarverslag 2000.* Brussel: Kind en Gezin.

Kind en gezin (2003*) Een toekomstvisie op kinderopvang. Brussel: Kind en Gezin.*

Knijn, T. *(1994)* 'Fish Without Bikes: Revision of the Dutch Welfare State and its Consequences for the (In) dependence of Single Mothers'. *Social politics,* vol. 1, no. 1: 83-105.

Knijn, T. (1998) 'Social Care in the Netherlands'. In J. Lewis (eds.) *Care and Welfare State Restructuring in Europe.* Ashgate: Aldershot.

Knijn, T. (2003) *Social and Family Policy: The Case of the Netherlands.* Available at http://www.york.ac.uk/inst/spru/research/summs/welempfc.htm.

Knijn, T. and M. Kremer (1997). 'Gender and the Caring Dimension of Welfare States: Towards Inclusive Citizenship'. *Social Politics* 3: 328-361.

Knijn, T. and F. van Wel (1999) *Zorgen voor de kost.* Amsterdam: SWP.

Knijn, T. and F. van Wel (2001a) *Een wankel evenwicht. Arbeid en zorg in gezinnen met jonge kinderen.* Amsterdam: SWP.

Knijn, T. and F. van Wel (2001b) 'Careful or Lenient? Welfare Reform for Lone Parents in the Netherlands'. *Journal of European Social Policy,* vol. 11, no. 3: 235-252.

Knijn, T. and F. van Wel (2004) 'Overgangsfase of nieuw evenwicht? Arbeid en zorg in gezinnen'. In W. Arts, H. Entzinger, and R. Muffels (eds.) *Verzorgingsstaat vaar wel.* Assen: Van Gorcum.

Knijn, T. and R. van Berkel (2003) 'Again Revisited Employment and Activiation Policies for Lone Parents on Social Assistance in the Netherlands'. In J. Millar and M. Evans (eds.) *Lone parents and employment: International Comparisons of What Works.* Department for Work and Pensions. Bath: Centre for Analysis of Social Policy.

Knijn, T. and A. Komter (eds.) (2004) *Solidarity Between the Sexes and the Generations: Transformations in Europe.* Cheltenham: Edward Elgar.

Koch-Nielsen, I. (1996) *Family Obligations in Denmark.* Copenhagen: SFI.

Kremer, M. (1994) *Interpretations of Citizenship: Gender, Care and the Obligation to Work in the British, Danish and Dutch Welfare State.* MA thesis. University of Utrecht. Unpublished.

Kremer, M. (1995) *Het Deense werkgelegenheidsoffensief. Kansen voor zorg en arbeid.* Utrecht: NIZW.

Kremer, M. (1997) *Hoe zorgt de verzorgingsstaat? Vlaamse zorgverhoudingen in perspectief.* Paper presented at the conference 'Wonen, Werken en Welzijn in Beweging'. March 7, 1997. Research school AWSB, University of Utrecht.

Kremer, M. (2000) *Geven en Claimen. Burgerschap en informele zorg in Europees perspectief.* Utrecht: NIZW.

Kremer, M. (2001) 'A Dutch Miracle for Women?' *Social Politics*, summer: 182-185.

Kremer, M. (2002) 'The Illusion of Free Choice: Ideals of Care and Child Care Policy in the Flemish and Dutch Welfare States'. In R. Mahon and S. Michel (eds.) *Child Care Policy at the Crossroads: Gender and Welfare State Restructuring.* New York: Routledge.

Kröger, T. (1997) 'The Dilemma of Municipalities: Scandinavian Approaches to Child Day-care Provision'. *Journal of Social Policy,* vol. 26, no. 4: 485-507.

Korpi, W. (1983) *The Democratic Class Struggle.* London: Routledge and Kegan Paul.

Kuhn, T. (2003, or. 1962). *De structuur van wetenschappelijke revoluties.* Amsterdam: Boom.

Kvist, J. and M. Jæger (2004) *Changing the Social Rights and Obligations of Social Citizenship in Europe.* Report for the initiative 'Strengthening the Security in Social Security' of the International Social Security Association under the UN.

KVLV (Katholieke Vrouwenbeweging van de Landelijke Vereniging) (1977) *Een dienst onthaalgezinnen in het kader van de v.z.w. Gezinszorg van de Landelijke Beweging.* Leuven.

Koopmans, I. et al. (2003) *Zorg in het huidige stelsel van sociale zekerheid en pensioen: een vergelijking tussen zes landen.* Utrecht: de Graaff.

Koven, S. and S. Michel (eds.) (1993) *Mothers of a New World.* London: Routledge.

La Valle, I., S. Finch, A. Nove, and C. Levin (2000) *Parents' Demands for Childcare.* London: Department for Employment and Education.

Lamb, M.E. (ed.) (2004, or. 1981) *The Role of the Father in Child Development* (fourth edition). Hoboken: John Wiley and Sons.

Lambrechts, E. and L. Dewispelaere (1980) *Het nationaal werk voor kinderwelzijn. Een overzicht van de ontwikkeling sinds 1957.* CBGS rapport 38. Brussel.

Lammertijn, F. and L. van Bavel (1996) *Het decor van de zorg. Sociale veranderingen en welzijn in Vlaanderen.* Acco: Leuven.

Land, H. (1998) 'New Labour, New Families?'. In H. Dean (ed.) *Social Policy Review 1998.* London: Longman.

Land, H. (2001) 'Lone Mothers, Employment, Child Care'. In J. Millar and K. Rowlingson (eds.) *Lone Parents Employment and Social Policy: Cross-national Comparisons.* Bristol: Policy Press.

Land, H. and H. Rose (1985) 'Compulsory Altruism for Some or an Altruistic Society for All?'. In P. Bean and J. Ferris and D. Whynes (eds.) *In Defence of Welfare.* London: Tavistock.

Land, H. and J. Lewis (1998) 'Gender, Care and the Changing Role of the State in the UK'. In J. Lewis (ed.) *Gender, Social Care and Welfare State Restructuring in Europe*. Avebury: Ashgate.

Langan, M. and I. Ostner (1991) 'Gender and Welfare'. In G. Room (ed.) *Towards a European Welfare State?* Bristol: Saus.

Leibfried, S. (1991) 'Towards a European Welfare State? On Integrating Poverty Regimes into the European Community'. In S.Ferge and J.E. Kolberg (eds.) *Social Policy in a Changing Europe*. Boulder: Westview.

Leira, A. (1990) 'Coping with Care: Mothers in a Welfare State'. In C. Ungerson (ed.) *Gender and Caring: Work and Welfare in Britain and Scandinavia*. Hemel Hempstead: Harvester Wheatsheaf.

Leira, A. (1992) *Welfare States and Working Mothers*. Cambridge: Cambridge University Press.

Leira, A. (1993) 'The "Woman-friendly" Welfare State? The Case of Norway and Sweden'. In J. Lewis (eds.) *Women and Social Policies in Europe. Work, Family and the State*. Aldershot: Edward Elgar.

Leira, A. (2002) *Working Parents and the Welfare State: Family Change and Policy Reform in Scandinavia*. Cambridge: Cambridge University Press.

Leira, A. and C. Saraceno (2002b) 'Care: Actors, Relationships and Contexts'. In B. Hobson et al. (eds.) *Contested Concepts in Gender and Social Politics*. Cheltenham/Northampton: Edward Elgar.

Leira, A. and C. Tobío and R. Trifiletti (2005) 'Kinship and Informal Support: Care Resources for the First Generation of Working Mothers in Norway, Italy and Spain'. In T. Knijn and A. Weckwert (eds.) *Working Mothers in Europe: A Comparison of Policies and Practices*. Cheltenham Edward Elgar.

Lewis, J. (1992a) 'Gender and the Development of Welfare Regimes'. *Journal of European Social Policy*, vol. 2, no. 3: 159-173.

Lewis, J. (1992b) *Women in Britain since 1945: Women, Family, Work and the State in the Post-War Years*. Oxford: Blackwell.

Lewis, J. (eds.) (1993) *Women and Social Policies in Europe: Work, Family and the State*. Aldershot: Edward Elgar.

Lewis, J. (1997a) 'Gender and Welfare Regimes: Further Thoughts'. *Social Politics*, summer: 160-207.

Lewis, J. (ed.) (1997b) *Lone Mothers in European Welfare Regimes: Shifting Policy Logics. London*: Jessica Kinsley Publishers.

Lewis, J. (ed.) (1998) *Gender, Social Care and Welfare State Restructuring in Europe*. Aldershot: Ashgate.

Lewis, J. (2001) 'Legitimising Care Work and the Issue of Gender Equality'. In M. Daly (ed.) *Care Work: The Quest for Security*. Geneva: ILO.

Lewis, J. (2003a) 'Developing Early Years Childcare in England, 1997-2002: The

Choices for (Working) Mothers'. *Social Policy and Administration*, vol. 37. no 3: 219-238.

Lewis, J. (2003b) 'Economic Citizenship: A Comment'. *Social Politics*, vol. 10, no. 2: 176-185.

Lewis, J. and S. Giullari (2005) 'The Adult Worker Model Family, Gender Equality and Care: The Search for New Policy Principles and the Possibilities and Problems of a Capabilities Approach'. *Economy and Society*, vol. 34, no. 1: 76-104.

Lijphart, A. (1968) *The Politics of Accommodation: Pluralism and Democracy in the Netherlands*. Berkeley: University of California Press.

Ligestillingsrådet/DS (1999) *Kvinder and Mænd*. Copenhagen: Danmarks Statistik Ligestillingsrådet.

LISO (1991) *Onderzoek kinderopvang in Limburg*, GOM-Limburg, Hasselt.

Lister, R. (1989) 'The Politics of Social Security: An Assessment of the Fowler Review'. In A. Dilnot and I. Walker (eds.) *The Economics of Social Security*. Oxford: Oxford University Press.

Lister, R. (1990) 'Women, Economic Dependence and Citizenship'. *Journal of Social Policy*, vol.19, no 4: 445-467.

Lister, R. (1992) *Women's Economic Dependency and Social Security*. Manchester: Equal Opportunities Commission.

Lister, R. (1994) '"She Has Other Duties" – Women, Citizenship and Social Security'. In S. Baldwin and J. Falkingham (eds.) *Social Security and Social Change*. Hemel Hemstead: Harvester Wheatsheaf.

Lister, R. (1996) 'Back to the Family: Family Policies and Politics under the Major Government'. In H. Jones and J. Millar (eds.) *The Politics of the Family*. Aldershot: Avebury.

Lister, R. (1997) *Citizenship: Feminist perspectives*. Hong Kong: Macmillan.

Lister, R. (2001) 'Foreword: Lone Parents: The UK Policy Context'. In J. Millar and K. Rowlingson (eds.) *Lone Parents, Employment and Social Policy: Cross-national Comparisons*. Bristol: Policy Press.

Lister, R. (2003) 'Investing in the Citizen-workers of the Future: Transformations in Citizenship and the State under New Labour'. *Social Policy and Administration*, vol. 37, no 5: 427-443.

Madsen, P. Kongshøj (1998) *Paid Leave Arrangements and Gender Equality: The Danish Experience in the 1990s*. Presentation for the OECD Conference Oslo October 12, 13.

Madsen, P. Kongshøj and P. Munch-Madsen, K. Langhoff-Roos (2001): 'All Hands on Deck! Fighting Social Exclusion in Denmark' in D. G. Mayes et al. (eds.) (2001) *Social Exclusion and European Policy*. Cheltenham: Edward Elgar.

Mahon R. and S.Michel (eds.) (2002) *Child care policy at the Crossroads: Gender and Welfare State Restructuring.* New York: Routledge.

March J. and Olsen, J. (1989) *Rediscovering Institutions: The Organizational Basis of Politics.* New York/London: Macmillan.

Marsh, A. and S.McKay (1993) *Families, Work and Benefits.* London: Policy Studies Institute.

Marsh, A. (2001) 'Helping British Lone Parents Get and Keep Paid Work'. In J. Millar and K. Rowlingson (eds.) *Lone Parents, Employment and Social Policy: Cross-national Comparisons.* Bristol: Policy Press.

Marshall, T.H. (1976, or. 1950) 'Citizenship and Social Class'. In T.H. Marshall *Citizenship and Social Development.* Westport: Greenwood Press Publishers.

Marshall, T.H. (1981) *The Right to Welfare and Other Essays.* London: Heinmann.

Marques-Pereira, B. and O. Paye (2001) 'Belgium: Vices and Virtues of Pragmatism'. In J. Jenson and M. Sineau (eds.) *Who Cares? Women's Work, Childcare, and Welfare State Redesign.* Toronto: University of Toronto Press.

Marx, I., K. Van den Bosch, B. Cantillon, and G. Verbist (1999) 'De uitkomsten in perspectief: armoede in de landen van de OESO'. In B. Cantillon et al. (eds.) *De welvaartsstaat in de kering.* Kapellen: Pelckmans.

Matheson, J. and C. Summersfield (2001) *Social Focus on Men.* National Statistics. London: The Stationary Office.

McLaughlin, E. and C. Glendinning (1996) 'Paying for Care in Europe: Is there a Feminist Approach?'. In L. Hantrais and S. Mangen (eds.) *Cross-National Research Methods in the Social Sciences.* London: Pinter.

McRae, S. (2003) 'Constraints and Choices in Mothers' Employment Careers: A Consideration of Hakim's Preference Theory'. *British Journal of Sociology,* vol. 53, no. 3: 317-38.

Mead, L.M. (1986) *Beyond Entitlement: The Social Obligation of Citizenship.* New York: Free Press.

Meyers, M.K., J.C. Gornick, and K.E. Ross (1999) 'Public Childcare, Parental Leave, and Employment'. In D. Sainsbury (eds.) *Gender and Welfare State Regimes.* Oxford: Oxford University Press.

Meulders, C. et al. (1990) *De gezins-en bejaardenzorg. De welzijnszorg in de Vlaamse gemeenschap. Voorzieningen en overheidsbeleid.* Leuven: KU Leuven.

Merton, R.K. (1968) *Social Theory and Social Structure.* New York: Free Press.

Millar, J. and A. Warman (1996) *Family Obligations in Europe.* London: Family Policy Studies Centre.

Millar, J. (1996) 'Poor Mothers and Absent Fathers: Support for Lone Parents in a Comparative Perspective'. In H. Jones and J. Millar (eds.) *The Politics of the Family.* Aldershot: Avebury.

Millar, J. and K. Rowlingson, K (2001) *Lone Parents, Employment and Social Policy: Cross-national Comparisons.* Bristol: Policy Press.

Ministry of Labour (1999) *The Labour Market Reforms – A Status.* Copenhagen: Abejdsministeriet.

Ministry of Labour/Ministry of Economic Affairs (2000) *National Action Plan for Employment 2000.* Copenhagen: Danish Government.

Ministerie van Sociale Zaken en Werkgelegenheid (1992) *Met het oog op 1995. Beleidsprogramma Emancipatie.* Den Haag: Vuga.

Ministerie van Sociale Zaken en Werkgelegenheid (1996) *Kansen op combineren.* Den Haag: Vuga.

Ministerie van Tewerkstelling en Arbeid (1996) *Het federaal werkgelegenheidsbeleid. Evaluatierapport 1996.* Brussel.

Ministerie van Tewerkstelling en Arbeid (1997) Loopbaanonderbreking: aflossing van de wacht? *Arbeidsblad*, nr 25, januari, februari, maart.

Ministerie van Tewerkstelling en Arbeid (2000). *Het federaal regeringsbeleid. Evaluatierapport 2000.* Brussel.

Ministerie van Welzijn, Gezondheid en Gelijke kansen (2000) *Blauwdruk voor een toekomstgerichte uitbouw van het kinderopvanglandschap in Vlaanderen – een totaalbeleidsplan kinderopvang.* Brussel.

Ministerie van Volksgezondheid, Welzijn en Sport/VWS (2002) Zorgnota 2002. Den Haag: VWS.

Mogensen, G. V. (ed.) (1995) *Work Incentives in the Danish Welfare State.* The Rockwell Foundation Research Unit. Aarhus: Aarhus University Press.

Montanari, I. (2000) 'From Family Wage to Marriage Subsidy and Child Benefits: Controversy and Consensus in the Development of Family Support'. *Journal of European Social Policy*, vol 10, 4: 307-333.

Morée, M. (1992) *'Mijn kinderen hebben er niets van gemerkt'. Buitenshuis werkende moeders tussen 1950 en nu.* Utrecht: Jan van Arkel.

Morée, M. (1990) *Een illusie van economische zelfstandigheid. Buitenshuis werkende moeders over hun inkomen: veranderingen en continuïteten.* Paper ten behoeve van het congres mannen/vrouwen. Amsterdam, 19 en 20 april. Unpublished.

Morgan, P. (1996) *Who Needs Parents? The Effect of Childcare and Early Education on Children in Britain and the USA.* London: IEA.

Morgan, K. J. and K. Zippel (2003) 'Paid to Care: The Origins and Effects of Care Leave Policies in Western Europe'. *Social Politics*, 10: 49-85.

Morris, J. (1991) *Pride Against Prejudice: Transforming Attitudes to Disability.* London: Women's Press.

Moss, P. (1991) 'Day Care for Young Children in the United Kingdom'. In E. Melhuish and P. Moss (eds.) *Day Care for Young Children: International Perspectives.* London/New York: Routledge.

Moss, P. et al. (1995) *Survey of Day Care Providers in England and Wales*. A working paper from the TCRU Children Act Project. London: Thomas Coram Institute.

Moss, P. et al. (2004) *Care Work in Europe: Current Understandings and Future Directions: A European Research Project on Paid Care*.

Naumann, I.K. (2005) 'Childcare and Feminism in West Germany and Sweden in the 1960s and 1970s'. *Journal of European Social Policy*, vol 15, no. 1: 47-63.

NS/National Statistics (1997) *Labour Market Trends*. London: NS.

Nievers, E. (2003) *'We moeten haar koesteren' Over de relatie tussen ouders en de betaalde kinderoppas aan huis*. Utrecht: de Graaff.

NRC *Handelsblad* (1998) 'Zalm wil voordeel voor kostwinner afschaffen'. 16 mei. Rotterdam.

Nussbaum, M.C. (2000) *Women and Human Development: The Capabilities Approach*. Cambridge: Cambridge University Press.

O'Connor, J and A.Orloff and S. Shaver (1999) *States, Markets, Families: Gender, Liberalism and Social Policy in Australia, Canada, Great Britain and the United States*. Cambridge: Cambridge University Press.

O'Donoghue, C. and H. Sutherland (1998) *Accounting for the Family: The Treatment of Marriage and Children in European Income Tax Systems*. Innocenti Occasional Papers. Economic and Social Policy Series, no. 65. Florence: UNICEF International Child Development Centre.

OECD (1991) *Shaping Structural Change: The Role of Women*. Paris: OECD.

OECD (1993) *Economic Survey. Denmark*. Paris: OECD.

OECD (1994a) *The OECD Jobs Study: Evidence and Explanations Part II*. Paris: OECD.

OECD (1994b) *Caring for Frail Elderly People: New Directions in Care*. Paris: OECD.

OECD (1995) *The Tax/Benefit Position of Production Workers 1991-1994*. Paris: OECD.

OECD (1996). *Economic Studies, no 26*. Paris: OECD.

OECD (2000a) *Taxing Wages*. Paris: OECD.

OECD (2000b) *Employment Outlook*. Paris: OECD.

OECD (2001) *Starting Strong – Early Childhood Education and Care*. Paris: OECD.

OECD (2002a) *Babies and Bosses: Reconciling Work and Family Life*. Vol 1. Australia, Denmark and the Netherlands. Paris: OECD.

OECD (2002b) *Employment Outlook*. Paris: OECD.

OECD (2002c) *Taxes and Benefits*. Paris: OECD.

OECD (2003) *Taxing Wages*. Paris: OECD.

OECD (2004) *Employment Outlook*. Paris: OECD.

Oppenheim, C. and R. Lister (1995) 'Ten Years after the 1986 Social Security Act'. In J. Baldock and M. May (eds.) *Social Policy Review 7*. Canterbury: SPA.

O'Reilly, J. and C. Fagan (1998) *Part-time Prospects: An International Comparison of Part-time Work in Europe, North America and the Pacific Rim*. London and New York: Routledge.

Orloff, A.S. (1993) 'Gender and the Social Rights of Citizenship: The Comparative Analysis of Gender Relations and Welfare States'. *American Sociological Review* 58: 303-328.

Orloff, S. (2006) 'From Materialism to "Employment for All": State Policies to Promote Women's Employment Across the Affluent Democracies'. In J. Levy (ed.) *The State After Statism New State Activities in the Era of Globalization and Liberalization*, Cambridge: Harvard University Press: 230-268.

Parker, H. (1995) *Taxes, Benefits and Family Life: The Seven Deadly Traps*. London: Insitute of Economic Affairs.

Pateman, C. (1989) *The Disorder of Women: Democracy, Feminism and Political Theory*. London: Polity Press.

Pauwels, K. (1978) *De arbeidsparticipatie van de gehuwde vrouw. Onderzoeksresultaten Nego 3 (1975-1976)*. Brussel.

Pedersen, L. H. and S. Weise and S.Jacobs and M. White (2000) 'Lone Mothers' Poverty and Employment'. In D. Gallie and S. Paugam (eds.) *Welfare Regimes and the Experience of Unemployment in Europe*. Oxford: Oxford University Press.

Peemans-Poulet, H. (1994) 'Wanneer rechtvaardigheid naar een financieel evenwicht in de sociale zekerheid leidt'. In M. Van Haegendoren and H. Moestermans (eds.) *Naar individuele rechten in de sociale zekerheid? De pensioenen en de werkloosheid in de kijker*. Leuven/Amersfoort: Acco.

Peemans-Poullet, H. (1995) *De sociale zekerheid hervormen?* Brussel: Christelijke Mutualiteit.

Peters, K. (1999) *Verdeelde macht. Een onderzoek naar invloed op rijksbesluitvorming in Nederland*. Amsterdam: Boom.

Pfau-Effinger, B. (1998) 'Gender Cultures and the Gender Arrangement – A Theoretical Framework for Cross-National Gender Research'. *Innovation*, vol. 11, no. 2: 147-166.

Pfau-Effinger, B. (1999) 'Change of Family Policies in the Socio-cultural Context of European Societies'. *Comparative Social Research*, vol. 18: 135-159.

Pierson, P. (1994) *Dismantling the Welfare State? Reagan, Thatcher, and the Politics of Retrenchment*. Cambridge: Cambridge University Press.

Pierson, P. (ed.) (2001) *The New Politics of the Welfare State*. Oxford: Oxford University Press.

Pittevils, I. and Timmermans, P. (1995) *Omvang van de belangrijkste directe en indirecte overheidstussenkomsten in het sociaal beleid.* Paper gepresenteerd op het 22ste Vlaams Wetenschappelijk Economisch Congres. De sociale zekerheid verzekerd? 20/21 oktober.

Plantenga, J. (1993). *Een afwijkend patroon. Honderd jaar vrouwenarbeid in Nederland en (West-) Duitsland.* Amsterdam: SUA.

Plantenga, J. (1996). 'For Women Only? The Rise of Part-time Work in the Netherlands'. *Social Politics*, spring: 57-71.

Plantenga, J. (1998) 'Double Lives: Labour Market Participation, Citizenship and Gender'. In J. Bussemaker and R. Voet (eds.) *Gender, Participation and Citizenship in The Netherlands.* Aldershot: Ashgate.

Plantenga, J., J. Schippers, and J. Siegers (1999) 'Towards an Equal Division of Paid and Unpaid Work: The Case of the Netherlands'. *Journal of European Social Policy*, vol 9, no 2: 99-110.

Plantenga, J. and M. Siegel (2004) 'Childcare in a Changing World'. Position Paper. The Hague: Ministry of Social Affairs and Employment. Available at www.childcareinachangingworld.nl.

Portegijs, W. and A. Boelens and S. Keuzenkamp (2002) *Emancipatiemonitor 2002.* Den Haag: SCP/CBS.

Portegijs, W. and A. Boelens and L. Olsthoorn (2004) *Emancipatiemonitor 2004.* Den Haag: SCP/CBS

Pott-Buter, H.A. (1993) *Facts and Fairy Tales about Female Labor, Family and Fertility: A Seven-country Comparison, 1850-1900.* Amsterdam: Amsterdam University Press.

Ragin, C. (2000) *Fuzzy-set Sciences.* Chicago: University of Chicago Press.

Rake, K. (2001) 'Gender and the New Labour's Social Policies'. *Journal of Social Policy*, vol. 30, no. 2: 209-231.

Randall, V. (1996) 'Feminism and Child Care in Britain'. *Journal of Social Policy*, 25: 485-505.

Randall, V. (2002) 'Child Care in Britain, or, How Do You Restructure Nothing?' R. Mahon and S. Michel (eds.) *Child Care Policy at the Crossroads: Gender and Welfare State Restructuring.* New York: Routledge.

Ravn, A.B. (2000) 'Gender Taxation and Welfare State in Denmark 1903-63'. Paper presented at the GEP International Conference 'New Challenges to Gender, Democracy, Welfare States – Politics of Empowerment and Inclusion'. Vilvorde KursusCenter, Denmark, August 18-20.

Rigter, D.P., E.A.M. van den Bosch, R.J. van der Veen, and A.C. Hemerijck (1995) *Tussen sociale wil en werkelijkheid. Een geschiedenis van het beleid van het ministerie van Sociale Zaken.* Den Haag: Vuga.

Ritzer, G. (2000) *Classical Sociological Theory*. Boston: McGraw Hill.

Rhodes, R.A.W. (1999) 'Traditions and Public Sector Reform: Comparing Britain and Denmark'. *Scandinavian Political Studies*, vol. 22, no. 4: 341-370.

Rostgaard, T and T. Fridberg (1998) *Caring for Children and Older People. A Comparison of European Policies and Practices*. Copenhagen: SFI.

Rostgaard, T. (2002) 'Setting Time Aside for the Father – Father's Leave in Scandinavia', *Community, Work and Family*, 5/3: 343-364.

Rostgaard, T. (2004) *With Due Care: Social Care for the Young and the Old across Europe*. Copenhagen: SFI.

Rothstein, B. (1998) *Just Institutions Matter: The Moral and Political Logic of the Universal Welfare State*. Cambridge: Cambridge University Press.

Rowlingson, K. (2001) 'The Social, Economic and Demographic Profile of Lone Parents'. In J. Millar and K. Rowlingson (eds.) *Lone Parents, Employment and Social Policy: Cross-national Comparisons*. Bristol: Policy Press.

Rubery, J. and M. Smith and C.Fagan (1999) *Women's Employment in Europe: Trends and Prospects*. London: Routledge.

Ruggie, M. (1984) *The State and Working Women: A Comparative Study of Britain and Sweden*. Princeton: Princeton University Press.

Sainsbury, D. (1996) *Gender, Equality and Welfare States*. Cambridge: Cambridge University Press.

Sainsbury, D. (ed.) (1999a) *Gender and Welfare State Regimes*. Oxford: Oxford University Press.

Sainsbury, D. (1999b) 'Taxation, Family Responsibilities, and Employment'. In D. Sainsbury (ed.) *Gender and Welfare State Regimes*. Oxford: Oxford University Press.

Salemink, T. (1991) *Katholieke kritiek op het kapitalisme. 1891-1991. Honderd jaar debat over vrije markt en verzorgingsstaat*. Amsterdam/ Leuven: Acco.

Sassoon, A. Showstack (1987) *Women and the State: The Shifting Boundaries of Public and Private*. London: Hutchinson.

Schippers, J (2004) 'Arbeid en zorg: tussen normering en keuzevrijheid'. In W. Arts, H. Entzinger and R. Muffels (eds.) *Verzorgingsstaat vaar wel*. Assen: Van Gorcum.

Schreuder, L. (2001) 'De Wet basisvoorziening kinderopvang. Mag het wat meer zijn?' *Tijdschrift voor de Sociale Sector*, 55, no.9: 10-13.

SCP (Sociaal Cultureel Planbureau) (2000) Nederland in Europa. Sociaal en Cultureel Rapport 2000. Rijswijk: SCP.

Sen, A. (1977) 'Rational fools: a critique of the behavioral foundations of economic theory'. *Philosophy and Public Affairs* 6, no 4: 317-344.

Sevenhuysen. S. (1998) *Citizenship and the Ethics of Care: Feminist Consideration on Justice, Morality and Politics*. London: Routledge.

Siaroff, A. (1994) 'Work, Welfare and Gender Equality: A New Typology' D. Sainsbury (ed.) *Gendering Welfare States* London: Sage.

Shaver, S. and Bradshaw, J. (1995) 'The Recognition of Wifely Labour by Welfare States' in *Social Policy and Administration*, vol. 29, no. 1: 10-25.

Siim, B. (1990) 'Women and the Welfare State: Between Private and Public Dependence: A Comparative Approach to Care Work in Denmark and Britain'. In C. Ungerson (ed.) *Gender and Caring: Work and Welfare in Britain and Scandinavia.* Hemel Hempstead: Harvester Wheatsheaf.

Siim, B. (1993) 'The Gendered Scandinavian Welfare States: The Interplay between Women's Roles as Mothers, Workers and Citizens in Denmark'. In J. Lewis (ed.) *Women and Social Policies in Europe: Work, Family and the State.* Aldershot: Edward Elgar.

Siim, B. (1998) 'Vocabularies of Gender and Citizenship: The Danish case'. *Critical Social Policy*, vol. 18, no 3: 375-96.

Siim, B. (2000) *Gender and Citizenship: Politics and Agency in France, Britain and Denmark.* Cambridge: Cambridge University Press.

Silva, E.B. (1996) (ed.) *Good Enough Mothering? Feminist Perspectives on Lone Motherhood.* London: Routledge.

Simoens, D. (ed.) (1991) *Ontwikkelingen van de sociale zekerheid 1985-1991.* Leuven: Die Keure.

Simoens, D. and J.Put (eds.) (1996) *Ontwikkelingen van de sociale zekerheid 1990-1996.* Instituut voor Sociaal Recht. Leuven: Die Keure.

Simon, H.A. (1957) *Models of Man.* New York: Wiley.

Singer, E. (1989) *Kinderopvang en de moeder-kindrelatie. Pedagogen, psychologen en sociale hervormers over moeders en jonge kinderen.* Proefschrift. Utrecht.

Skocpol, T. (1979) *States and Social Revolutions: A Comparative Analysis of France, Russia and China.* Cambridge: Cambridge University Press.

Skocpol, T. (1992) *Protecting Soldiers and Mothers.* Cambridge: Harvard University Press.

Skocpol, T. and M. Somers (1980) 'The Uses of Comparative History in Macrosocial Inquiry'. *Comparative Studies in Society and History*, vol. 22: 174-197.

Snijders-Borst, H. (1985) 'Terug naar het fornuis.Tweeverdienerswetgeving een nodeloze ravage'. *Intermediair*, vol. 21, no. 15, april: 69-75.

Socialkomissionen (1993) *Reformer. Socialkommissionens samelede forslag.* Copenhagen.

Somers, A. and J. Peeters (1991) *Over slechte moeders, goede kinderopvang en vice versa. Grasduinen in de geschiedenis van de visie op moederschap en kinderopvang.* GSO Jaarboek: Gent.

Sørensen, A. (2001) 'Gender Equality in Earnings at Work and at Home'. M. Kautto et al. (eds.) *Nordic Welfare States in the European Context.* London: Routledge.

Standaard Magazine (1995) Interview with Miet Smet, February, 10.

Steunpunt wav (Werkgelegenheid, Arbeid, Vorming) (1994) *Regionaal-sectoriële spreiding van deeltijdarbeid*. Nieuwsbrief, no 1.

Steunpunt wav (Werkgelegenheid, Arbeid, Vorming) (1995) *Beroepsbevolking naar gewest*. Nieuwsbrief, no 4.

Steunpunt wav (Werkgelegenheid, Arbeid, Vorming) (1996) *Hoe lang is te lang? De recente evolutie van het aantal geschorsten omwille van abnormaal langdurige werkloosheid* Nieuwsbrief 4.

Stolk, B. and C. Wouters (1982) 'De gemoedsrust van de verzorgingsstaat'. *Maandblad Geestelijke Volksgezondheid*, 37/6: 599-613.

Storms, B. (1995). *Het matteüs-effect in de kinderopvang*. csb berichten. Universiteit van Antwerpen/ufsia: Centrum voor Sociaal Beleid.

svr (Sociale Verzekerings Raad) (2001) *Kroniek van de sociale verzekeringen*. Zoetermeer: svr.

Swaan, A. de (1990) *Zorg en de staat. Welzijn, onderwijs en gezondheidszorg in Europa en de Verenigde Staten in de nieuwe tijd*. Amsterdam: Bert Bakker.

Swiddler, A. (2001) *Talk of Love: How Culture Matters*. Chicago: University of Chicago Press.

Sztompka, P. (1988) 'Conceptual Frameworks in Comparative Inquiry: Divergent or Convergent?'. *International Sociology*, vol. 3, no. 3: 207-218.

Taylor-Gooby, P. (1991) 'Welfare State Regimes and Welfare Citizenship'. *Journal of European Social Policy* vol. 1, no. 2: 93-105.

Thomas, C. (1993) 'De-constructing Concepts of Care'. *Sociology* vol. 27, no. 4: 649-669.

Tester, S. (1996) *Community Care for Older People: A Comparative Perspective*. London: Macmillan.

Teulings, C. and R. van der Veen and W. Trommel (1997) *Dilemma's van sociale zekerheid. Een analyse van 10 jaar herziening van het stelsel van sociale zekerheid*. Den Haag: Vuga.

Thomson, K (1995) 'Working Mothers: Choice or Circumstance?'. In R. Jowell et al. (eds.) *British Social Attitudes: The 12th Report*. Aldershot: Dartmouth Publishing Co.

Tinker, A. et al. (1994) *The Care of Frail Elderly People in the United Kingdom*. London: hmso.

Titmuss, R. (1958) "The Social Division of Welfare: Some Reflections on the search for Equity" *Essays on the Welfare State*. London: Allen and Unwin.

Titmuss, R. (1974) *Social Policy*. London: Allen and Unwin.

tk (Tweede Kamer) (1979-1980) *Op weg naar gelijke benadeling voor de loon- en inkomstenbelasting van de (werkende) gehuwde vrouw en haar man, en van deel-*

genoten aan vormen van samenleving en samenwonen. 'De nota Nooteboom', 15835, nrs 1-2.

TK (Tweede Kamer) (1980-1981) 49ᵉ *Vergadering Vaste Commissie voor Financiën en voor Emancipatiebeleid,* over de nota 'Op weg naar gelijke fiscale behandeling van de (werkende) gehuwde vrouw en haar man,en van deelgenoten van samenleven en samenwonen' 16 maart.

TK (Tweede Kamer) (1993-1994) *Memorie van Antwoord, ivm wetsvoorstel De Korte en Van Rey.* 23231, nr. 5.

Trommel, W. and R. van der Veen (eds.) (1999) *De herverdeelde samenleving. Ontwikkeling en herziening van de Nederlandse verzorgingsstaat.* Amsterdam: Amsterdam University Press.

Tronto, J.C. (1993) *Moral Boundaries: A Political Argument for an Ethic of Care.* London: Routledge.

Ungerson, C. (1987) *Policy is Personal: Sex, Gender and Informal Care.* London: Tavistock.

Ungerson, C. (1990) 'The Language of Care: Crossing the Boundaries'. In C. Ungerson (ed.) *Gender and Caring: Work and Welfare in Britain and Scandinavia.* Hemel Hempstead: Harvester Wheatsheaf.

Van Buggenhout, B. (1994) 'Inleiding tot debat' Van Haegendoren and H. Moestermans (eds.) *Naar individuele rechten in de sociale zekerheid? De pensioenen en de werkloosheid in de kijker.* Leuven/Amersfoort: Acco.

Van der Veen, R. (1994) 'De wankele verzorgingsstaat. Een vergelijkende analyse van verzorgingsstaten in het licht van internationaliseringsprocessen'. In G. Engbersen et al. (eds.) *Zorgen in het Europese huis. Verkenningen over de grenzen van nationale verzorgingsstaten.* Amsterdam: Boom. Van Doorn, J.A.A. (1978) 'De verzorgingsstaat in praktijk.' J.A.A. van Doorn and C.J.M. Schuyt (eds.) *De stagnerende verzorgingsstaat* Meppel: Boom.

Van Haegendoren M. and H. Moestermans (1996) *Vrouwen, Gezinnen en Fiscaliteit.* Brussel: NVR.

Van Haegendoren, M. (1994) 'Inleiding'. In Van Haegendoren and H. Moestermans (eds.) *Naar individuele rechten in de sociale zekerheid? De pensioenen en de werkloosheid in de kijker.* Acco/leuven/Amersfoort.

Van Haegendoren,M. and B. Bawin-Legros (1996) *Solidariteit en familie.* Brussel: Koning Boudewijnstichting.

Van Kersbergen, K. (1995) *Social Capitalism: A Study of Christian Democracy and the Welfare State.* London/New York: Routledge.

Van Lieshout (1994) *Zorgen en laten zorgen.* Oratie. Universiteit Utrecht.

Van Luijn, H and S. Keuzenkamp (2004) *Werkt verlof? Het gebruik van regelingen voor verlof en aanpassing van de arbeidsduur.* Den Haag: SCP.

Van Oorschot, W. (2003) *Over de Culturele Analyse van Sociaal beleid.* Oratie. Universiteit van Tilburg.

Van Peer, C. and H. Moors (1996) 'Perceived Obstacles to Fertility: Opinions on Family Policies in Flanders and in the Netherlands'. In H. van den Brekel and F. Deven (eds.) *Population and Family in the Low Countries 1995.* Dordrecht: Kluwer Academics.

Van Rijswijk-Clerkx, L.E. (1981) *Moeders, kinderen en kinderopvang. Veranderingen in de kinderopvang in Nederland.* Nijmegen: SUN.

Vanistendael, F. (1989) 'Gezinsfiscaliteit'. *Algemeen Fiscaal Tijdschrift.* De hervorming van 1988. jrg, 40, no 1: 12-20.

Vanpée, K. and L. Sannen and G. Hedebouw (2000) *Kinderopvang in Vlaanderen. Gebruik, keuze van de opvangvorm en evaluatie door ouders.* Leuven: HIVA.

Vedel-Petersen, J. (1992) *Daycare Institutions for Children Under School Age in Denmark.* Copenhagen: SFI.

Visser, J. and A. Hemerijck (1997) *'A Dutch Miracle': Job Growth, Welfare Reform and Corporatism in the Netherlands.* Amsterdam: Amsterdam University Press.

Visser, J. (1999) *De sociologie van het halve werk.* Oratie. Amsterdam: Vossiuspers AUP.

Visser, J (2002) 'The First Part-time Economy in the World: A Model to be Followed?'. *Journal of European Social Policy*, vol. 12, no. 1: 23-42.

Voet, R. (1998) 'Citizenship and Female Participation'. In J. Bussemaker and R. Voet (eds.) *Gender, Participation and Citizenship in the Netherlands.* Aldershot: Ashgate.

Voorn, M. C. and P. Meijer (1999) *Nederland wordt ouder. Meningen over ouderenzorg en ouderdom.* Amsterdam: NIPO.

Vrouwenalliantie (1998) *Verslag en Advies Werkconferentie Belastingen in de 21ᵉ eeuw.* 26 maart. Utrecht.

Wheelock, J. and K. Jones (2002) '"Grandparents Are the Next Best Thing": Informal Childcare for Working Parents in Urban Britain'. *Journal of Social Policy*, vol. 31, no. 3: 441-463.

Wehner, C. and P. Abrahamson (2003) *Labour Supply: The Case of Denmark.* Available at http://www.york.ac.uk/inst/spru/research/summs/welempfc.htm.

Welzijnszakboekje 1992-1993 (1993) *Overzicht/wetgeving/adressenregister.* Zaventum: Kluwer.

Wentholt, K.(1990) *Arbeid en Zorg. Een verkenning vanuit het gelijkheidsbeginsel van werknemers met gezinsverantwoordelijkheid.* Amsterdam: Thesis Publishers.

Werkgroep Vlaamse Diensten voor Opvanggezinnen (1992) *Wie zijn de opvanggezinnen?* Unpublished.

Waerness, K. (1984) 'Caring as Women's Work in the Welfare State'. In H. Holterman (ed.) *Patriarchy in a Welfare Society.* Oslo: Universitetsforlaget.

Wilson, E. (1977) *Women and the Welfare State.* London: Tavistock.

Wilkinson, H. (ed.) (1998) *Time Out: The Costs and Benefits of Paid Parental Leave.* London: Demos.

Witte, H. de (1992) *Tussen optimisten en teruggetrokkenen.* Leuven: HIVA.

Woldring, H.E.S (2003) *Politieke filosofie van de christen-democratie.* Budel: Damon.

Wolfe, A. (1989) *Whose Keeper? Social Science and Moral Obligation.* Berkeley: the University of California Press.

WRR (Wetenschappelijke Raad voor het Regeringsbeleid) (1990) *Een werkend perspectief. Arbeidsparticipatie in de jaren negentig.* Den Haag: SDU.

Zijderveld, A. (1988) *De culturele factor. Een cultuursociologische wegwijzer.* Culembourg: Lemma.

Index of Names

Index of Subjects

CHANGING WELFARE STATES

PREVIOUSLY PUBLISHED

Jelle Visser and Anton Hemerijck, *A Dutch Miracle. Job Growth, Welfare Reform and Corporatism in the Netherlands*, 1997 (ISBN 978 90 5356 271 0)

Christoffer Green-Pedersen, *The Politics of Justification. Party Competition and Welfare-State Retrenchment in Denmark and the Netherlands from 1982 to 1998*, 2002 (ISBN 978 90 5356 590 2)

Jan Høgelund, *In Search of Effective Disability Policy. Comparing the Developments and Outcomes of the Dutch and Danish Disability Policies*, 2003 (ISBN 978 90 5356 644 2)

Maurizio Ferrera and Elisabetta Gualmini, *Rescued by Europe? Social and Labour Market Reforms from Maastricht to Berlusconi*, 2004 (ISBN 978 90 5356 651 0)

Martin Schludi, *The Reform of Bismarckian Pension Systems. A Comparison of Pension Politics in Austria, France, Germany, Italy and Sweden*, 2005 (ISBN 978 90 5356 740 1)

Uwe Becker and Herman Schwartz (eds.), *Employment 'Miracles'. A Critical Comparison of the Dutch, Scandinavian, Swiss, Australian and Irish Cases Versus Germany and the US*, 2005 (ISBN 978 90 5356 755 5)

Sanneke Kuipers, *The Crisis Imperative. Crisis Rhetoric and Welfare State Reform in Belgium and the Netherlands in the Early 1990s*, 2006 (ISBN 978 90 5356 808 8)

Anke Hassel, *Wage Setting, Social Pacts and the Euro. A New Role for the State*, 2006 (ISBN 978 90 5356 919 1)

Ive Marx, *A New Social Question? On Minimum Income Protection in the Postindustrial Era*, 2007 (ISBN 978 90 5356 925 2)